Read this book online today:

With SAP PRESS BooksOnline we offer you online access to knowledge from the leading SAP experts. Whether you use it as a beneficial supplement or as an alternative to the printed book, with SAP PRESS BooksOnline you can:

• Access your book anywhere, at any time. All you need is an Internet connection.
• Perform full text searches on your book and on the entire SAP PRESS library.
• Build your own personalized SAP library.

The SAP PRESS customer advantage:

Register this book today at *www.sap-press.com* and obtain exclusive free trial access to its online version. If you like it (and we think you will), you can choose to purchase permanent, unrestricted access to the online edition at a very special price!

Here's how to get started:

1. Visit *www.sap-press.com*.
2. Click on the link for SAP PRESS BooksOnline and login (or create an account).
3. Enter your free trial license key, shown below in the corner of the page.
4. Try out your online book with full, unrestricted access for a limited time!

Your personal free trial **license key**
for this online book is:

ra8x-gdju-2c54-9mzv

Maximizing Cash Management with SAP® ERP Financials

 **PRESS**

SAP PRESS is a joint initiative of SAP and Galileo Press. The know-how offered by SAP specialists combined with the expertise of the Galileo Press publishing house offers the reader expert books in the field. SAP PRESS features first-hand information and expert advice, and provides useful skills for professional decision-making.

SAP PRESS offers a variety of books on technical and business related topics for the SAP user. For further information, please visit our website: *www.sap-press.com*.

Shivesh Sharma
Maximizing SAP General Ledger
2010, app. 550 pp.
978-1-59229-306-3

Eric Bauer, Jörg Siebert
The SAP General Ledger
2010, app. 500 pp.
978-1-59229-350-6

Mitresh Kundalia
Segment Reporting with Document Splitting in the SAP General Ledger
2009, app. 150 pp.
978-1-59229-265-3

Naeem Arif, Sheikh Muhammad Tauseef
SAP ERP Financials: Configuration and Design
2008, app. 450 pp.
978-1-59229-136-6

Eleazar Ortega Van Steenberghe

Maximizing Cash Management with SAP® ERP Financials

Galileo Press

Bonn • Boston

Galileo Press is named after the Italian physicist, mathematician and philosopher Galileo Galilei (1564–1642). He is known as one of the founders of modern science and an advocate of our contemporary, heliocentric worldview. His words *Eppur se muove* (And yet it moves) have become legendary. The Galileo Press logo depicts Jupiter orbited by the four Galilean moons, which were discovered by Galileo in 1610.

Editor Kelly Grace Harris
Copyeditor Julie McNamee
Cover Design Graham Geary
Photo Credit Image Copyright OfiPlus. Used under license from Shutterstock.com.
Layout Design Vera Brauner
Production Manager Kelly O'Callaghan
Assistant Production Editor Graham Geary
Typesetting Publishers' Design and Production Services, Inc.
Printed and bound in Canada

ISBN 978-1-59229-324-7

© 2011 by Galileo Press Inc., Boston (MA)

1st Edition 2011

Library of Congress Cataloging-in-Publication Data
Ortega Van Steenberghe, Eleazar.
  Maximizing cash management with SAP ERP financials / Eleazar Ortega Van Steenberghe. —
1st ed.
    p. cm.
  ISBN-13: 978-1-59229-324-7
  ISBN-10: 1-59229-324-7
  1. Cash management — Computer programs. 2. SAP ERP. I. Title.
  HG4028.C45O78 2011
  658.15'2028553—dc22
2010031415

Contents at a Glance

Dear Reader,

More than ever before, corporations must maintain sophisticated cash management systems that enable them to optimize both their investments and their daily cash. SAP customers can take advantage of the myriad cash management products offered in the SAP ERP Financials, Treasury and Risk Management, and FSCM components, but the real-world aspects of maximizing the existing solutions can be hard to understand, navigate, and implement without experienced, practical guidance.

Thanks to the expertise of Eleazar Ortega Van Steenberghe, reading this book will put you in the best possible position to truly maximize your use of SAP's cash management systems. Building off 20 years of experience working with Fortune 500 companies such as Nike, Target, and Aflac, Eleazar's clear, detailed explanations and numerous examples will teach you exactly what you need to know about this complex topic. Throughout the course of writing his manuscript, Eleazar continually impressed me with his knowledge of this subject and dedication to his work. You are now the recipient of this knowledge and dedication, and I'm confident that you'll benefit greatly from both.

We always look forward to praise, but are also interested in critical comments that will help us improve our books. We encourage you to visit our website at *www.sap-press.com* and share your feedback about this work.

Thank you for purchasing a book from SAP PRESS!

Kelly Grace Harris
Editor, SAP PRESS

Galileo Press
Braintree, MA

kelly.harris@galileo-press.com
www.sap-press.com

Contents

The expectations of life depend upon diligence; the mechanic that would perfect his work must first sharpen his tools.

— Confucius

Preface

Why This Book Was Written

Ever since I began implementing treasury applications from SAP, I've faced the same questions from my clients:

▶ How should a modern treasury operate?

▶ What are the current trends?

▶ What are the best practices?

▶ Is the way I run it today the best way?

▶ How can I use new technologies to make my work easier?

▶ What exactly is covered by the functionality in SAP Treasury and Risk Management?

▶ What are the differences among SAP Treasury and Risk Management, Corporate Finance Management (CFM), and SAP Financial Supply Chain Management (SAP FSCM)?

▶ What is Financial Supply Chain Management?

Unfortunately, a lot of confusion about treasury applications from SAP arises from a number of sources and circumstances:

▶ **Name changes**
The name of the treasury functionalities included in SAP has changed a number of times as new versions are launched. Back in version 3.0, it was known as *TR-CM for Cash Management* and *TR-TM for Treasury Management;* at the time,

this included money markets, loans, and so on. In versions 4.5 and 4.6, the product became *Corporate Finance Management (CFM)*, which included both Cash Management and Treasury Management. In the current SAP ERP 6.0 version, it is part of SAP Financial Supply Chain Management (SAP FSCM), which also includes other applications related to receivables and payables.

► **SAP marketing materials**
SAP marketing materials sometimes mention functionality that is meant for future releases but is not available at the time the brochures and materials are given to clients. Although this is stated somewhere in the brochures, it causes a lot of confusion and sometimes disappointment among clients and prospective clients. This was particularly true in the 1990s but is still true to some extent today.

► **Few implementations of treasury applications from SAP**
The treasury applications from SAP are usually part of a second or third phase in the implementation cycle, which means it is often canceled due to expenditures in consulting.

► **Lack of standard naming conventions**
There is no standard name for some of the business functions in a treasury department, so each software company tends to give the functions different names. As with a lot of SAP terms, this makes it difficult to understand for potential customers and new implementation team members.

► **Incorrect implementations**
Because, in the past, treasury has been a relatively uncommon functionality to implement, very few consultants knew it well, which led to companies implementing it without proper knowledge. Naturally, this has lead to poor results and given the product an unfairly negative reputation.

Despite these misunderstandings, the role of the treasury applications from SAP has evolved significantly during the last two decades, mainly due to the adoption of integrated software, connectivity to the Internet, and the evolution of the financial markets. This has caused treasury to move from a back office function into a critical business function that has resulted in a whole new set of processes, rules, and best practices.

This book answers all of the questions presented at the beginning of this section, while also explaining some of the main issues and alternatives for resolution of problems.

How the Book Is Organized

A modern treasury has several main processes, and this book explains how they work and how can they be set up in SAP. **Chapters 1** and **2** cover local and international treasury business processes and issues. **Chapters 3** and **4** focus on inbound and outbound cash flows that take place electronically using SAP functionality. **Chapter 5** explains how to set up your banks and bank accounts, as well as how to manage all of the information and processes between your company and your bank. It also covers some of the new features of SAP, such as the Integration Package for SWIFNET. **Chapter 6** describes SAP In-House Cash, including the benefits of using it and how it is configured. **Chapter 7** covers Liquidity Planner, how to track actual cash flows, and provides an overview of the planning process. **Chapter 8** is about how other components of SAP and the business processes outside of finance integrate with the different treasury functionalities. **Chapter 9** summarizes all of the previous chapters and shows how the integrated treasury will ultimately work. **Chapter 10** gives a review of general SAP implementation methodology and some treasury-specific lessons. Finally, **Chapter 11** closes the book by providing an overview of new and future functionalities of SAP, and how they will complement the existing ones to provide a more integrated treasury functionality.

Intended Audience

This book is aimed at financial executives who deal with treasury issues on a daily basis and want to find better ways to organize and run their treasury departments. The book is also applicable to those who are considering an implementation of treasury applications from SAP.

The book will also help information technology executives who are weighing the possibility of implementing either SAP ERP in general or treasury applications from SAP in particular, as well as those who are already engaged in it and want to know how to organize the project and the project's most important aspects.

Finally, the book will help those consultants who want to learn treasury and SAP FSCM, or who are already working on an implementation project and want to enhance knowledge or resolve specific issues and questions.

How to Use This Book

Every author dreams that those who buy the book will read it cover to cover. If you bought this book and have that intention, congratulations. A more realistic approach, however, is to provide readers with a table of contents and some guidance on how to use this book.

With that in mind, consider the following information:

▶ If you are a technical consultant who wants to understand the treasury applications from the perspective of the treasury business and processes, read Chapters 1 and 2, and then browse through the other chapters to see if there are particular areas you want to learn.

▶ If you are a financial executive who is exploring functionality, read Chapters 1 and 2, then read Sections 3.1, 4.1, 5.1, 6.1, 7.1, 8.1, 9.1, and all chapter summaries.

▶ If you are an IT executive considering an implementation of treasury applications from SAP, read Chapters 1, 2, and 10.

▶ If you are an SAP consultant working on a specific project and struggling with a particular issue, read Chapters 1 and 2, and then use the table of contents to find the particular section relevant to your project or issue.

▶ If you can't find the answer you're looking for, you can always find me on Facebook or LinkedIn. I may be able to give you the answer you need, or point you in the right direction.

With that said, I wish you good luck in your learning experience; I hope you find what you are looking for in this book. Let's get started....

Acknowledgments

Thanks to my loving and supportive wife Andrea, and my beloved kids, Paulina and David, for their enormous patience during the many weekends and nights I spent working on the book.

Thanks to my parents Lourdes and Eleazar for their love and for supporting my education and growth.

Thanks to my grandmother Maria Luisa for teaching me the first things about money and banks, and for her love and support.

Thanks to Craig Jeffery, who has become recognized as an expert in treasury technology and strategy and is a very active thought leader on LinkedIn and other websites (like his firm's at *www.strategictreasurer.com*), for kindly providing information about many of the treasury technology platforms available on the market.

Eleazar Ortega Van Steenberghe

This chapter covers the importance of international cash management and the impact of the global liquidity crisis on the role of the treasurer.

1 Business and Functional Overview

In this chapter, we discuss the importance of international cash management and the impact of the global liquidity and credit crisis on strategic, operational, governance, and regulatory issues, including how technology can be used as an enabler.

1.1 International Cash Management

This section explains why treasurers should understand international treasury processes, including what those processes are and how the recent financial crisis made their importance more evident.

1.1.1 Growing Importance of International Cash Management

The financial crises of the past 15 years have shown how economies and markets are connected. Those who have chosen to ignore the international environment and focus on their local markets have been blindsided when new challenges or opportunities arise and had to pay big premiums due to a lack of liquidity in their domestic markets; those who had liquidity and ignored the global markets missed out on good investment returns.

To understand the global financial markets, take advantage of them effectively, and minimize financing costs, it is fundamental to understand how they work, who the main players are, and where they are located. It is also important to understand the following:

▶ **Regulatory factors**
International markets are often subject to particular regulations that control the transfers of cash between banks, companies, and countries.

▶ **Tax factors**
Cash flows and profits can be taxable in your local country or in the country where the transactions took place, and sometimes both.

▶ **Risk factors**
In addition to those risks associated with investing in a particular security, international transactions pose the risk of currency fluctuations that can significantly hurt or improve the margins on a transaction.

▶ **Technological factors**
Payment systems such as SWIFT, EDI, and others can make a big difference in the way cash flows are executed and tracked.

▶ **Accounting factors**
Norms such as the International Financial Reporting Standards (IFRS) can look at valuations, profits, losses, and hedging in a different way than your local accounting rules. This may affect how these transactions are reflected in financial statements and how are they perceived by shareholders and other interested parties.

Beginning with this chapter, this book will give you a reasonable overview of all of these factors in a way that will help you understand what your options are and where to go when you have additional questions.

1.1.2 Key Business Processes in International Cash Management

All treasury departments around the world have to perform the following functions, regardless of whether they operate locally or internationally:

▶ **Bank relationship management**
This involves opening bank accounts, negotiating fees and rates, and setting up accounts in the treasury and accounting systems. It also involves setting up communications with the bank, either electronically or over the phone.

▶ **Cash management**
Although the accounts payable and receivable functions are segregated from

treasury in most companies, treasury has some oversight activities, such as making sure the banking infrastructure enables customers to pay and collectors to recover accounts efficiently. It also helps accounts payable departments to process urgent payment transactions and to obtain confirmation that international payment transfers were successful.

Other important cash management activities involve reviewing daily cash balances, incorporating the liquidity forecast, and deciding whether to invest or borrow.

▶ **Cash concentration**
After the decision of whether to invest or borrow has been made, it is necessary to transfer money from those accounts that have funds or cash surpluses to those that need funding. This is critical to ensure the success of all payments and investments.

▶ **Liquidity forecasts**
This involves determining the expected cash flow for the day, based on purchase orders, budget, and information coming from receivable and payable accounts.

▶ **Investments**
This involves trading, confirmation, and settlement of money markets and security transactions.

▶ **Borrowings**
This involves trading, confirmation, and settlement of loans.

▶ **Month-end processes**
This involves valuation and accruals processing and posting.

▶ **Banking reconciliation**
This involves comparing the transactions reflected in the bank statement to the ones in accounting and then resolving any differences.

In addition to these functions, international cash management involves the following:

▶ **Interest rate risk management**
This involves the mark to market valuation of interest rate transactions and the updating of accounting records.

▶ **Foreign exchange risk management**
This involves the mark to market valuation of foreign currency transactions and the updating of accounting records.

▶ **International cash flow management**
This involves managing international payments and transfers, and may also include managing intercompany loans and funding acquisitions and payments.

When dealing with international operations, it's important to understand that currency and interest rate fluctuations are closely related; a negative fluctuation in exchange rates automatically decreases the real interest rate, and a negative variation in interest rates can turn into a rate better than a local rate when the currency value fluctuates in a positive way.

Also remember that depending on the country in which you operate, you will have to comply with one or several of the following accounting standards:

▶ FAS 133: United States

▶ IAS 39: Multinational companies

▶ IFRS 7 and 39: European companies today, US companies starting in 2014, and most companies in the world after that

SAP can assist in automating the implementation of these accounting standards, performing the mark to market valuation, and providing you with valuable reports.

1.1.3   The Global Liquidity Crisis and the Treasury Department

Next we discuss the historical roles of the treasury department in business and the impacts of the global liquidity crisis on this role.

Historical Role of the Treasury Department

Historically, and up to a decade ago, treasury was considered a back-office function. The treasurer was the bean counter; his job was to make sure there was enough money to pay the bills and fund payroll, tell the owners or shareholders how much cash was left at the end of the day, deal with bank executives, and answer the questions of accountants in charge of writing the bank reconciliation. Besides these functions, key business executives largely ignored Treasury.

Depending on the industry, some companies regularly have excess cash and invest it, while others have cash needs and borrow it; the treasurer must find the safest ways to invest and the cheapest ways to borrow. However, in the past, interest returns were always considered an almost irrelevant part of the P&L statement, and interest expenses were considered unavoidable. Thus, in spite of its impact on the bottom line, treasury was not considered a strategic part of business.

This is no longer the case. The recent fluctuations in interest rates, the large variation in currency exchange rates, and the recent global liquidity crisis have made it clear that having access to enough cash, either owned or borrowed, can make a big difference between staying in business and going out of the business.

Effects of the Global Liquidity Crisis

At a very high level, this is the story of the 2007-2010 global liquidity crisis. Right before 2008, leveraged buyouts had become one of the most popular ways to acquire, develop, and sell companies. A *leveraged buyout* consists of a group of investors, typically with a lot of business experience in a particular industry, who identify companies that, in their opinion, are publicly traded for a stock price that amounts to a company price and market capitalization significantly below what the business is worth. To put it in simple terms, they then take advantage of this opportunity to buy low, fix, and sell high; this is similar to flipping properties but on a massive scale. The companies that enter into this business are called *private equity firms*.

When these executives identify such companies, which are usually worth billions, they must raise capital or obtain one or several loans to pay for them, after which they take control of the company (via majority ownership), take the company off the market (privatizing it), and then make the necessary adjustments in management, assets, and capital structure to increase the value of the company. Then, after a reasonable period, they take the company public again, hopefully at a much higher stock price, or sell the company to either a larger competitor or to another group of investors.

During the past decade, the economies of China, India, Russia, and Brazil grew at unprecedented rates, generating enormous profits, which made large volumes of cash available to investors willing to lend it. Most of those investors saw the United States as a safe place to put their capital, and therefore cash became available at very low rates. This enabled private equity firms to execute very large acquisition deals, taking over entities that, in theory, could be turned in a reasonably short time into valuable companies.

Meanwhile, low rates caused investors who owned liquid assets to search for the highest return. Some firms saw this as an opportunity and created a form of derivatives called *credit default swaps*, which bundled real estate loans into large amounts of debt that was then split into derivative instruments that offered large returns. The returns were then backed by AIG, and, as a result, rating agencies gave them high grades.

What very few predicted was that the availability of cash at low rates would also fuel the real estate bubble, which started in 2000 and burst in late 2007. The burst took place when subprime borrowers started having record default rates; this lowered the price of real estate properties and caused the banks to have record losses coming from the mortgage loans they gave to borrowers. This then produced the "default" on the credit default swaps, which in turn caused AIG to have large losses. As a result, credit default swaps lost value, creating another source of losses for the banks and for the investors who bought them, which included many large corporations and pension funds. This forced many banks to cut the loans they offered and increase the rates they charged to borrowers.

Taken all together, the situation spiraled into a massive volume of foreclosures. At the same time, companies with large amounts of debts, many of which were the companies acquired by private equity firms, faced financial expenses that were never projected, which caused them not only to never become the valuable companies that had been predicted but to go bankrupt or out of business due to their inability to cover restructuring costs, private equity fees, and costs of debt — all in addition to their normal operating costs. This became even worse when the recession hit, and sales in most businesses plummeted. The recession also affected the rest of the world and continues to do so as major financial crises in countries such as Greece, Spain, and others have raised concerns about how quickly the world economy is going to recover.

What has been obvious to some for years has now become clear for everyone: An organization that traditionally has a cash surplus can very quickly turn into an organization that depends on financing to survive; and an organization that has large profits can quickly be affected by its customers becoming insolvent or going out of business, leaving large irrecoverable debts and little profits to offset them.

1.1.4   Challenges and Opportunities for the Treasury Department

All of the developments described in the previous section make evident the importance of having a tight control of cash, finding low-cost financing, properly monitoring investments and receivables, assessing the exposure of potential customers and counterparties correctly, finding key financial partners and negotiating the best rates, streamlining payment and collection processes, monitoring and forecasting cash flows, and automating all of these processes to make operations less expensive. As a result, over the past decade, treasurers went from bean counters to key executives that hold the power to keep their companies afloat, save them millions in financial costs, and earn significant interest income. This dramatically changed the demands of the treasury business team processes and systems, which now must be best in class to properly support their companies.

This brings us to this book, which, among other things, intends to provide treasurers with enough information to understand the main areas that offer potential improvements, explain how they can be designed and set up, and describe how SAP can be leveraged to enable and automate these new processes.

1.2   Regulatory Compliance and Governance Issues

This section explains some of the main regulatory, legal, and governmental bodies, initiatives, and laws that shape the way international treasuries work.

1.2.1   SEPA

The topic of payments and cash transfers across borders has always been difficult. It traditionally deals with foreign exchange rates, considering the risks associated with currency exchange rate fluctuations and the way those can affect investments and debt, taxes, legal reporting requirements, bank fees, and confirmation processes.

Because of its multiple countries and currencies within a relatively small territory, Europe has traditionally been one of the most complex regions in the planet when it comes to payments and transfers of cash. Over the past few decades, Europe has taken the initiative to remove some of these complexities by integrating itself, and eliminating customs issues, currency differences, labor regulations, and so on. Part of their efforts include the creation of the *Single Euro Payment Area* (SEPA), whose purpose is to unify currency (Euro), conditions, rights, and obligations to simplify payments and cash flows between people or companies living in the member countries.

SEPA consists of the 27 European Union (EU) member states, in addition to Iceland, Liechtenstein, Monaco, Norway, and Switzerland. It also includes the following territories that are considered to be part of the EU in accordance with Article 299 of the Treaty of Rome: Martinique, Guadeloupe, French Guiana, Reunion, Gibraltar, Azores, Madeira, Canary Islands, Ceuta, Melilla, and Aland Islands. The authority that regulates SEPA is the European Payments Council (EPC), which was established in 2002 and consists of 74 members, composed of banks and banking associations. More than 300 professionals are directly engaged in the work program of the EPC from 30 countries representing all sizes and sectors of credit institutions within the European market.

This organization has launched several schemas to facilitate different forms of payment:

▶ **SEPA Credit Transfer Schema**
This is a credit transfer service that enables single or bulk payments in Euros within SEPA countries, as long as the banks are schema participants. One of its main characteristics is *straight-through processing* (STP), or, in other words, same-day processing.

▶ **SEPA Direct Debit (SDD)**
Traditionally, direct debit payments have been limited to domestic transactions. However, this new schema allows international direct debits in Euros throughout the SEPA area.

► **Single Euro Cash Area (SECA)**

Cash seems to continue to be the preferred method of payment for consumers in Europe; however, the issuance and control of coins and notes is very costly to governments. SECA has two primary functions; first, to encourage consumers to use alternative forms of payment such as payment cards, and so on, and second, to standardize cash processing across the Euro zone and improve the handling and security of bills and coins.

For more information on SEPA, visit the European Payment Council website: *www. europeanpaymentscouncil.eu.*

1.2.2   International Accounting Standards (IAS)

Global operations, particularly when it comes to treasury transactions, have always been complex. This is due, among other reasons, to the different accounting standards that prevail in different parts of the world. What could be perceived as a reserve in one country could be perceived as a loss in another, and the financial statements for each must reflect the correct version according to which country they belong to. Consolidating these financial statements poses significant challenges and can also have tax implications.

In the interest of facilitating global operations and supporting multinational companies and international transactions, the International Accounting Standards Board has created a set of International Financial Reporting Standards (IFRS) for general-purpose financial statements. European countries already migrated to IFRS, and public American companies are now required by the SEC to migrate to IFRS by 2015. These standards will affect the treasury department in areas such as foreign exchange rate gains, mark to market valuation of currencies and financial instruments, hedging, and so on. Migration to these standards should make international transactions easier to register in accounting and their results easier to valuate.

In general, IFRS provide guidance, but the criteria of each accountant has more weight, as opposed to GAAP, which are more specific and restrictive.

For more information on the International Accounting Board log, visit *www.iasb. org*; for more information on IFRS, visit *www.iasb.org/IFRSs/IFRS.htm.*

1.2.3 Bank Secrecy Act

In response to the September 11, 2001 terrorist attacks, the US Congress approved the Patriot Act, which, among other things, intends to reinforce US efforts to detect, prevent, and prosecute international money laundering and the financing of terrorism. One of the main changes in the financial system is that this act amends the Bank Secrecy Act, allowing the government to inquire about certain information when deemed pertinent for terrorist or money laundering investigations.

As a result of the Act, financial institutions and any person that could be considered a futures commission merchant, an introducing broker, a commodity pool operator, or a commodity trading advisor may be required to establish anti–money-laundering programs, reporting suspicious activity, verifying the identity of customers, and applying enhanced due diligence for certain foreign persons. The Act names some particular institutions as money laundering concerns and prohibits them from having an office or correspondence with US institutions. It also requires the reporting of any foreign account with a value of $10,000 USD or more, and of any person traveling with more than $10,000 USD. Finally, it enforces financial institutions to comply with any information requests from the US Department of the Treasury.

For more information on anti–money-laundering and terrorist financing, visit *www.cftc.gov/industryoversight/antimoneylaundering/index.htm*.

1.2.4 Stimulus Package

The recession that resulted from the financial crisis of 2008 caused a decrease in liquidity in the global financial markets, paralyzing credit and forcing many companies to downsize or simply go out of business, resulting in the loss of millions of jobs in the United States and the rest of the world. On February 13, 2009, Congress passed the American Recovery and Reinvestment Act of 2009. Four days later, President Obama signed the legislation into law. The Recovery Act's three main goals are listed here:

▶ Create and save jobs.

▶ Spur economic activity and invest in long-term economic growth.

▸ Foster unprecedented levels of accountability and transparency in government spending.

The $787 billion stimulus package and the $700 billion financial institution rescue package (approved in October by Congress and President Bush) helped to avoid the bankruptcy of banks due to losses resulting from mortgage defaults and investments in mortgage derivatives, returning confidence to investors and bringing back liquidity to the financial system.

The results of this legislation can already be seen at the time this book is being written. The stock market has returned from a Dow Jones index of 6,500, existing house values have increased, and unemployment is increasing at a slower pace. Several large banks have returned to profitability and started to pay back the funds to the government. Obviously, there is some debate as to whether those benefits will be permanent, but clearly there has been improvement. The Act includes several initiatives, which, in addition to generating jobs and economic activity in the short term, should improve the infrastructure of the United States and aid in future economic development for many years.

For more information about the Recovery and Reinvestment Act, go to *www.recovery.gov/About/Pages/The_Act.aspx*.

1.2.5   Regional Tax and Legal Requirements

One of the sources of complexity in international treasury operations is the need to comply with very diverse regulations, reporting requirements, and tax laws. Mexico, for example, which is the destination of the largest volume of international money orders coming from the United States, has launched its own anti–money-laundering laws as part of the fight against drug dealers; it now taxes cash transactions exceeding 25,000 pesos. Financial institutions are required to track these transactions and to withhold tax. Similarly, many other countries have established regulations on cash flows with different purposes, ranging from economic to political to security-related.

Whenever you design international treasury operations, you should include both the accounting and legal departments in the design to ensure that your process doesn't ignore any of those regulations.

1.2.6 Sarbanes-Oxley Act

One of the most important legal reforms of the last years is the Sarbanes-Oxley Act of 2002 (SOX), which was created as a reaction to major accounting scandals (e.g., Enron, Tyco, Adelphia, and Worldcom). The Act establishes the creation of a Public Company Accounting Oversight Board that oversees audit firms, establishes new rules for auditor independence, lists all of the responsibilities of public corporations, and establishes rules about fraud and white collar crimes. For public companies, the treasury department is particularly affected because this department controls the flows of cash to the outside world, and SOX contains several principles — such as segregation of duties, risks, and controls — that affect this process.

Most implementation teams either have SOX teams or are supplemented by an internal audit team, which uses a set of questionnaires provided by the Act itself to evaluate whether the new process contains proper controls. Usually the security teams on a project work in coordination with the SOX team to make sure controls are properly incorporated into the system security. SAP created its BusinessObjects governance, risk, and compliance solutions (GRC) to address all of these requirements.

1.3 Technology as an Enabler

This section explains some of the drivers of implementing a treasury system and some of the additional advantages of using a treasury system that is part of an enterprise resource planning (ERP) system.

1.3.1 Treasury Systems and Technology

There is a system and process design principle that can be expressed in a mathematical expression: $OO + NT = OONT$. To spell it out, Obsolete Organization plus New Technology equals Obsolete Organization with New Technology.

As simple as it sounds, this formula has sold billions of dollars in business process reengineering projects and convinced most organizations not to implement a new software package unless all of their processes were redesigned. Indeed, the implementation of new technology should go hand-in-hand with a design review process.

Technology can help facilitate the following outcomes:

- A more efficient use of resources
- Improved execution
- Improved security and process controls
- Improved reporting and decision making
- Improved historical analysis

1.3.2 The Case for ERP Treasury Systems

A number of standalone treasury systems, usually labeled "treasury workstations," are available today. Although most of them can carry out the main treasury functions, only those that are part of an ERP system can execute in real time all process functions, such as trading, funding, payments, cash position report generation, payment media creation, and accounting updates. In other words, only an ERP system (such as SAP ERP) can execute multiple functions at the same time in real time and fulfill all of the functions associated with cash management, payment execution, accounting updates, and forecast updates. This reason alone makes the treasury applications from SAP a much better option than using a nonintegrated treasury workstation.

1.3.3 Key Drivers and Benefits of a Global ERP Treasury System

Implementing a global ERP system has many business benefits, making it easy to justify their implementation. Among the many benefits is the integration of frontend application functions, such as supply chain and customer relationships, with backend application functions, such as accounting, inventory management, human resources, and cost planning. This integration results in the ability to analyze costs in more detail and ultimately reduce them, to plan purchasing more in alignment with demand, to plan and control labor and human resource costs, and to make sure available labor is in line with existing work. Other benefits of global ERP systems include the ability to perform multicompany, multicurrency transactions, and to standardize processes across multiple regions. As such, controlling processes and reporting on them becomes much easier.

All of these benefits apply to global treasury ERP implementations. The ability to perform risk management across the globe; to hedge multicurrency transactions; to control flows of cash across banks, countries, and currencies; to plan cash requirements; and to evaluate credit exposure are all reasons it is hard to conceive of an efficient global treasury system that doesn't incorporate an ERP system.

1.4   Summary

In this chapter, we covered the main business processes of an international treasury and explained how they work. We also explained how the treasury department has evolved from a back-office function into a strategic business function that can determine whether a company survives or not. We then proceeded to explain some of the main initiatives to standardize accounting rules across the globe, gave an example of how Europe has simplified cross-border payments, discussed how the war on terror has affected international transactions, explained the impact of the stimulus packages, and provided an introduction to tax implications. Lastly, we explained how technology is required to move treasury functions into their highest level of efficiency, speed, visibility, and control. In the next chapter, we will review the main banking and treasury practices across the globe, the authorities that regulate those practices, and the main issues that exist today.

This chapter covers international and regional banking and payment systems, and gives an overview of the different SAP ERP functionalities available to meet these requirements. It also covers relevant regulatory and governance issues specific to geographical regions.

2   Global Banking and Payment Systems and Practices

In this chapter, we explain the different practices and entities that regulate international banking and payment systems. We also explore some alternatives you can use to manage global treasury processes, such as centralized and decentralized systems, as well as integrated and standalone systems. Finally, we review the different treasury functionalities available in SAP ERP and discuss how to leverage them to achieve a best-in-class operation.

2.1   Overview of International and Regional Banking

In this section, we offer a brief overview of both international and regional banking systems and practices.

2.1.1   International Banking

The Bank for International Settlements (BIS) promotes cooperation between banks across the globe. Established on May 17, 1930, the BIS is the world's oldest international financial organization. Its main offices are in Basel, Switzerland, but it has representative offices in Hong Kong and Mexico. Following are the main functions of BIS:

▶ To analyze and review monetary and financial policy between central banks

▶ To perform research in monetary topics

▸ To serve as an agent or counterparty in international banking transactions

In addition to BIS, the Committee on Payment and Settlement Systems (CPSS) helps central banks supervise domestic and international payment, settlement, and clearing systems.

2.1.2 Regional Banking

The Central Bank is the main authority that regulates payment systems in each country, and the CPSS and BIS have published descriptions of these payment systems. The Red Book contains sections that describe the payment systems of the North America and EMEAP (Europe, Middle East, and Arab Peninsula) regions; the Green Book describes the payment systems of most African countries; the Yellow Book, published in cooperation with CEMLA (Centro de Estudios Monetarios Latinoamericanos), describes the payment systems of Latin American countries; the Silver Book was written under the auspice of the World Bank and contains the practices for the Commonwealth states; and the Blue Book contains the relevant publications by the European Central Bank. You can access these publications by visiting the website of the Bank for International Settlements: *www.bis.org*.

In addition to national Central Banks, there are other organizations that strongly influence the system.

▸ **International Monetary Fund (IMF)**
The IMF groups representatives of 186 countries and promotes financial cooperation between countries to achieve international economic growth and poverty reduction.

▸ **European Central Bank (ECB)**
The European Central Bank (ECB) is the official Bank for the Euro; its objective is to maintain a strong currency in international markets and to achieve price stability in affiliated countries.

▸ **Centro de Estudios Monetarios Latinoamericanos (CEMLA)**
CEMLA promotes discussion and analysis of monetary policy across Latin America.

▸ **American Bankers Association (ABA)**
The ABA groups all American banks and promotes competitiveness of the

American banking system to help develop the economy across all communities.

▸ **Society for Worldwide Interbank Financial Telecommunications (SWIFT)**
SWIFT is a member-owned cooperative that provides technology products and services to exchange financial information across the globe and helps define best practices, standards, and solutions for financial transactions. SWIFT's main objective is to be a carrier of messages; as such, it doesn't act as a bank or clearing house. Its headquarters are in Belgium, but it has representative offices in most financial markets..

2.1.3   Universal Elements of a Payment Process

Independently of country, system, or payment method, following are some universal elements of a payment process (Figure 2.1):

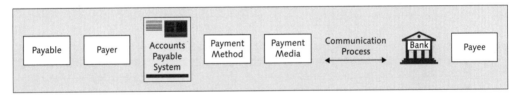

Figure 2.1   Elements of a Payment Process

▸ **Payable**
The invoice due or reason for the payment.

▸ **Payer**
The company or individual making the payment.

▸ **Accounts Payable system**
This can be as simple as a clerk writing a manual check or as sophisticated as an SAP system.

▸ **Payment method**
The form of payment determines the nature of the payment media and the communication method.

▸ **Payment media**
This can be a check, a wire, or an ACH.

▶ **Communication method**

This can be EDI, FTP, RFC, SWIFTNET, or another method. It usually includes encryption or other security methods to protect the information being transmitted. In the case of checks, the communication method is usually the mail. SAP NetWeaver Process Integration (PI) is often used to format the files before they go to the bank.

▶ **Bank**

The bank executes payments by either cashing checks or delivering an electronic transfer.

▶ **Payee**

The vendor or institution receiving the funds.

Throughout the rest of the book, we describe some of the multiple alternatives for each of these elements, how they work, and how to set them up in SAP ERP.

2.2 Challenges for Global Treasury Management

When trying to manage a global treasury, some challenges are inherent:

▶ Operating in multiple time zones and languages

▶ Transferring cash across different banks and countries

▶ Managing transactions in multiple countries

▶ Dealing with different regulations, payment systems, and communications methods

▶ Accurately valuating different currencies

▶ Taking the risk of interest and exchange rate fluctuations

▶ Having the necessary security and controls

▶ Having lead time for payment delivery on international payments

▶ Having to operate across companies that have different technology platforms

▶ Deciding whether to keep Treasury departments in different regions or to centralize all treasury operations

▶ Selecting an integrated package or running treasury applications in a stand-alone system

In this section, we focus specifically on technology platforms, the advantages and disadvantages of centralization, and the pros and cons of integration.

2.2.1 Treasury Technology Platforms

The core topic of this book is SAP ERP and its treasury functionalities; however, for the sake of a complete discussion, here we briefly list some of the other well-known technology systems (at least those most commonly used in North America).

The consulting firm Strategic Treasurer lists some of them in their presentation "Ten Essentials of Treasury Technology," which is available at *www.strategictreasurer.com*. Figure 2.2 was extracted from that presentation with permission of its author, Craig Jeffery:

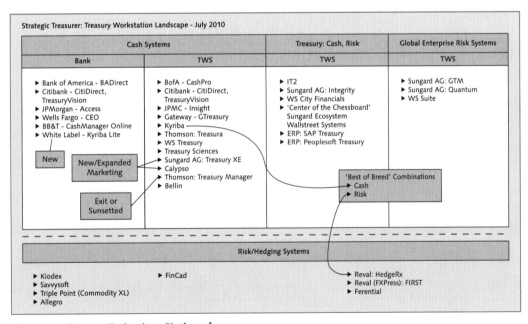

Figure 2.2 Treasury Technology Platforms[1]

---

1 Content adapted from *The Strategic Treasurer: A Partnership for Corporate Growth*, Craig A. Jeffery; Copyright © 2009 John Wiley & Sons. Used with permission of John Wiley & Sons, Inc.

As you can see in the diagram, several cash management applications are provided by different banks, as well as several treasury workstations. Usually, companies use a combination of one or several bank-provided systems and one treasury workstation. Figure 2.2 also shows some systems that combine a treasury workstation and a risk management system.

The main function of a treasury workstation is to calculate cash balances and funding requirements, execute cash concentrations, facilitate cash accounting, and enable the daily decision of whether to invest or borrow cash. Risk management systems, on the other hand, deal with hedging to protect against interest and exchange rate fluctuations, calculate mark-to-market valuations, and facilitate FASB133 and IAS 39 accounting postings.

2.2.2 Centralized versus Decentralized Treasury Operations

Because global companies have to deal with multiple time zones, languages, payment systems, banks, and currencies, the decision about whether to have a global central treasury or multiple treasury centers is an important one.

Some pros of a global treasury are as follows:

▸ The ability to perform payments from one entity on behalf of all of the other legal entities reduces the number of accounts payable clerks that is required.

▸ Less overhead occurs due to a smaller headcount.

▸ Standard processes are used for trading, payments, and accounting.

▸ A single treasury system is used across different regions (not necessary, but common).

▸ Only one cash management process, one cash position, and one liquidity forecast are necessary.

▸ Global cash position is easier to control.

▸ Information flow is easier to control, and access restricted to a smaller number of users in a single location makes it easier to design security.

▸ One source of cash reporting and accounting is used.

Some cons are as follows:

▶ A global treasury usually means that 24-hour support is required, which means you would need three shifts of employees.

▶ Employees must be versed in different payment systems.

▶ Consolidation of cash balances in different countries, currencies, banks, and time zones can be very difficult because it is a moving target.

▶ Multilingual support is often required.

▶ Intercompany accounting becomes more complex.

Figures 2.3 and 2.4 illustrate a centralized and a decentralized treasury process, respectively.

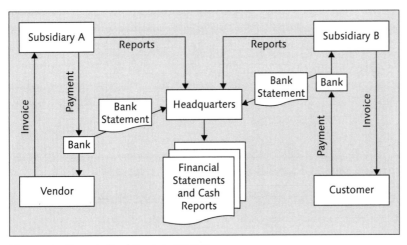

Figure 2.3 Decentralized Treasury Process

As shown in Figure 2.3, the main characteristic of a decentralized treasury is that each subsidiary sends invoices to customers, receives invoices from vendors, runs its own AP and AR departments, and executes all treasury functions.

As shown in Figure 2.4, the main feature of a centralized process is that payable invoices are usually forwarded to a Shared Service AP center, which handles payments on behalf of all subsidiaries. Cash received from customers is forwarded to a corporate bank account, so only the person in charge of that corporate account performs treasury functions; the subsidiaries are limited to intercompany accounting.

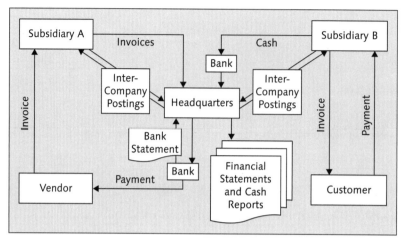

Figure 2.4 Centralized Treasury Process

Typically, most large global companies set up several treasury departments. They usually have one in North America, which funds all of the other centers, covers Latin America (same time zone), and operates the transactions that take place in the United States and Canada (which often represent the largest volume). They then also have one for Europe and one for Asia-Pacific, which handle the transactions in their regions and report to the central treasury department.

2.2.3 Integrated versus Standalone Treasury Operations

Another important decision is whether to run a treasury system that is standalone or integrated. Some pros of an integrated treasury are as follows:

▶ AP and AR information is automatically fed into the Treasury Workstation for liquidity forecasting purposes.

▶ Accounting is automatically done within the same system, making bank reconciliation much easier.

▶ There are fewer interfaces and control figures to validate, and potentially fewer employees.

▶ An integrated process is more secure because there is visibility to all steps prior to payments (quotation, purchase order, goods receipt, and invoice are all inside the same system); as a result, double payment of invoices is easier to avoid.

▶ Reporting of an integrated process and document flow is enabled.

Some cons include the following:

▶ If the subsidiaries don't have the same SAP ERP or accounting and AR/AP systems, an integrated process requires multiple interfaces and is sometimes impossible.

▶ Cash management is a dynamic process that has to be completed before noon in most cases, while accounting is a more static process that can be completed one or several days after the fact. Integrating these functions can cause delays to the cash management process, although design measures can be taken to avoid this. Often, the advantages of an integrated system heavily outweigh the disadvantages.

2.3   Leveraging SAP ERP Treasury Functionality

Now that we've discussed some of the main issues of a global treasury, we should discuss what functionalities are available in SAP, and how they can be leveraged to address some of the main concerns and achieve most of the desired benefits. In this section, we briefly describe each functionality and then expand that explanation in the following chapters.

2.3.1   Cash and Liquidity Management

This functionality is divided into Cash Management and Liquidity Planner. Cash Management is used to update bank balances and items, to perform bank reconciliation, to decide whether there is a deficit or surplus of cash for the day, and to review potential inflows and outflows of cash coming from the AR and AP functionalities.

Liquidity Planner is used to estimate cash flows over a 12-month period or longer. It runs on an SAP NetWeaver Business Warehouse (SAP NetWeaver BW) server — or, in the latest version, on SAP BusinessObjects Planning and Consolidation — and its functionality consists of multiple upload, data entry, and formula features to calculate projected cash flows for each month. It also has a cash accounting functionality that runs in ECC and is used to calculate actual cash flows after they take place.

2.3.2 Treasury and Risk Management

This functionality is divided into four parts:

▶ **Transaction Manager**

The Transaction Manager is used to perform investment and borrowing transactions, as well as foreign exchange operations. It serves to register the trade, settle it, and carry out the accounting postings associated with it. It can also generate trade confirmation letters.

▶ **Market Risk Analyzer**

The Market Risk Analyzer is used to perform mark-to-market valuations of the instruments entered in the Transaction Manager, determine values at risk, and then calculate FAS 133 or IAS 39 postings.

▶ **Credit Risk Analyzer**

The Credit Risk Analyzer is used to measure credit exposure coming from existing transactions, and report on potential credit risks.

▶ **Portfolio Analyzer**

The Portfolio Analyzer is used to calculate the rate of return of those investments and loans entered in the Transaction Manager or in the loans functionality. It can use different methods for the calculation.

2.3.3 SAP In-House Cash

SAP In-House Cash is used to create a virtual bank inside SAP ERP, which is then used to provide several services that are usually provided by external banks. SAP In-House Cash can be used to centralize treasury operations and payment and collections processes, and, at the same time, provide detailed reports on how much of the centralized cash belongs to each of the member companies.

2.3.4 SAP Bank Communication Management

SAP Bank Communication Management's main components are the Batch and Payment Monitor, the Bank Statement Monitor and SAP Integration Package for SWIFT. As a whole, it is used to ensure bank files are imported and posted correctly into SAP, to facilitate payment media creation and transmission outside of SAP, and to connect SAP ERP with the SWIFTNet infrastructure, thus streamlining the processing of payments; increasing traceability, control, and compliance; and reducing costs.

2.3.5 Bank Communications and Interfaces

If you don't use SAP Bank Communication Management, you still need to set up communications with the banks for different processes. First, you need to be able to send wire and ACH files to the bank; second, you need to send positive pay files for issued checks; and third, you need to receive the electronic bank statement and check clearing files every day.

To do this, SAP ERP provides ALE functionality in which you set up IDocs (intermediate documents). IDocs are SAP file layouts that can be used to create Wire, ACH, or other required files. ALE is one of the main components in SAP ERP used to send and receive files from SAP software.

After the files are created, they are usually saved in a directory in the SAP ERP server. From there, the files need to be transferred to the bank, and for this there are several options:

▶ Transform the IDoc into an EDI file, move the file from the SAP ERP server into an EDI server, and then transmit the file using EDI.

▶ Transform the IDoc into the Wire or ACH file directly, and run an encrypted FTP to send it to the bank.

▶ Transform the IDoc into the Wire or ACH file, save it in a specific server, and then have the bank run an RFC to retrieve the file periodically.

With the creation of the SAP Bank Communication Management functionality, SAP made another processing option available:

▶ Use the Payment Media Workbench to produce the payment media file, encrypt it and format it in the Integration Package for SWIFT (which uses SAP Netweaver PI), and then transmit it to the bank using SWIFTNet.

This is only a sampling of the possible options; more details on each will be discussed later in the book.

2.3.6 SAP ERP Tools and Architecture

In addition to SAP ALE functionality, other functionalities are useful for treasury processes, including the following:

▶ **Business partners**
This type of master data is widely used in the treasury functionality to create counterparties such as banks, trading counterparties, and so on.

▶ **Bank accounting**
This functionality is used to configure the accounting postings that correspond to the transactions included in the electronic bank statement.

▶ **Job scheduling and monitoring**
In Transaction SM37, you can schedule batch jobs and review the logs.

▶ **IDoc list**
In Transaction WE05, you can review the log for the execution of IDocs.

▶ **Role-based security**
This can be used to set up processes so that there is a segregation of duties and compliance with Sarbanes-Oxley (SOX) regulations.

2.4 Summary

In this chapter, we began by discussing specific country details about banking and payment systems, and also listed some of the organizations that manage or influence them. Then we reviewed some of the main global treasury issues, such as whether to centralize a treasury, and whether to implement a standalone or integrated system. Finally, we reviewed the different SAP functionalities available for treasury processes. In the next several chapters, we get into the specific details of how all of these pieces fit together, and the business and technical considerations of each.

This chapter reviews the main inbound processes in electronic banking, including the most common practices, systems, and file formats, as well as the business processes and the configuration required to use them.

3 Advanced Inbound Electronic Banking in SAP ERP

When working in a treasury department, the main business partners are always the banks. As part of that working relationship, numerous transactions result in multiple documents being exchanged between companies and banks. Information can flow from the bank to the company (inbound) or from the company to the bank (outbound), and the most efficient way to do either is via electronic methods. This chapter covers the main electronic inbound processes that bring information into SAP, for either creating master data or for updating SAP General Ledger.

Section 3.1 gives a business process overview, Section 3.2 provides a more detailed explanation of how those processes work in SAP ERP (with screen shots and examples), and Section 3.3 provides detailed step-by-step configuration instructions.

3.1 Business Process Overview

Inbound electronic banking in SAP ERP consists of four major processes:

- Importing bank master data
- Importing bank statements
- Uploading cashed checks files
- Processing lockbox files

3.1.1 Importing Bank Master Data

From the business process point of view, importing master data is just a means to an end, where the end is that payments, payroll, and cash records are properly updated without having to manually enter bank details on each transaction.

Bank master data files can be obtained from Accuity in the United States, which is the routing number registrar for the Federal Reserve. For international banks, the BIC Directory is published in Europe. Both directories have a cost associated with them.

> **Note**
>
> The steps for creating bank master data are covered in Section 3.2.1, Importing Bank Master Data, of this chapter.

3.1.2 Importing Electronic Bank Statements

There are three major reasons to import electronic bank statements into SAP: First, so that you know your daily cash balances (your *cash position*) at the beginning and end of every day; second, so that you can update your accounting and bank reconciliation to differentiate items in transit from items that already cleared, and take action on those items that are either wrong or pending; and third, so that you can integrate cash position and banking reconciliation into the same process and system so that you don't duplicate functions.

Bank reconciliation is the process of identifying the differences between the cash balance reported in a bank statement and the cash balance in a general ledger, and then taking corrective measures to resolve these differences. A typical bank reconciliation report looks like the one shown in Figure 3.1.

Without SAP ERP, bank reconciliation is usually accomplished by manually uploading the items in the general ledger and the items in the bank statement into a database — such as Excel or SQL — and then comparing both lists. This manual process looks like the diagram shown in Figure 3.2.

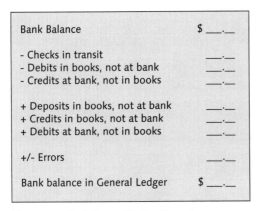

Bank Balance	$ ___.__
- Checks in transit	___.__
- Debits in books, not at bank	___.__
- Credits at bank, not in books	___.__
+ Deposits in books, not at bank	___.__
+ Credits in books, not at bank	___.__
+ Debits at bank, not in books	___.__
+/- Errors	___.__
Bank balance in General Ledger	$ ___.__

Figure 3.1 Bank Reconciliation Report

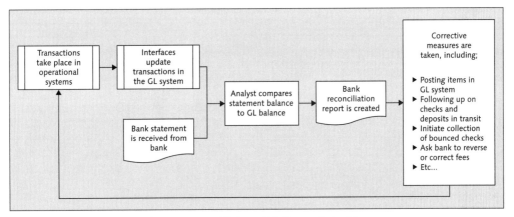

Figure 3.2 The Bank Reconciliation Process Without SAP Electronic Banking

In addition to not being automated, another disadvantage of manual bank reconciliation is that you must manually follow up on each item, which means that there is no log of the actions taken. For example, if an item needs to be posted in the general ledger (e.g., a bank fee), the posting has to be done separately, and there is no direct link between the general ledger document and the reconciled item. Another disadvantage is that the cash position has to be updated in an entirely separate process.

Some software offerings in the market aim to automate the comparison between bank and company records — ReconNet from Trintech is probably the main one.

However, the disadvantages of not being integrated with SAP General Ledger and the cash position report still apply to these solutions.

The aim of the SAP bank reconciliation process is to integrate bank transactions, bank statements, bank reconciliation, and cash position in the same system. When you implement the process in SAP ERP, it looks like the diagram in Figure 3.3.

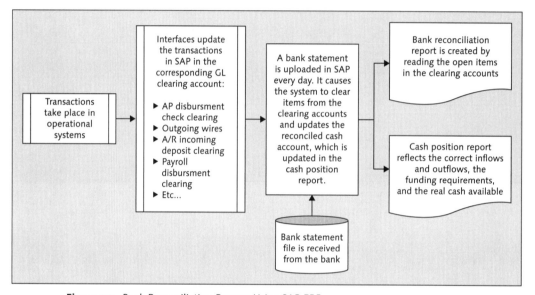

Figure 3.3 Bank Reconciliation Process Using SAP ERP

> **Note**
>
> When we refer to *cash position* in relationship to electronic bank statements and bank reconciliation, we really mean *initial cash balances* (the previous day's ending balances). The cash position is usually a forecast for the same day, and is based on intraday bank statements, as well as the liquidity forecast report and manual forecasts for the same day. The rest of the electronic bank statement contains items for the previous day's activity, and, as such, is not relevant for the current day's cash position.

As you can see, by integrating the accounting and the electronic bank statement into the same repository and connecting the general ledger accounts and the bank statement with the cash position, you can process the bank reconciliation and update the cash position initial balances within the same task. An important change in the process is that the general ledger accounts associated with each bank account have to change, as shown in Figure 3.4.

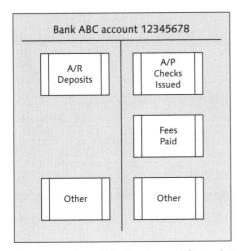

Figure 3.4 General Ledger Account for Bank Account

As you can see, traditionally, a single general ledger account is created for each bank account, and all activity related to this account is posted to it. However, for bank reconciliation to work in SAP ERP, the best practice is that several general ledger accounts have to be created for each bank account, as shown in Figure 3.5. These accounts have to be created to post all of the activities related to a single bank account. At the same time, a planning level is assigned to each account for proper display in the cash position report.

> **Note**
>
> Usually, the only clearing accounts that can affect the cash position for the current day are the ones that reflect wire transfers issued that day, and the ones that reflect ACH payments issued the previous day. The remaining clearing accounts are not relevant, because they will be reflected in the cash position several days later.

```
       ABC Bank account 12345678

  GL Account Name          Number    PL
  Reconciled cash          113100    F0
  Inbound checks           113101    F1
  Inbound wires            113102    F2
  Miscellaneous debits     113103    F3
  Outbound checks          113104    F4
  Outbound wires           113105    F5
  Miscellaneous credits    113106    F6
  Payroll outgoing checks  113107    F7

  A planning level is assigned to each account. ↑
  This level determines how the account is shown
  in the cash position report.
```

Figure 3.5 Multiple General Ledger Accounts and Planning Levels per Bank Account

As you can see, each type of activity (e.g., inbound wires or inbound checks) has its own bank account, which makes the reconciliation process easier and also allows you to track cash flows according to each type of activity. The number of accounts that should be opened for each bank account depends on the number of activities done on the account (e.g., control disbursement accounts will get outbound checks, inbound wires, and ACHs only), and also on the level of detail desired by the accountant and the treasurer. Some companies only create an account for outgoing activity, incoming activity, and reconciled cash, whereas other companies may create 12 or more general ledger accounts for each type of item. Figure 3.6 shows an example of how these accounts are posted.

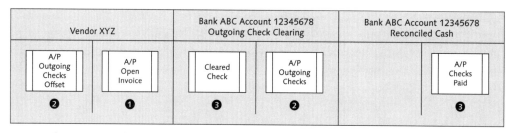

Figure 3.6 Bank Postings in SAP ERP

As you can see, each stage in the process has different postings:

❶ Original vendor payable invoice

❷ Posting at the time of check payment

❸ Posting at the time of electronic bank statement upload

Don't be surprised if the accountants in your company oppose this design. Two common arguments, and good responses to these arguments, are listed here:

▶ **It is a best practice to reduce the number of general ledger accounts, not increase them.**
Although this is generally true, cash accounts in SAP ERP are an exception. SAP recommends this setup, and most Fortune 500 Companies have implemented it.

▶ **Accountants are not comfortable entering non-reconciled activity in the books.**
Although some activity isn't reconciled yet, the general ledger account is specifically labeled as non-reconciled and is clearly a bank reconciliation account, so no confusion should result. This setup is the only way to automate bank reconciliation using SAP ERP.

You will likely experience pushback at some companies, but with patience and persistence, you can get your message across and succeed in implementing this model. Use the previous diagrams to back up these facts.

After the proper general ledger accounts are opened and a planning level has been assigned to them, the cash position report can be updated and displayed according to the type of cash activity, as shown in Figure 3.7. Each account shows the type of activity, while the reconciled cash report shows the real balance, comprised of those items that have already been confirmed by the bank statement.

ABC Bank ABC Bank Account 12345678				
	092109	092209	092309	092409
F1 Inbound Checks	9000			
F2 Inbound Wires		45	37	15
F3 Miscellaneous Debits				
F4 Outbound Checks	800	723		800
F5 Miscellaneous Credits	27	27		27
F0 Reconciled Cash	9827	10622	10659	11501

Figure 3.7 Cash Position Report

3.1.3   Importing the Cashed Checks File

The Accounts Payable (AP) department mails checks to its vendors once or twice a week, and usually several days go by before the check arrives in the vendor's mailbox and is deposited in the bank. The bank then either cashes the check from an account within itself or sends the check to the Federal Reserve to be cashed by another bank. If the cashing fails, there is a second attempt at 11am the next day (usually known as the *second presentment*).

After the bank cashes the check, the bank updates its records and produces a file in which it indicates what checks were cashed, from what account, and for what amount. This information can be included in the electronic bank statement, and it usually is in the US. Separate cashed check files are not processed; however, for reasons related to the specific bank set up or to specific company systems, some US companies — and many companies in other countries — use a separate cashed checks file for checks and exclude this information from the bank statement.

3.1.4   Processing Lockbox Files

Customers in the United States and other developed countries tend to pay by check. To accommodate large volumes of check payments by customers and also give some extra security to the process, banks offer a lockbox service, which consists of customers mailing their payments to a certain address. This address corresponds to a mailbox where these envelopes containing checks and payment advices (a record of what is being paid) are deposited. The bank employee then receives the mailbox, opens the envelopes it contains, reads the payment advices, and types the invoice numbers and amounts into an electronic file.

There are two main file formats that contain lockbox information in the United States, BAI and BAI2. BAI2 gives a subtotal by invoice, and BAI doesn't; most companies use BAI2. This file is imported into SAP to update the cash receipt records, and, at the same time, clear the receivable invoices from the Accounts Receivable (AR) component.

3.2 Inbound Processes: Screens and Examples

In this section, we explain the following processes in more detail, showing examples of SAP screens:

▶ Importing bank master data

▶ Importing electronic bank statements

▶ Importing cashed checks files

▶ Importing lockbox files

3.2.1 Importing Bank Master Data

To do businesses with a bank in SAP ERP, whether it is to import the bank statement, issue a wire payment, or run a payroll, SAP needs to have information about that bank. This necessary information includes the routing number, SWIFT number, bank address, and more, and can be manually provided in Transaction FI01 (Figure 3.8). This transaction is accessed via SAP Menu • Accounting • Financial Accounting • Banks • Master Data • Bank Master Record • F101 – Create.

On the master data creation screen, enter the necessary bank information: routing number (bank key), bank name, address, SWIFT code, bank number, and so on.

As you can imagine, the process can be time consuming, especially if you consider that there are thousands of banks around the world. If you've come to the conclusion that there must be a better way, you are correct. SAP provides programs to import files with large quantities of banks in a few minutes. Access these programs via the following menu path: SAP Menu • Accounting • Financial Accounting • Banks • Master Data • Bank Master Record • BAUP – Transfer Bank Data. This takes you to the screen shown in Figure 3.9.

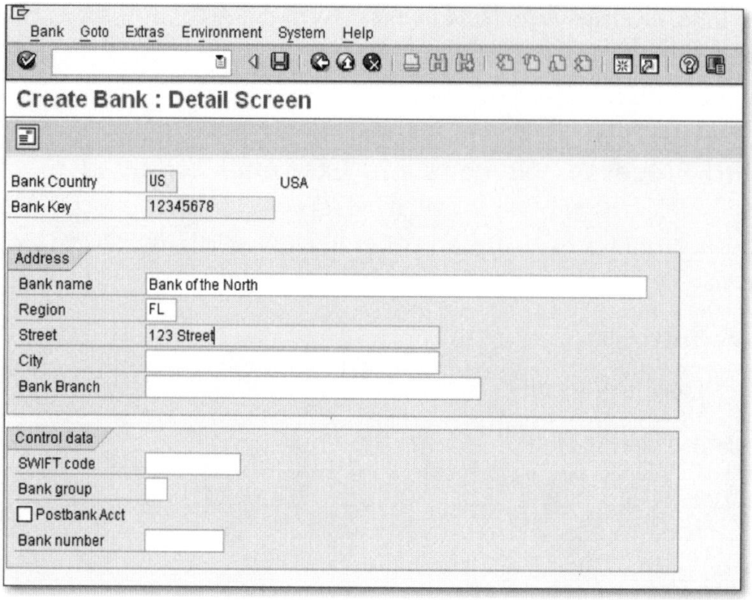

Figure 3.8 Bank Master Data Creation

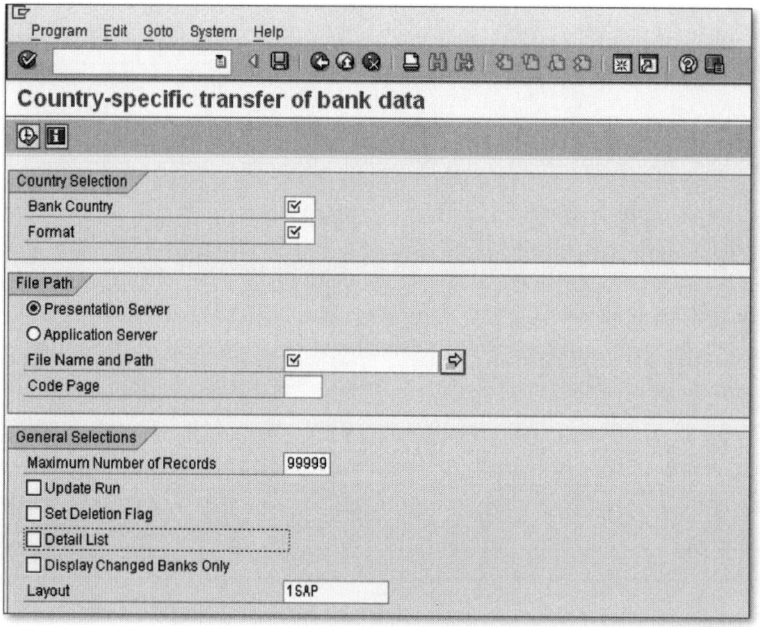

Figure 3.9 Execution Screen for Importing Bank Data

Enter the bank country, file name and path, and output options — such as whether you are doing an update run or an initial load, whether you want to set a deletion flag, or whether you want to see a detailed list of the loaded data. Then, in the Format field, select the format that corresponds to your file, and execute. SAP ERP has programs for the formats shown in Figure 3.10.

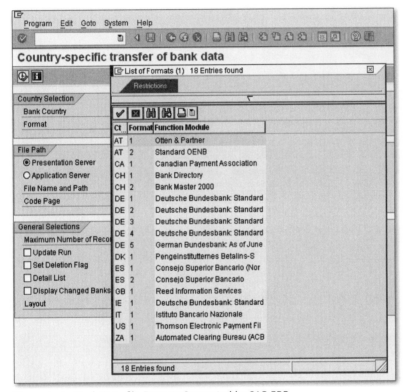

Figure 3.10 Bank Data file Formats Supported by SAP ERP

3.2.2 Importing Electronic Bank Statements

As we explained in Section 3.1, importing electronic bank statements are fundamental to having the correct cash balances and processing bank reconciliation. To do this, access the following menu path: SAP MENU • ACCOUNTING • FINANCIAL ACCOUNTING • BANKS • INCOMINGS • BANK STATEMENT • FF_5 – IMPORT; the screen shown in Figure 3.11 appears.

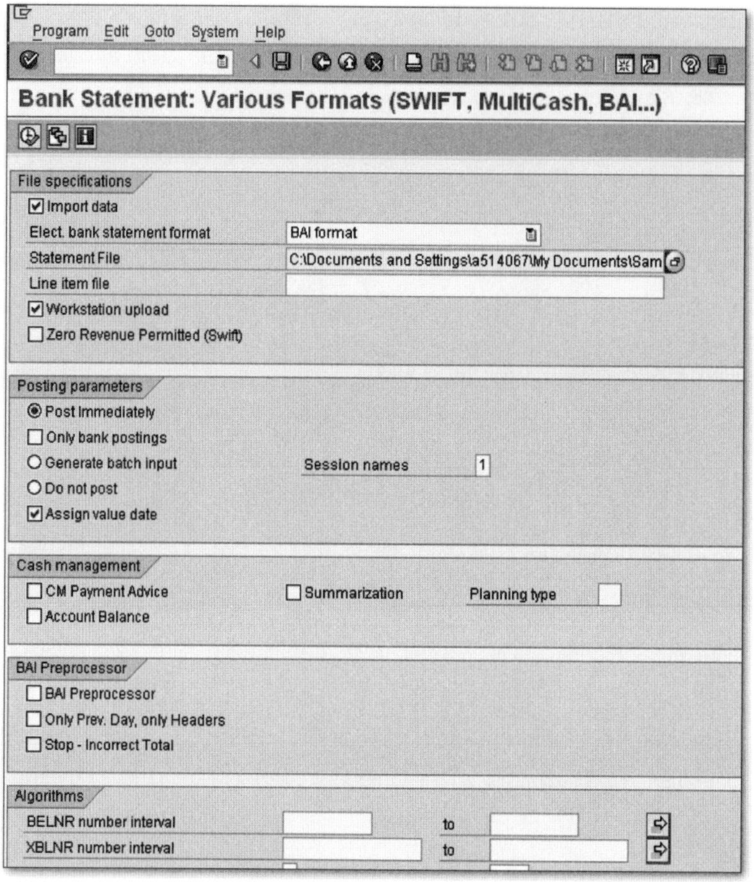

Figure 3.11 Importing Bank Statements

On this screen, select Import Data, and then select the statement format. Select Workstation Upload, unless you are loading it from a server. In the Posting Parameters section, select Post Immediately if you want the Financial Accounting documents to be created right away. Otherwise, select Generate Batch Input to post in batches, or Do Not Post if you want to post it later.

Batch Input Functionality

SAP batch input functionality is used in all components of SAP ERP. In the example at hand, it consists of gathering all of the information related to the desired postings in a batch file and then processing it to create the postings.

It is important to correctly decide when to post, so let's discuss this in more detail. Most treasurers like to update the electronic bank statement of the previous day — which is updated in accounting — but some also like to update the electronic bank statement the same day, which is called an *intraday bank statement*. However, if you post intraday bank statements in SAP ERP and then post previous day statements, the system duplicates the entries in SAP General Ledger. To avoid this situation, SAP ERP offers the Do Not Post option. If you select this option, and, at the same time, select the CM Payment Advice option in the Cash Management section, the system creates memo records instead of general ledger postings. This updates the cash position, but it won't update the general ledger; you can then import the previous day bank statement the next day, update it in accounting, and thus avoid duplicate accounting entries.

Another posting option determines whether to update only bank postings, or subledger accounts as well. If you don't select the Only Bank Postings checkmark, the system tries to clear customer and vendor open items in addition to creating bank postings.

If you are testing and need to delete a bank statement from the system, you can use program RFEBKA96. Access the ABAP Editor screen (Transaction SE38) and execute as shown in Figure 3.12.

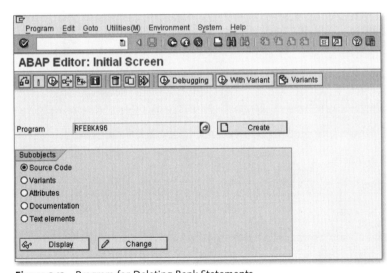

Figure 3.12 Program for Deleting Bank Statements

The screen shown in Figure 3.13 appears.

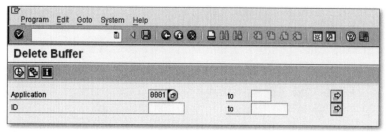

Figure 3.13 Delete Bank Statement Screen

When you click Execute, the program shows you a list of all of the imported bank statements, and you can select the one you want to delete.

International Electronic Bank Statement Formats

One of the issues of managing a global treasury is that you have to deal with multiple banks in different countries. Unfortunately, there is not yet a global standard for electronic bank statements, which means that you must use a number of resources to upload all your statements into SAP ERP. Some of these resources are as follows:

▶ **SAP-supported formats**

The following formats are currently supported:

- ▶ MultiCash (format AUSZUG.TXT and UMSATZ.TXT)
- ▶ SWIFT MT940 International
- ▶ SWIFT MT940 with field 86 structured
- ▶ SWIFT MT940 with field 86 structured and recognized automatically
- ▶ ETEBAC format (France)
- ▶ DTAUS format (Germany)
- ▶ CSB43 format (Spain)
- ▶ CSB43 format (Spain); reference fields together
- ▶ Cobranza/Pagar Itau (Brazil)

- Cobranza/Pagar Bradesco (Brazil)

- BAI format (United States)

- TITO format (Finland)

- **SAP conversion programs**

   In some cases, SAP already provides programs to convert country-specific formats into MultiCash or other supported formats. According to SAP documentation, the following conversions are available:

   - Program RFEBBE00: Converts CODA, the Belgium bank statement format, to the MultiCash format.

   - Program RFECFI00: Converts Finnish bank statements that specify reference payments from customers or bank collections to the MultiCash format.

   - Program RFEBDK00: Converts Danish bank statements to the MultiCash format.

   - Program RFEBNO00: Converts Norwegian bank statements to the MultiCash format.

   - Program RFEBSE00: Converts Swedish bank statements to the MultiCash format.

- **User-developed conversion programs**

   You can develop your own conversion program by mapping the available layout to the MultiCash layout, and creating the conversion program. Tools such as SAP NetWeaver Process Integration (SAP NetWeaver PI) are useful for this purpose.

- **ETL (extract, transform, and load) tools**

   There are many ETL tools on the market, and some countries have tools recommended by the local SAP office or SAP-certified user groups. If this is not available in your country, you can pick one of the tools available in your market, use the ETL to extract the bank statement data as text, and then format it to conform to either MultiCash or some other format.

If you want to access the SAP provided conversion programs for international bank statement formats, use the following menu path: SAP MENU • ACCOUNTING • FINANCIAL ACCOUNTING • BANKS • INCOMINGS • BANK STATEMENT • FEBC – CONVERT. On the resulting screen (Figure 3.14), select your desired format.

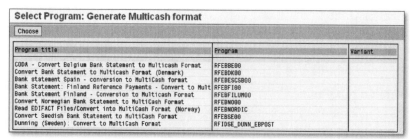

Figure 3.14 Available Bank Statement Conversion Programs

Additional Processing Functions

If you selected Do Not Post when you imported your bank statement, you can post it later using the following path: SAP MENU • ACCOUNTING • FINANCIAL ACCOUNTING • BANKS • INCOMINGS • BANK STATEMENT • FEBP – POST. The screen shown in Figure 3.15 appears.

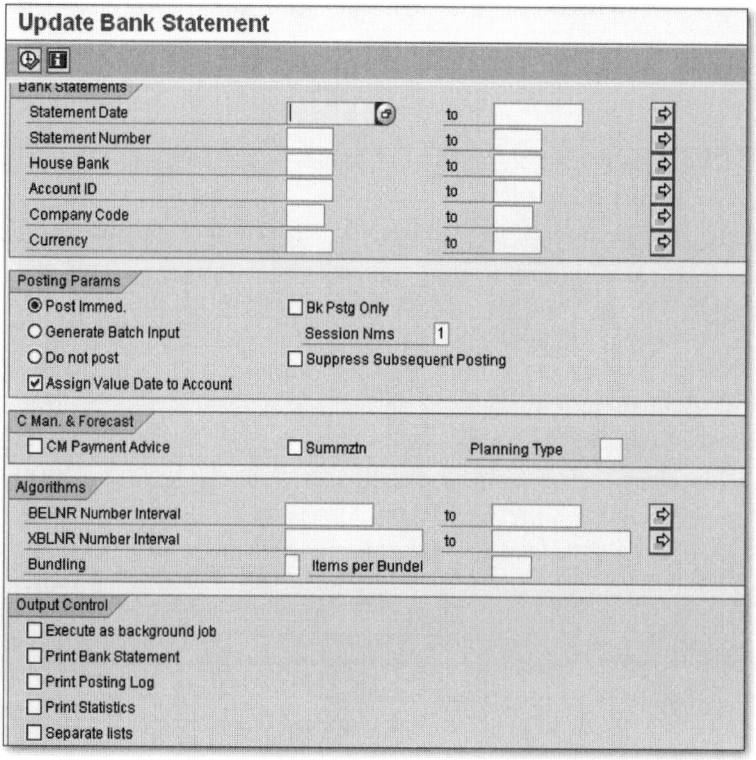

Figure 3.15 Post Bank Statement Screen

Enter the statement parameters, such as date, statement number, house bank and account ID, company code, and currency. Then select Post Immediately and indicate whether you want to post only bank postings, or subledger postings as well. Select Print Posting Log if you want to see the general ledger documents that are created.

In some cases, it may be necessary to reprocess a bank statement as a result of an error, or because you want to process bank and subledger postings separately. To do this, use the following menu path: SAP MENU • ACCOUNTING • FINANCIAL ACCOUNTING • BANKS • INCOMINGS • BANK STATEMENT • FEBA_BANK_STATEMENT — REPROCESS. The screen shown in Figure 3.16 appears.

In this screen, you can enter parameters to identify the bank statement that you want to reprocess, and then select whether you want to correct bank or subledger postings, as well as the document number to be corrected. Click Execute.

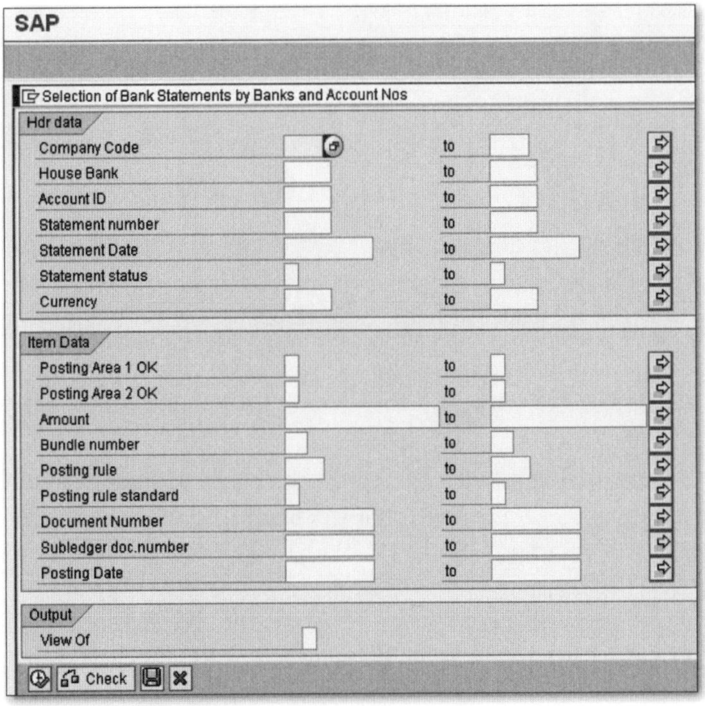

Figure 3.16 Reprocessing Bank Statements Screen

If your bank does not provide you with an electronic bank statement, you can obtain a hard copy or print it from the website, and then manually enter your bank statement in SAP. To do this, access the following menu path: SAP MENU • ACCOUNTING • FINANCIAL ACCOUNTING • BANKS • INCOMINGS • BANK STATEMENT • FF67 – MANUAL ENTRY. The screen shown in Figure 3.17 appears.

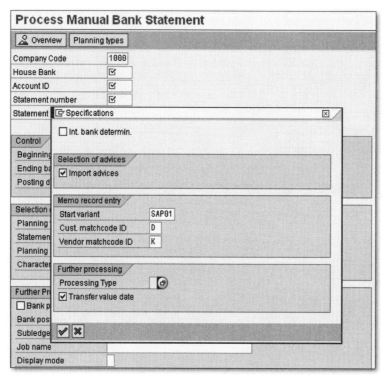

Figure 3.17 Manual Bank Statement Parameters

Select Internal Bank Determination if you want to use the house bank and account ID to find the correct general ledger accounts. For the processing type, you have the options presented in Figure 3.18.

These options allow you to choose whether to post the statement online, or use batch input. After you have entered these parameters, click Enter, and you see a screen where you can type all of the items that appear on the bank statement with the corresponding code.

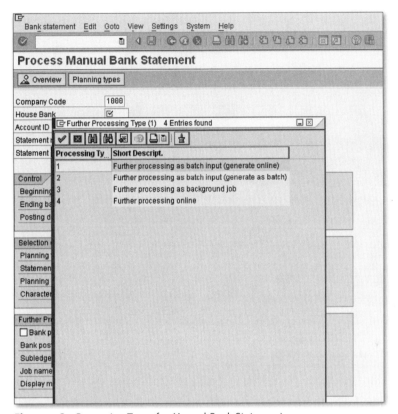

Figure 3.18 Processing Types for Manual Bank Statements

3.2.3 Importing Cashed Checks Files

In some cases, the bank separates the bank statement from the cashed checks format. This can happen because the details on what checks were cashed by whom are not always finalized by the next day (some countries require banks to place holds on checks with large amounts), so the check cashing details are extracted from the electronic bank statement and included in another file.

To import this file into the system, SAP ERP provides a standard transaction, Transaction FCKR. When you access the transaction, the screen shown in Figure 3.19 appears.

On this screen, select the path to the file location. Then indicate whether the file contains prenumbered checks, specify the way the file needs to be posted (immediately or in batch), and check the appropriate boxes in the Output Control area.

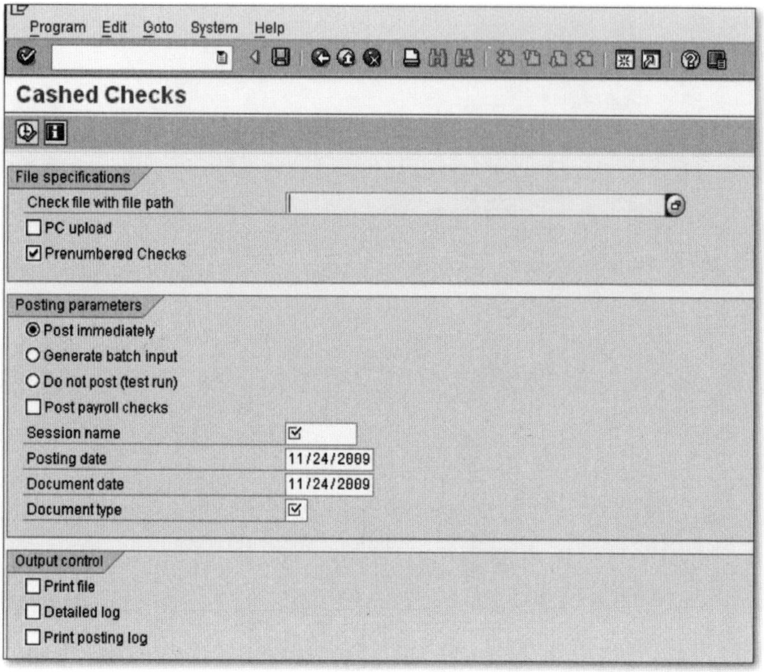

Figure 3.19 Import Cashed Checks Screen

3.2.4 Importing Lockbox Files

In this process, you set up a lockbox at the bank where your customers will submit their payments together with a remittance form. The bank clerk captures both the payment amount and the invoices listed in the remittance.

If the BAI format is used, the bank does not provide a subtotal for each invoice paid; it only provides a total per check, and then a list of invoices included. If the total amount matches the total open items listed, the items are cleared; otherwise, the payment is posted "on account" (a term for payments not specifically assigned to any invoice), or it is not processed.

If the BAI2 format is used, the system provides a total for the check received and a subtotal for each invoice, which makes it possible to match some items and post the remaining amounts on account, allowing a higher matching rate. If the payment is posted on account, the clerks have to manually clear it against the open items. For example, consider a situation where a BAI2 is imported that contains a total payment of $1000 USD, including: eight separate invoices for $100 USD (with a separate invoice number and subtotal for each one), and one invoice for $200 USD (with no invoice number). In this situation, the system finds and clears the eight invoices, and then creates a new credit posting for the remaining $200 USD, which will have to be manually applied to invoices by the AR clerk.

You access the lockbox import transaction via the following menu path: SAP MENU • ACCOUNTING • FINANCIAL ACCOUNTING • BANKS • INCOMINGS • LOCKBOX • FBL2 – IMPORT. The screen shown in Figure 3.20 appears.

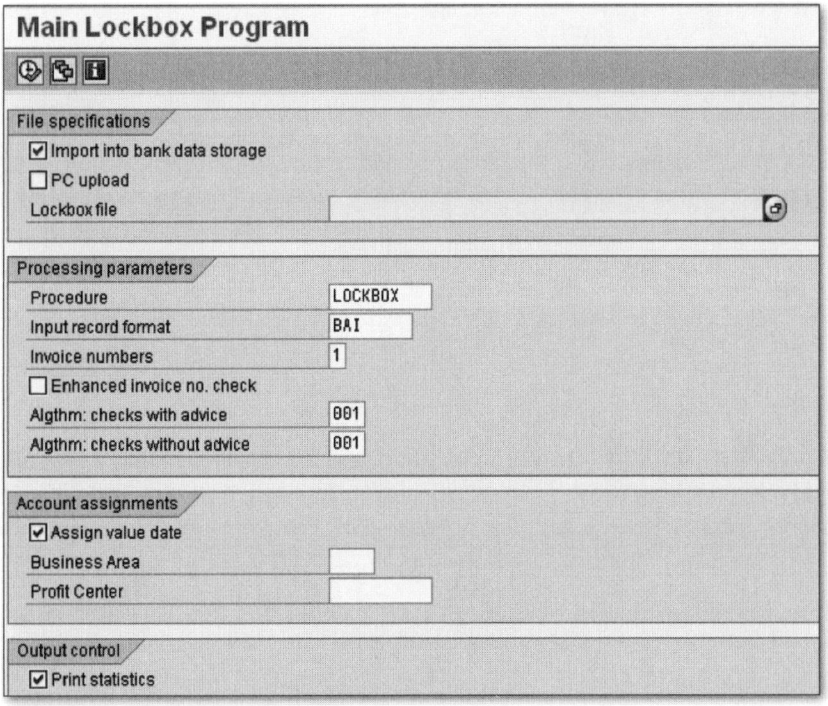

Figure 3.20   Import Lockbox File Screen

On this screen, select the file path, indicate whether it is a BAI or BAI2, and execute. This imports the file into the bank data storage. To post the lockbox file after it has been imported, access the following menu path: SAP MENU • ACCOUNTING • FINANCIAL ACCOUNTING • BANKS • INCOMINGS • LOCKBOX • FLBP – POST. The screen shown in Figure 3.21 appears.

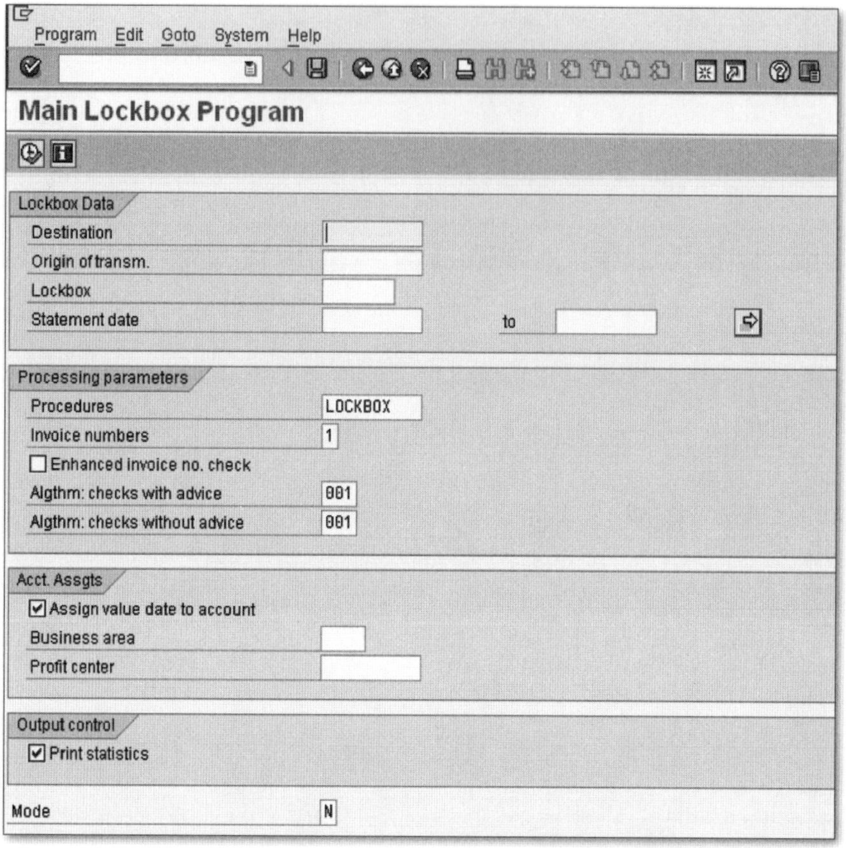

Figure 3.21 Lockbox Post Program

Executing the preceding transaction reads the information imported into the bank statement tables and creates payment advices that include payment amounts, invoice numbers, and customer numbers. With this data, the system produces two types of documents: First it creates a general ledger entry to reflect the cash inflow; second, it creates an AR subledger entry to clear the open invoice.

Sometimes the system cannot find a match initially but is able to at a later time (after more information has been entered in the system). In this case, you can run the post-processing program. The menu path for this transaction is the following: SAP MENU • ACCOUNTING • FINANCIAL ACCOUNTING • BANKS • INCOMINGS • LOCK-BOX • FEBA_LOCKBOX - REPROCESS When you access this path, the screen shown in Figure 3.22 appears.

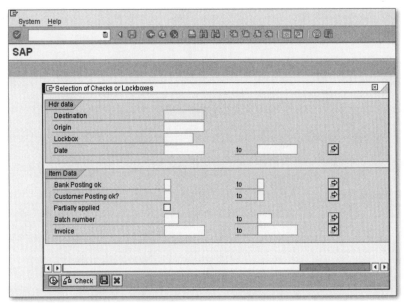

Figure 3.22 Lockbox Post Process

When the lockbox file is not processed successfully the first time, you can try several more times; this is called *post processing*.

On this screen, select the date that you want to perform the post process, and whether you want to correct bank or customer postings. If possible, also provide the invoice number; if there is enough information in the system, it will match payments and invoices.

3.3 Configuration and Integration of Inbound Processes

In this section, we explain the necessary configuration steps for making inbound processes work.

3.3.1 Importing Bank Master Data

If SAP ERP supports the format you are importing, either because it is one of the standards or because you have access to a conversion program, you don't need to perform any configuration. If you need to use a different format, however, you must write a conversion program to transform your file into one of the standard formats.

3.3.2 Importing Electronic Bank Statement

After you have created the bank master data, either by using Transaction FI01 or by importing a file, the first configuration step is to create your *house banks*, that is, the banks in which your company has bank accounts. You can access this via the following IMG menu path, or via Transaction FI12: SAP CUSTOMIZING IMPLEMENTATION GUIDE • FINANCIAL ACCOUNTING (NEW) • BANK ACCOUNTING • BANK ACCOUNTS • DEFINE HOUSE BANKS.

Because house banks are specific to each company code, when you access the path, you must make a selection in the screen shown in Figure 3.23.

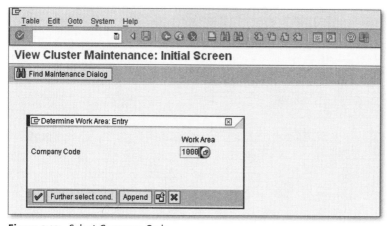

Figure 3.23 Select Company Code

In the screen shown in Figure 3.24, enter the four digits that identify the particular house bank, as well as the bank country and the bank key. (The bank key is the key you created in the system when you created the bank master data.)

The next step is to configure the account IDs, which are the bank accounts that your company holds in a particular house bank. This screen is shown in Figure 3.25, which you access by using Transaction FI12, entering a company code, and then clicking on Bank Accounts on the menu on the left.

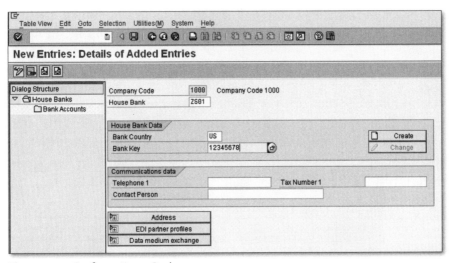

Figure 3.24 Configure House Bank

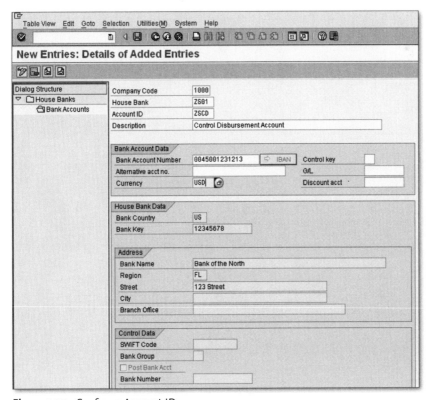

Figure 3.25 Configure Account ID

On this screen, you enter the house bank, the four digits that identify the account ID, the description, the bank account number, the currency, and the main general ledger account.

The next step is to perform the configuration for the electronic bank statement. To access the IMG or configuration guide, execute Transaction SPRO, and use the following menu path: SAP Customizing Implementation Guide • Financial Accounting (New) • Bank Accounting • Business Transactions • Payment Transactions • Electronic Bank Statement • Make Global Settings for Electronic Bank Statement. On the next screen (Figure 3.26), select a chart of accounts.

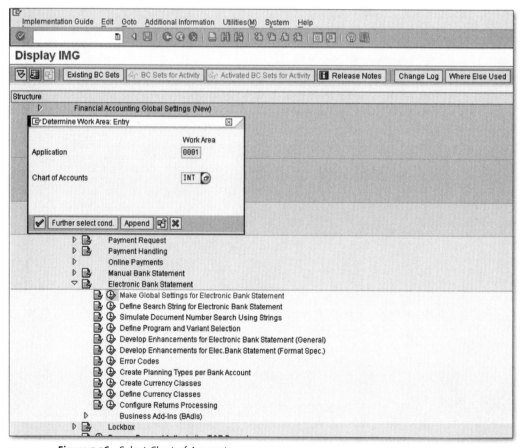

Figure 3.26 Select Chart of Accounts

After you select the chart of accounts, press Enter. Click on Assign Bank Accounts to Transaction Types on the left menu, and the screen shown in Figure 3.27 appears.

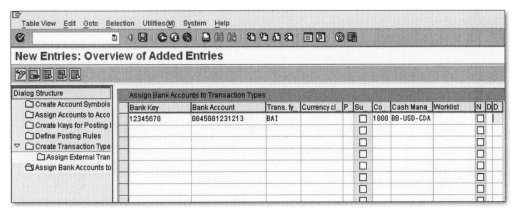

Figure 3.27 Assign Bank Accounts to Transaction Types

In this screen, enter the bank key previously configured, the bank account number, the transaction type (in this example, BAI), and the company code to which the bank account belongs. Then click on Create Account Symbols, and the screen shown in Figure 3.28 appears.

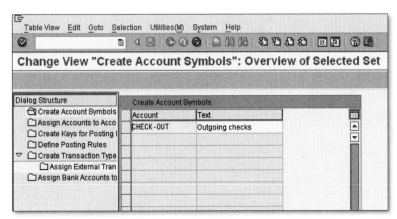

Figure 3.28 Create Account Symbols

The bank statement generates general ledger postings when it's uploaded and posted into SAP ERP. For that to happen, you must configure such postings by assigning symbols to each side of each posting (i.e., to the accounts that are to be posted to on both the debit and credit sides).

In the example shown in Figure 3.29, the posting created when a check clears would debit outgoing checks and credit cash, so a symbol is needed for the outgoing checks account. We called this symbol "CHECK-OUT." After all of the symbols have been created, click on Assign Accounts to Account Symbols (Figure 3.29).

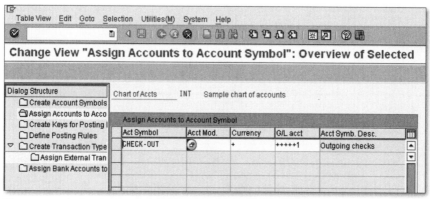

Figure 3.29 Assign Accounts to Account Symbols

On this screen, assign the symbol to an account. Note that, in this case, I did not use a general ledger account number but entered "+++++1" instead; this is called a *mask*. Later in this chapter, you'll see that the system can replace this mask with an account number, using other parameters available in configuration and master data. At this point, all you need to know is that "+" means "any number on the specified position." This indicates that the system will accept any number entered here but the last one, which will be always replaced with a "1".

After you've assigned all accounts or masks to the symbols, click on Create Keys for Posting Rules (Figure 3.30).

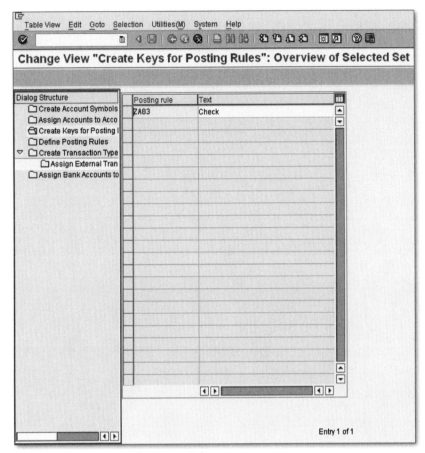

Figure 3.30 Create Keys for Posting Rules

On this screen, define the name of the different automatic postings to be configured, and give each a name; the remaining details are defined later. In the example in Figure 3.31, we want to create a posting rule for the checks that appear in the bank statement, so we selected Check.

After you create all of the required keys, click on Define Posting Rules (Figure 3.31).

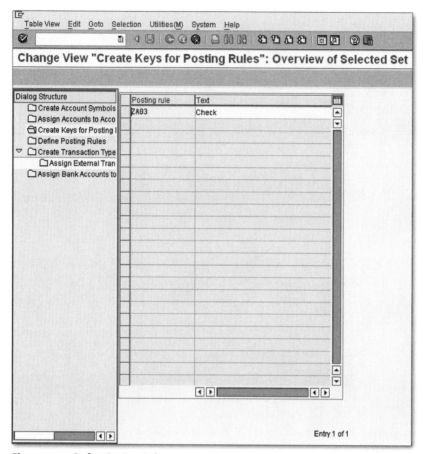

Figure 3.31 Define Posting Rules

On this screen, enter the details for the posting rule. In the example in Figure 3.31, the settings indicate that the system should try to match and clear the check number on the debit side and post to the general ledger cash account on the credit side. We also indicated the document type to use and the posting type.

There are eight options for the posting type:

▶ **Post to GL Account**
Post a transaction to the general ledger account (i.e., the main account and the respective expenses account) without affecting any other subledger accounts.

▶ **Post Subledger A/C Debit**
This option is used for postings that need to affect a subledger (customer or vendor) account with a debit, for example, a check payment to a vendor.

▶ **Post Subledger A/C Credit**
This option is used for postings that need to affect a subledger account on the credit side, for example, check receipts.

▶ **Clear Debit GL Account**
This option posts the transaction to the debit of the account, as specified in the debit column, and clears the transaction from that account.

▶ **Clear Credit GL Account**
This option posts the transaction to the credit of the account, as specified in the credit column, and clears the transaction from that account.

▶ **Clear Debit Subledger A/C**
This option means that the subledger account will be debited, and the open item corresponding to the entry will get cleared.

▶ **Clear Credit Subledger A/C**
This option means that the subledger account will get credited, and the open item corresponding to the entry will also get cleared.

After selecting the posting time, click on the Simulate button at the bottom of the screen.

Because a mask was entered for the CHECK-OUT symbol, the system searches for the appropriate general ledger account by reading the bank account number being posted from the BAI file, finding the bank account configuration (account ID), and using the general ledger account number entered there (Figure 3.32). After the account is identified, the system uses the correct general ledger account number instead of the mask.

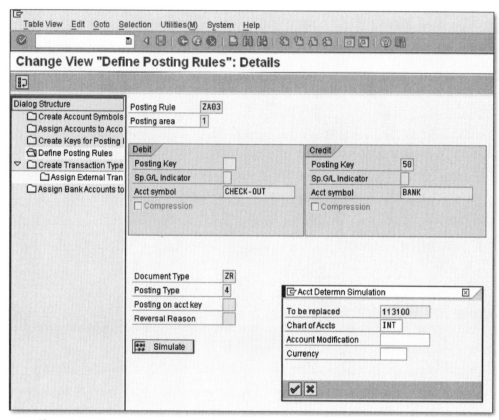

Figure 3.32 Enter Account to be Replaced and Chart of Accounts

Because this is only a simulation, we enter account "113100". The system replaces it with "113101" by using the mask (Figure 3.33).

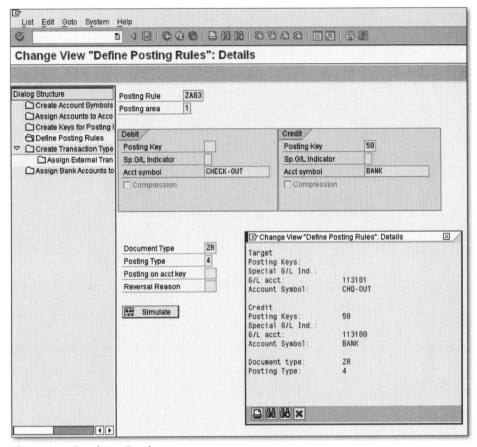

Figure 3.33 Simulation Results

As shown in Figure 3.33, the system creates the posting debit to account 113101, and credit to account 113100, using document type ZR. Now click on Create Transaction Type (Figure 3.34).

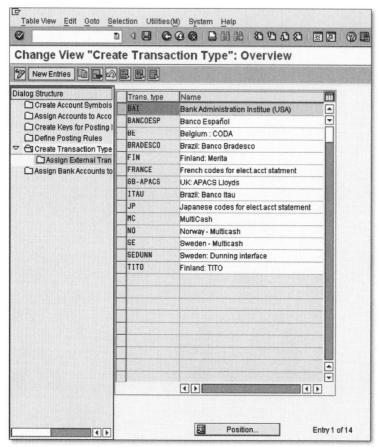

Figure 3.34 Create Transaction Types

In our example, the BAI transaction type already exists. If you are using a different one, select from the existing ones or create a new one. Then click on Assign External Transaction Types to Posting Rules (Figure 3.35).

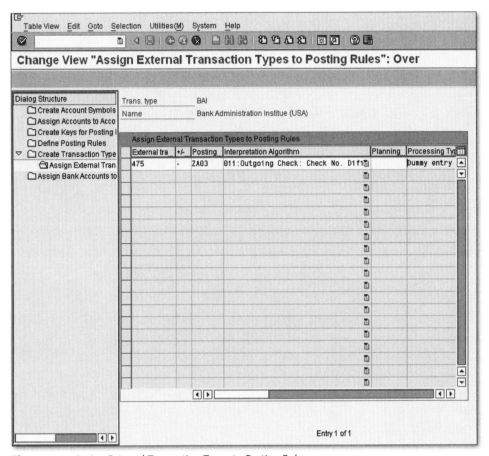

Figure 3.35 Assign External Transaction Types to Posting Rules

On this screen, assign the external transactions (in this example, the BAI codes, which are the codes that correspond to each transaction in the bank statement) to the posting rules created. In our example, we mapped 475, which in BAI standard means Check Cleared, to posting rule ZA03, which is the rule we configured to post checks contained in the bank statement. Now the system will know what general ledger accounts to post to and how to proceed when the bank statement contains a 475, a check number, and an amount.

In addition to all of the preceding configuration steps, many companies find it useful to use text strings contained in the electronic bank statement to find the correct posting rule or to match the correct invoice or check. This can be particularly helpful if you configure the subledger part of the postings, which you can do via the following menu path: SAP CUSTOMIZING IMPLEMENTATION GUIDE • FINANCIAL ACCOUNTING (NEW) • BANK ACCOUNTING • BUSINESS TRANSACTIONS • PAYMENT TRANSACTIONS • ELECTRONIC BANK STATEMENT • DEFINE SEARCH STRING FOR ELECTRONIC BANK STATEMENT. When you access this path, the screen shown in Figure 3.36 appears.

Figure 3.36 Search String Configuration Screen

On the right side of this screen, click on Search String Definition. The screen shown in Figure 3.37 appears.

On this screen, enter the text in the BAI file that you want to use to determine the posting rule. In this example, we entered "Payment from Client 1 – Reference." After you enter the text, click on the Test button. The system uses the mapping and shows the hits on the right corner of the screen.

After this, you must configure the use of the string; in other words, you must specify in what company, bank account, and BAI code this string should appear. To do this, click on Search String Use. The screen shown in Figure 3.38 appears.

On this screen, enter the company code, the house bank, the account ID, and the external transaction (in this example, the BAI code) on which the string will be contained within the bank statement file.

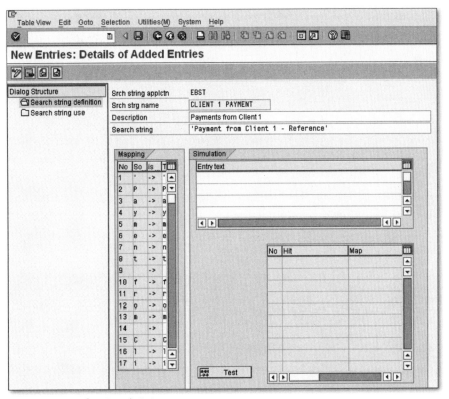

Figure 3.37 Define Search String

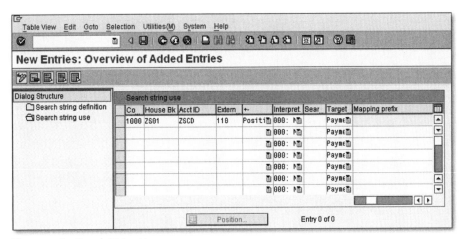

Figure 3.38 Search String Use

3.3.3 Importing Cashed Checks Files

The configuration for importing cashed checks files is the same as the configuration for the electronic bank statement; the only difference is that you must configure the subledger part of the posting rules.

3.3.4 Importing Lockbox Files

Access the lockbox configuration via the following menu path: SAP Customizing Implementation Guide • Financial Accounting (New) • Bank Accounting • Business Transactions • Payment Transactions • Lockbox • Define Control Parameters. The screen shown in Figure 3.39 appears.

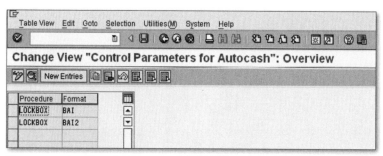

Figure 3.39 Lockbox Configuration Screen

On this screen, choose whether the file you will use is in the BAI or BAI2 format. If the file is in BAI format, double-click on BAI; the screen shown in Figure 3.40 appears.

Because the lockbox BAI file does not have a subtotal amount for each invoice — only a total amount for the check and then a list of the invoices contained — you must define how many digits the document number has and also how many invoice numbers will appear on record types 6 and 4. (You can find more information on record types on the BAI website; such a discussion is beyond the scope of this book.) Indicate whether the file should be used to update the general ledger only or AR subledgers as well. Finally, indicate the posting type to be used.

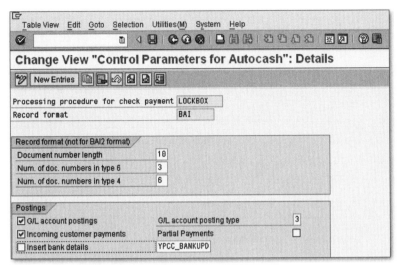

Figure 3.40 Lockbox BAI Configuration

If your file is in the BAI2 format, access the BAI2 option on the previous screen (Figure 3.40), and configure it as shown in Figure 3.41.

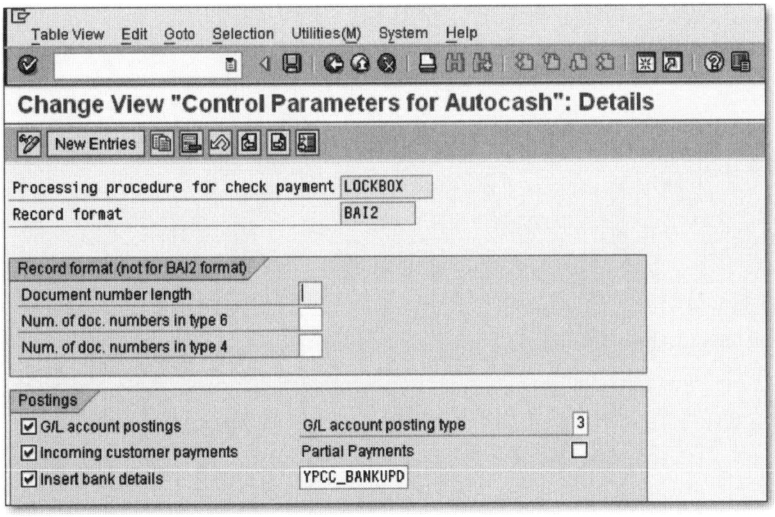

Figure 3.41 Lockbox BAI2 Configuration

Because the BAI2 format contains a subtotal for each invoice paid, in addition to the total per check, you don't need to configure the Record Format section of the screen (which is used for BAI files without this subtotal); you only need to indicate whether you will post to the general ledger only, or subledgers as well. Indicate the posting type, and select Insert Bank Details to populate the appropriate tables.

After this is done, you must configure the posting data. Use the following menu path: SAP CUSTOMIZING IMPLEMENTATION GUIDE • FINANCIAL ACCOUNTING (NEW) • BANK ACCOUNTING • BUSINESS TRANSACTIONS • PAYMENT TRANSACTIONS • LOCKBOX • DEFINE POSTING DATA. The screen shown in Figure 3.42 appears.

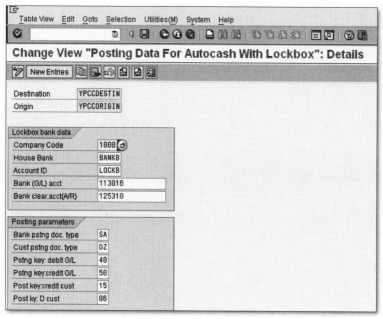

Figure 3.42 Configure Lockbox Posting Data

On this screen, enter the company code, house bank, and account ID associated with the lockbox. Then enter the bank general ledger account and the bank clearing account for AR. Finally, enter the corresponding document types and posting keys.

3.4   Summary

In this chapter, we reviewed the business process for uploading and reconciling bank statements into SAP ERP, as well as different bank statement formats and conversion programs supported by the system. In this context, we reviewed four inbound processes: importing bank master data, importing electronic bank statements, importing cashed checks files, and importing lockbox files. For these processes, we explained the business processes and provided step-by-step instructions for configuration. In the next chapter, we discuss the other side of electronic banking: outbound processes.

This chapter covers the key components of domestic and international outbound banking/payment functionality provided in SAP ERP, including SWIFT, positive pay, and other payment methods.

4 Advanced Outbound Electronic Banking in SAP ERP

There are two sides to electronic banking: *inbound,* in which information flows from outside the company into SAP; and *outbound,* in which information flows from the company into the bank. This chapter explains the main outbound processes, namely those related to payments via check, wire, and ACH, as well as the cash concentration process.

Section 4.1 contains a business process overview, Section 4.2 explains system configuration, and Section 4.3 provides business process examples with SAP ERP screenshots and demonstrations.

4.1 Business Process Overview

In this section, we provide a business process description of the outbound processes discussed in this chapter. To begin, let's recall the main elements of the payment process, which we discussed in Chapter 2, Global Banking and Payment Systems and Practices, and which are shown in Figure 4.1. (Of course, these elements differ slightly for each of the payment methods, but the basic concepts are similar enough for comparison.)

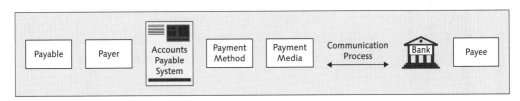

Figure 4.1 Payment Process Elements

In this chapter, we describe the following processes:

► Checks payment processing and positive pay file generation

► ACH: domestic and international

► Wire transfers: domestic and international

► Cash concentration

4.1.1 Check Payment Processing and Positive Pay File Generation

In many countries, the check is the preferred and most common payment method for the following reasons:

► Usually the cheapest option

► Allows for some time between when the payment is sent and when the check is cashed, providing some float that can be used to finance other payments

► Commonly accepted as the standard by customers and vendors

> **Note**
>
> We say "in *many* countries," not "in *most* countries" because in countries where forgery and fraud are common, customers, vendors, and banks prefer electronic transfer methods (which are considered safer). In some countries, banks even incentivize this behavior by making checks more expensive than electronic methods; because of this, electronic funds transfers in those countries are the preferred method, if not the only method, accepted by large corporations.

In the United States and many other countries, banks avoid forgery by having check issuers provide the bank with a file that contains a list of all of the checks issued, with amounts, and, in some cases, payee information. Using these details, the bank can verify that file, called the *positive pay file*, against the checks at the time of cashing them, thus avoiding fraud. Figure 4.2 shows the specific elements of the payment process for check payments, including the positive pay file. For the check, the communications method is mail; for the electronic transmission, it is the positive pay file. Note that in the communications process, the diagram oversimplifies the description and nature of the communications among companies, banks, and vendors. We will cover this topic in more detail in Chapter 5, Overview of Bank Communication Management.

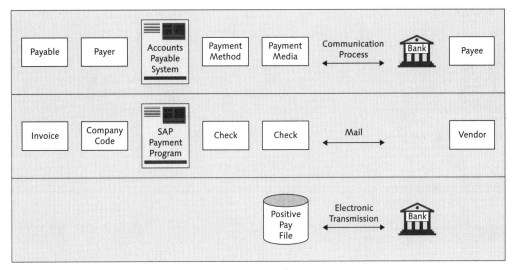

Figure 4.2 Elements of the Payment Process for Check Processing

Next we discuss the check payment processing and positive pay file generation in more detail.

Check Payment Processing

Figure 4.3 illustrates the different steps and players involved in performing a check payment.

The process starts when a vendor submits an invoice for payment. Accounts Payable (AP) then does what is commonly referred to as *invoice verification*, in which the invoice is compared to both the purchase order and the goods receipt for a *three-way match*. This ensures that both the price and the quantity in the invoice are correct. When the invoice is related to services instead of goods, it is usually compared to a service receipt in SAP Supplier Relationship Management (SAP SRM).

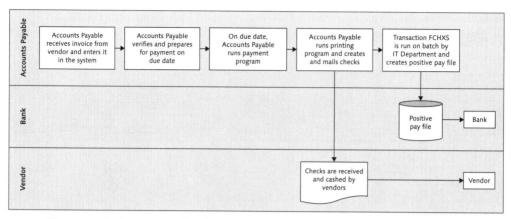

Figure 4.3 Business Process for Check Payments

After the invoice has been verified, it is created as a payable, where it remains until the due date. On this date, the AP team executes the payment program and uses the printing program to produce the checks, which are usually mailed immediately. Every time a check is created, SAP stores information in Table PAYR; the report that reads this table is known as the check register.

Later on the same day that the checks are created, IT processes a batch job that executes the program linked to Transaction FCHX. This program reads the check register for the checks created that day and produces a positive payment file, which is then sent to the bank.

Note

In our example, we chose to assign the steps in Transaction FCHX to IT for the sake of simplicity. Although they *can* be performed by AP, they are performed by IT in most companies.

Positive Pay File Generation

Unfortunately, there is no standard format for a positive pay file; each bank has its own. As a result, the standard program available in Transaction FCHX can be used to extract the information from the check register, and an additional ABAP program needs to be written to create the specific file in the required format. For the sake of simplicity, we use Transaction FCHX to refer to the process that generates this file; however, it will ultimately be done with a custom program. If you don't want to use the standard program, you can create your own to read Tables PAYR, REGUP, and REGUV. (We won't go into the details on how this file is sent because we cover it in the next chapter.)

The bank receives the file and stores the details on its own system to be validated by the bank teller when someone shows to cash the check. A few days later, the vendor receives the check and presents the check at the bank for cashing. The process that follows this step was covered in Section 3.3.3, Importing Cashed Check Files.

4.1.2 ACH Payments: Domestic and International

ACH (*automated clearing house*) is a payment method facilitated by NACHA, the Electronic Payments Association (formerly known as the National Automated Clearing House Association). NACHA was created in 1974 to enable the exchange of ACH payments among banks across the United States with a single set of rules. The Funds Management Division of the Department of the Treasury oversees ACH payments.

> **Note**
>
> ACH payments are also referred to as direct deposit payments. They are commonly used both to pay vendors and by payroll processors to pay salaries.

An ACH is a form of electronic funds transfer. One of the differences between an ACH and a wire is that the ACH usually cashes one or two days after it's sent, whereas the wire is immediate. The price is also different; an ACH can cost a quarter of what a wire costs — perhaps even less. Another difference is that the ACH is considered safer for the issuer because there is more time to detect errors and correct the payment, if necessary. And the last difference is that the ACH file format sent to the bank is different from the format for wires.

Figure 4.4 shows how the elements of the payment process change for ACH payments. In the diagram, the method is ACH, and the media is the ACH file, which is then sent to the bank. The bank performs the last part of the process, in which it gives the funds to the vendor.

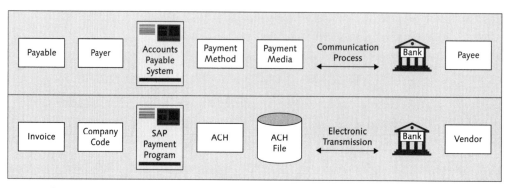

Figure 4.4 Elements of the ACH Payment Process

One of the requirements for processing ACH payments is that you must have the bank account number of the vendor you are paying. This must be entered on the SAP ERP vendor master record. You must also have authorization from the vendor receiving the payment to post ACHs to the vendor's bank account.

In those countries in which the ACH payment method is available, it is considered safe and effective. Although it is usually not free, the prices depend on the volume, the issuer negotiating power with the bank, and the bank's interest in using this type of payment (as opposed to checks and wires).

A typical ACH file contains the following sections:

▶ **File header**
Contains information on the originator, date, and processing bank.

▶ **File trailer**
Provides record and amount totals to validate file integrity.

▶ **Batch header**
Contains the entry class (CTX, PPD, etc.), effective date, and purpose.

▶ **Batch trailer**
Contains record and amount totals.

▶ **Detailed transaction records**
Contains ABA/routing number, account number, amount, receiver ID, and transaction code.

▶ **Addendum records**

Contain important information pertinent to a transaction; the most common example is an invoice number, but it can also be an employee number, vendor number, and so on. For CCD and PPD ACHs, there can be only one addendum record, whereas CTX can have up to 9,999.

Besides the number of addendum records, the main difference between the CTX, PPD, and CCD formats is the application. The PPD format is for consumer use and is typically for payroll direct deposit, pensions, dividends, and utility payments. The CCD format is for corporate use, which normally includes cash concentration, intercompany transfers, collections from distributors, and so on. The CTX format is also for corporate use — such as direct debit and intercompany transfers — and it is very useful for scenarios in which one payment needs to be issued to pay multiple invoices from the same vendor because the multiple addendum records can be used to place the references for each invoice. The file format for CTX can be an EDI 820 format or a text file for companies that are not EDI enabled.

Starting on September 18, 2009, NACHA put in place a new ACH format for international ACH transactions (IAT). This format is used for ACH payments entering or exiting the United States. The aim of these new rules is to stop terrorist and narcotics trafficking organizations from moving funds across borders to finance their operations. The Office of Foreign Assets Control (OFAC) regulates these efforts. The IAT format has a mandatory addendum that should contain the following fields:

▶ Originator name and address

▶ Beneficiary name and address

▶ Originating bank name/ID/branch code

▶ Foreign correspondent bank name/ID/branch code

▶ Reason for payment

Figure 4.5 shows the steps performed to execute an ACH payment. The rows show the typical players that execute each step.

Even though the process starts when a vendor submits an invoice, the pre-requisites for the process are that an agreement to use the ACH payment method exists between the issuer and the payee, that authorization has been given to the issuer to posts ACHs to the payee account, and the correct routing and bank account numbers of the payee has been provided to the issuer. Note that many banks have different routing numbers for ACH and wire payments, so it is important that the correct one is used for each method.

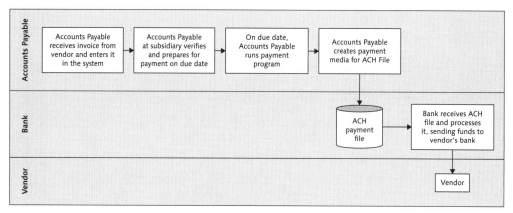

Figure 4.5 Business Process for ACH Payments

If the invoice is approved, AP executes the payment program on the day the invoice is due. Many companies only run payment proposals once or twice a week. After the payment proposal is processed; AP creates the payment media, which goes to the bank.

> **Note**
>
> We discuss SAP Bank Communication Management (BCM) details for this process in the next chapter.

4.1.3 Wire Transfers

When a payment has to be made with urgency or for a very large amount, companies often use the wire transfer method, mainly because the funds arrive very quickly (same day in the United States and Europe, one or two days in some other countries or across regions), and because it is safe and predictable — as opposed to mailing a check that can be stolen, forged, or lost. Figure 4.6 illustrates the elements of the payment process for wire payments.

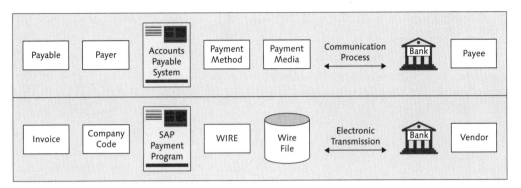

Figure 4.6 Elements of the Payment Process for Wire Transfers

As in other payment methods, the process starts with a payable invoice processed by a payer on the AP system. The only differences are that the payment method to use here is wire transfer, and the payment media is a wire file, which is sent through a bank connection to a bank. (The details of this transmission are covered in the next chapter.)

There are two main types of wire transfers. In the United States, the method of choice is the Fedwire, which can be used for both domestic and international wire transfers, and is operated by the Federal Reserve; most banks in the United States are affiliated with it.

Table 4.1 shows the structure of a Fedwire file at a high level.

Mandatory Tags	
Field Tag	**Elements**
{1500}	Sender-supplied information
{1510}	Type code (2 characters)
	Subtype code (2 characters)
{1520}	Input message accountability data (IMAD)
{2000}	Amount (up to a penny less than $10 billion)
{3100}	Sender FI
{3400}	Receiver FI
{3600}	Business function code

Table 4.1 The Structure of a Fedwire File

Other Transfer Information	
Field Tag	**Elements**
{3000}	Adjustment
{3320}	Sender reference number (16 characters)
{3500}	Previous message IMAD
{3700}	Charges
{3710}	Instructed amount
{3720}	Exchange rate (12 numeric, including one comma)
Beneficiary Information	
Field Tag	**Elements**
{4000}	Intermediary FI
{4100}	Beneficiary's FI
{4200}	If identifier is provided, ID-code must be present
{4200}	Beneficiary
{4320}	Reference for beneficiary (16 characters)
{4400}	Account debited in drawdown
Originator Information	
Field Tag	**Elements**
{5000}	Originator
{5100}	Originator's FI
{5000}	If identifier is provided, ID-code must be present
{5200}	Instructing FI
{5400}	Account credited in drawdown
{6000}	Originator to beneficiary information

Table 4.1 The Structure of a Fedwire File (Cont.)

FI-to-FI Information	
Field Tag	**Elements**
{6100}	Receiver FI information
{6110}	Drawdown debit account advice information
{6200}	Intermediary FI information
{6210}	Intermediary FI advice information
{6300}	Beneficiary's FI information
{6310}	Beneficiary's FI advice information
{6400}	Beneficiary information
{6410}	Beneficiary advice information
{6420}	Method of payment to beneficiary
{6430}	Payment limitation (BONL is the only valid option)
{6500}	FI to FI information (6 lines of 35 characters each)
Service Message Information	
Field Tag	**Elements**
{9000}	Service message information
Information Appended by Fedwire	
Field Tag	**Elements**
{1100}	Message disposition
{1110}	Acceptance time stamp
{1120}	Output message accountability data (OMAD)
{1130}	Error field

Table 4.1 The Structure of a Fedwire File (Cont.)

SAP doesn't directly produce Fedwire files; instead, the payment program produces an IDoc, which is then converted into the Fedwire format via ABAP. However, if you are using SAP BCM, SAP ERP uses a format created using the Payment Media Workbench instead of the IDoc. SAP ERP comes with some predelivered formats, and you can develop new ones as necessary.

> **Note**
>
> Instructions on how to map payment media formats to payment runs in SAP BCM are provided in the next chapter.

To map files into the Fedwire format, you need to obtain the detailed file description of the Fedwire file at *www.frbservices.org/campaigns/fedwireformat/index.html*. Outside of the United States, the prevalent system is the SWIFT wire, which can be used within the same country or for international wires. SWIFT (Society for World Interbank Financial Telecommunications) is a communications vendor that offers message exchange through a network of banks and financial institutions. SWIFT also produces software and financial services; within SWIFT, the most common format is the MT103.

Table 4.2 shows the structure of the MT103 file at a high level.

Tag	Field Name
20	Sender's Reference
13C	Time Indication
23B	Bank Operation Code
23E	Instruction Code
26T	Transaction Type Code Value Date/Currency/Interbank/Settled
32	Amount
33B	Currency/Instructed Amount
36	Exchange Rate
50a	Ordering Customer
51A	Sending Institution
52a	Ordering Institution
53a	Sender's Correspondent
54a	Receiver's Correspondent
55a	Third Reimbursement Institution

Table 4.2 Structure of the MT103 File

Tag	Field Name
56a	Intermediary Institution
57a	Account with Institution
59a	Beneficiary Customer
70	Remittance Information
71A	Details of Charges
71F	Sender's Charges
71G	Receiver's Charges
72	Sender to Receiver Info
77B	Regulatory Reporting
77T	Envelope Contents

Table 4.2 Structure of the MT103 File (Cont.)

As with Fedwires, SAP ERP doesn't automatically produce an MT103 format, so it is necessary to map the IDoc format to the MT103. And, again as with Fedwire, if you are using SAP BCM, SAP doesn't use the IDoc and needs to use a format created using the Payment Media Workbench.

> **Note**
>
> Instructions on how to assign payment media formats to payment runs in SAP BCM are provided in the next chapter.

> **Note**
>
> You can get more information about MT103 and all other SWIFT formats at *www. SWIFT.com*.

Figure 4.7 shows the steps involved in executing a wire transfer payment. The rows show the typical players that execute each step. Although the figure shows the process for wire payments that originate from a payable invoice, wire transfers are also used for many other purposes, such as cash concentration, real estate acquisitions, company acquisitions, tax payments, and so on.

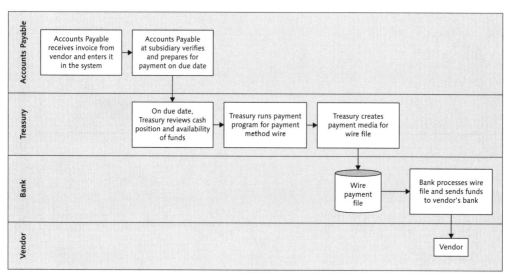

Figure 4.7 Business Process for Wire Payments

Even though the wire payment process starts when a vendor submits an invoice, a prerequisite for this process is that the correct routing and bank account number of the payee has been provided to the issuer. Note that many banks have different routing numbers for ACH and wire payments, so it is important that the correct one is used for each method.

Two important considerations make wire processing different from ACH processing:

▶ Wire transfers move cash out of your bank account immediately after being processed by the bank, so you must make sure the bank from where the funds are coming has enough cash to cover it. The cash position report is usually reviewed before the payment takes place to ensure this happens.

▶ In most companies, the treasury department prefers to handle wire payments due to the reason just listed and because, in many cases, if the wrong wire transfer is made, it is difficult to get the cash back. (This changes from country to country, depending on the specific regulations and circumstances.)

On the day the invoice is due, the treasury department reviews the cash position to make sure the account has the required funds and then executes the payment program. After the proposal is processed, the treasury department creates the payment media, which then goes to the bank.

> **Note**
>
> As with ACH, we won't cover SAP Bank Communication Management (SAP BCM) details for this process in this chapter because they are covered in Chapter 5, Overview of Bank Communication Management.

4.1.4 Cash Concentration

Cash concentration is the process that results from reviewing projected inflows and outflows of cash from each bank account, and then deciding how much cash has to go into or out of each account. This process also removes funds that are in excess of the minimum required at each account and places them into a controlled disbursement or investment account.

Figure 4.8 shows the main steps in the cash concentration process.

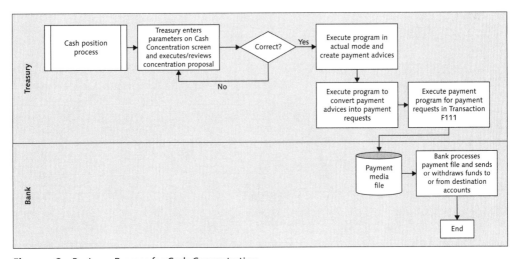

Figure 4.8 Business Process for Cash Concentration

As shown in the diagram, the last part of the cash position process consists of moving the cash between accounts to leave the correct balance everywhere. (For more information on the cash position process, please see Chapter 9, Global Cash Position Reporting and Management.) There are two main ways to do this. First, you can ask the bank to automatically sweep everything that exceeds a certain balance from each account (when that desired balance is zero, this process is called ZBA, for *zero balance account*). Alternatively, you can process your cash concentration in your treasury system (i.e., SAP ERP) and send the instructions to the bank via a wire transfer file or an ACH file.

Your choice of either option depends on the accuracy of your cash forecast. If your cash forecast is just an order of magnitude of where you will be every day, it is better to have the bank run an automatic sweep every evening and invest your leftover cash in an overnight money market fund. If your cash forecast is reasonably accurate on most days, it is better to try to close your cash position around noon, and negotiate the best possible rate either to invest or borrow at that time. Companies that have accurate cash forecasts have the best chance of obtaining good interest revenue or reducing their financial costs.

The cash concentration program in SAP ERP allows you to do a test run and create a concentration proposal. If you review it and agree to it, you run it in Actual mode. After you do this, the system creates payment advices, which can be turned into payment requests by another program. Those are then paid using the Payment Program for Payment Requests, Transaction F111.

The cash concentration process always results either in wire transfers or ACHs, which are sent to the bank. The bank then moves the funds into the destination accounts.

4.2 System Configuration

In this section, we describe the necessary configuration for each of the processes described in the previous section.

> **Note**
>
> Bank master data creation was covered in the previous chapter, so it is not discussed here.

The section is divided into the following subsections:

▶ House bank and account ID creation, including ALE configuration

▶ Payment program configuration

4.2.1 House Bank and Account ID Creation (Including ALE Configuration)

> **Note**
>
> Although house bank configuration was covered in the previous chapter, this section contains additional specific details that are unique to outbound processes.

A house bank is a bank at which your company has a bank account. It is different from bank master data because you need bank master data for all of your vendors' and employees' banks, or at least for those for which you issue ACHs or wire transfers — regardless of whether you have an account with them or not. House banks, on the other hand, are only required if your company *has* an account with the bank. Create a house bank via the following menu path: SAP CUSTOMIZING IMPLEMENTATION GUIDE • FINANCIAL ACCOUNTING • BANK ACCOUNTING • BANK ACCOUNTS • DEFINE HOUSE BANKS. When you access the menu path, the screen shown in Figure 4.9 appears.

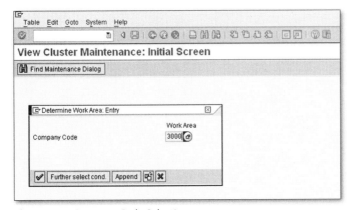

Figure 4.9 Company Code Selection

Because house banks are always associated with the company code in which you have the account, you need to select the company code before you access the creation screen. Enter the company code, and press Enter. The screen shown in Figure 4.10 appears.

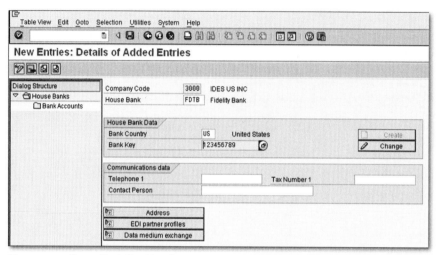

Figure 4.10 House Bank Creation Screen

Enter a three- or four-digit identifier for the house bank; common examples are BOA (Bank of America) and CITI (Citibank). (When a company deals with hundreds or even thousands of banks, it may be necessary to enter a consecutive number from 0001 to 9999; however, this is fairly rare.) Enter the country key in the Bank Country field, and the routing number in the Bank Key field (which is usually the ABA number for the bank). If you want to enter additional address details, you can do so by clicking on the Address button; however, if you updated the bank master data with the address information, this will already be populated.

Now click on the EDI Partner Profiles button, and the screen shown in Figure 4.11 appears.

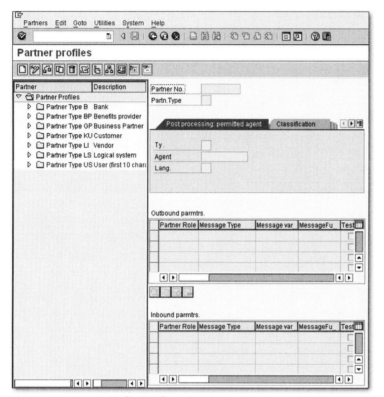

Figure 4.11 Partner Profile Configuration

On the left side of the screen, open the folder for Partner Type B. Enter the partner type and number, and go to the Post Processing Permitted Agent tab, which is shown in Figure 4.12.

On this tab, you can enter the user ID of the person responsible for answering questions and postprocessing IDocs related to the payment. After that, create another session, and execute Transaction WE21 (Figure 4.13).

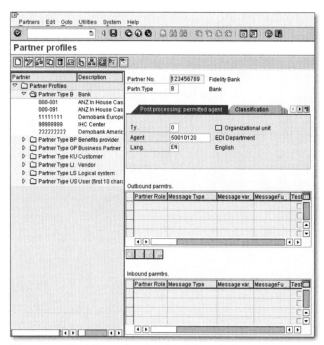

Figure 4.12 Post Processing Permitted Agent Tab

Figure 4.13 IDoc Port Creation Screen

In the resulting screen, click on the Create button. The screen shown in Figure 4.14 appears.

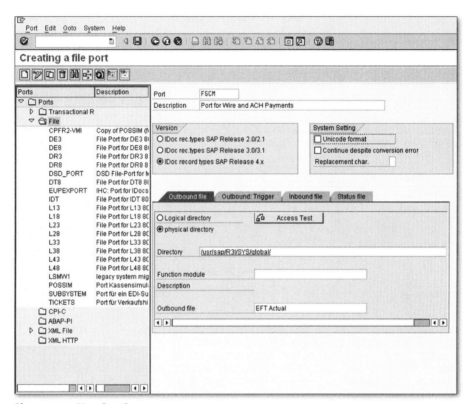

Figure 4.14 New Port Screen

A *port* represents a location in a directory (usually secured) and a file name. In this case, enter the path to the directory in the Directory field, and then enter the file name in the Outbound File field. (The same applies if you need to configure it for inbound files, but outbound is what is relevant in this chapter.) After you complete this step, go back to the previous session, where you had opened the ALE partner profile for the house bank (Figure 4.15).

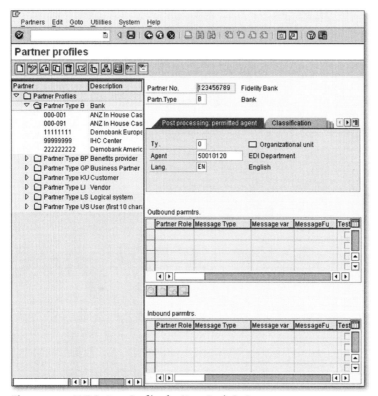

Figure 4.15 ALE Partner Profiles for New Bank Partner

On this screen, click on the Create Outbound Parameters button. The screen shown in Figure 4.16 appears.

In ALE, a message type defines the type of IDoc to be processed, in other words, the type of file layout and processing that needs to be used. On this screen, select message type PAYEXT, which is the most common message type used when processing payments. On the receiver port screen, enter the port that you just created in the previous step. In the Basic Type field, enter "PEXR2002", which is also the most common type for bank payments. Now select the Transfer IDoc Immediately button. Save the parameters, and click the Back button, which brings you to the screen shown in Figure 4.17.

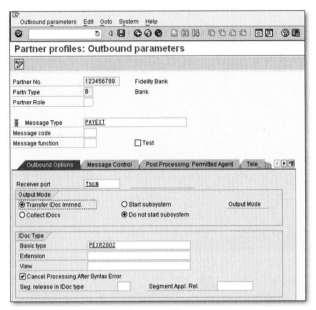

Figure 4.16 Outbound Parameter Screen

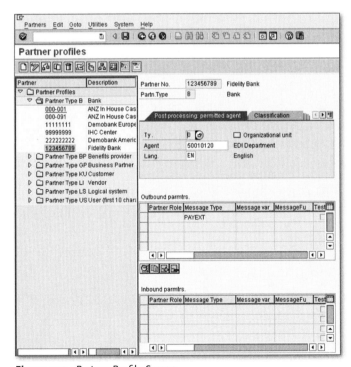

Figure 4.17 Partner Profile Screen

On this screen, click the + button on the Outbound Parameter section of the screen to add another parameter (Figure 4.18).

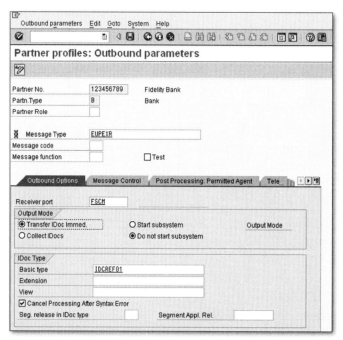

Figure 4.18 Additional Outbound Parameter

In the Message Type field, use Message Type EUPEXR and use Basic Type IDCREF01, which is a required reference message for electronic signature. Select the Transfer IDoc Immediately button, save, and go back. The next step is to add inbound parameters (Figure 4.19).

On this screen, select message type EUPEXR, process code FI04, and the Trigger Immediately radio button. At the end, your partner profile screen should look like the one shown in Figure 4.20.

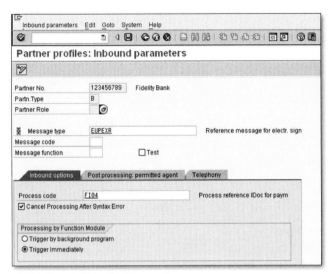

Figure 4.19 Inbound Parameter Screen

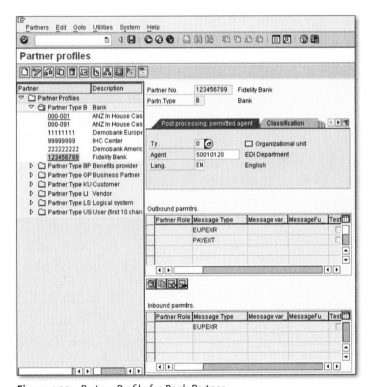

Figure 4.20 Partner Profile for Bank Partner

Now save your work, and go back to the house bank creation screen (Figure 4.21). If you accidentally closed the session, you can use Transaction FI12 to get back.

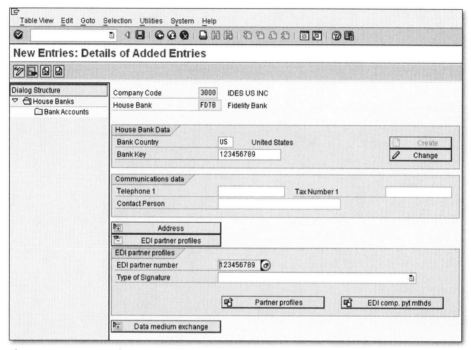

Figure 4.21 House Bank Creation Screen

Now click on the EDI Comp. Pyt Methods button. The screen shown in Figure 4.22 appears.

Enter the payment methods for wire transfers and ACHs. If the payment program is not yet configured, make a note to come back and do this after you are done. (Payment program configuration is covered in Section 4.2.2, Payment Program Configuration.) When completed, the screen should look like the one shown in Figure 4.23.

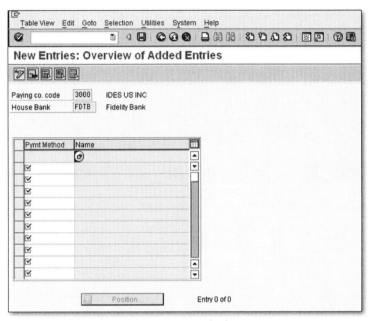

Figure 4.22   EDI Compatible Payment Methods

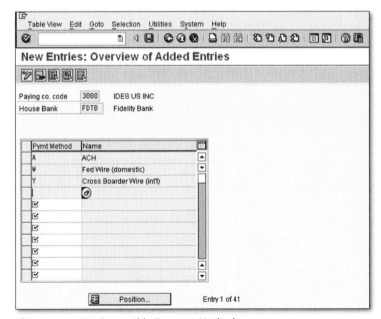

Figure 4.23   EDI Compatible Payment Methods

After this is done, go back to the house bank creation screen (Figure 4.24).

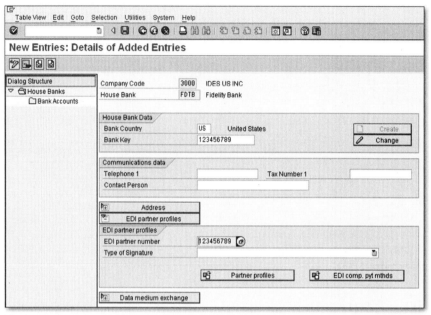

Figure 4.24 House Bank Creation Screen

Click on the Data Medium Exchange button, and the section of the screen shown in Figure 4.25 appears.

In the Bank Receiving DME field, enter the SWIFT code of the bank. Depending on the particular bank and country, you may need to fill some of the other fields as well. Click on each field, press [F1] for an explanation of each field, and then ask your bank which fields are required. Most banks provide specific instructions to configure SAP ERP to send payments to them. After this step is done, save, and then click on House Banks (Figure 4.26).

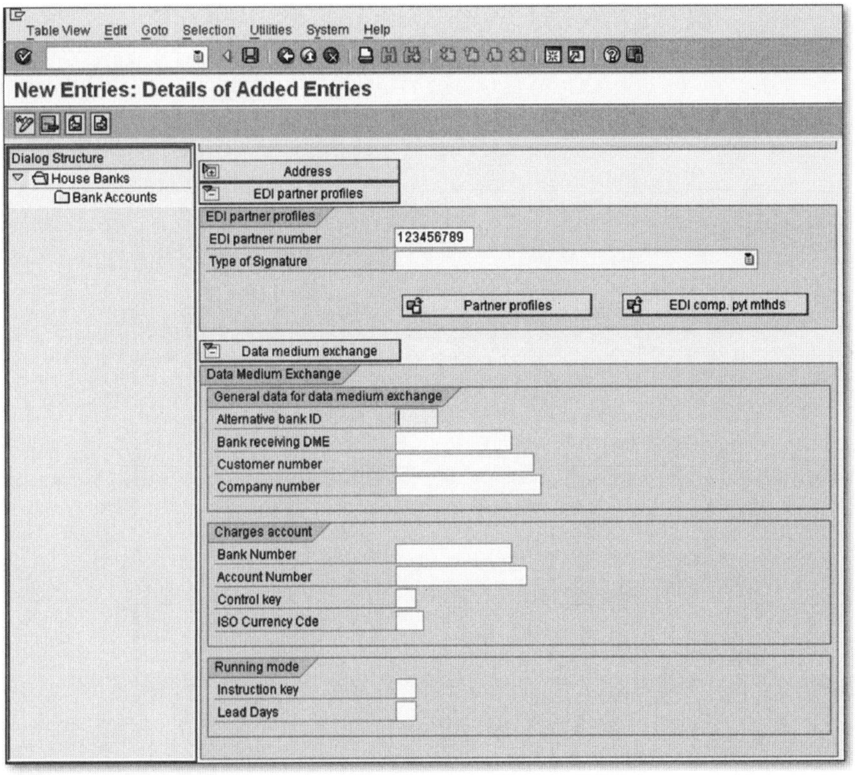

Figure 4.25 Data Medium Exchange for House Bank

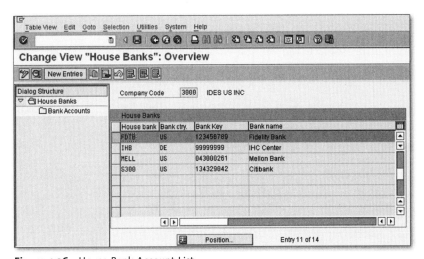

Figure 4.26 House Bank Account List

Select the corresponding house bank, and then click on Bank Accounts (Figure 4.27).

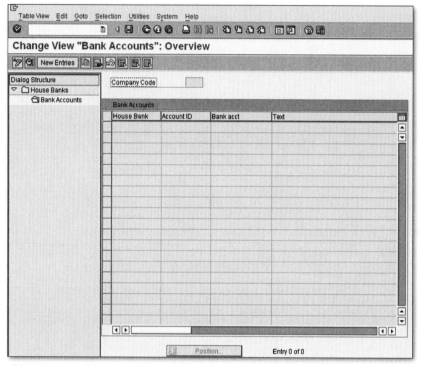

Figure 4.27 Bank Account Creation Screen

Click the New Entries button, and the screen shown in Figure 4.28 appears.

On this screen, the three most important fields are Bank Account Number, G/L, and Currency.

4.2.2 Payment Program Configuration

When configuring the payment program, most of the steps required can be done in Transaction FBZP. When you access it, the screen shown in Figure 4.29 appears.

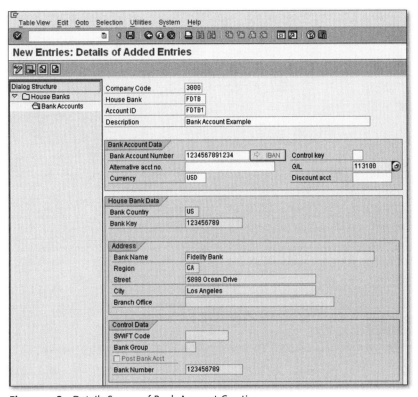

Figure 4.28 Details Screen of Bank Account Creation

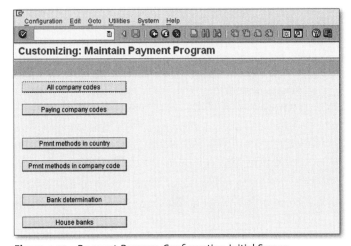

Figure 4.29 Payment Program Configuration Initial Screen

Click on All Company Codes, and the screen shown in Figure 4.30 appears.

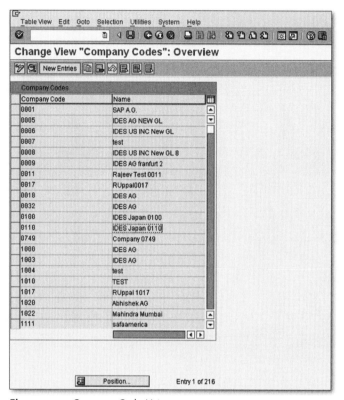

Figure 4.30 Company Code List

Select your company code, and click on the magnifying glass icon. The screen shown in Figure 4.31 appears.

Unless you are using a payment-on-behalf scenario (e.g., when a shared services center is paying on behalf of all other company codes), enter the same company code for the Sending Company Code and Paying Company Code fields. Enter the tolerance days for payments if you want the system to incorporate extra days in the due date calculation, and the special general ledger transactions to be paid for customers and vendors, if any. Now click on Paying Company Code, and the screen shown in Figure 4.32 appears.

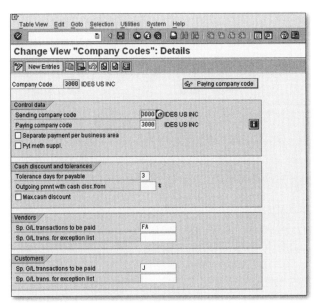

Figure 4.31 Company Code Parameters

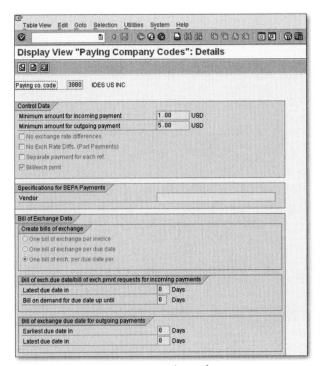

Figure 4.32 Paying Company Code Configuration

On this screen, enter the minimum amounts for incoming and outgoing payments. These are the amounts at which the payment program will kick in — lower amount invoices won't be read by the program. Then save, and go back to the previous screen (Figure 4.33).

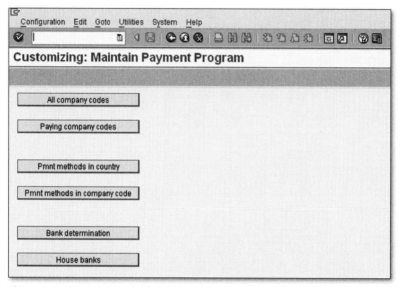

Figure 4.33 Payment Method Configuration Screen

Click on Payment Methods in Company Code (Figure 4.34).

On the screen shown in Figure 4.35, select the payment method for ACH.

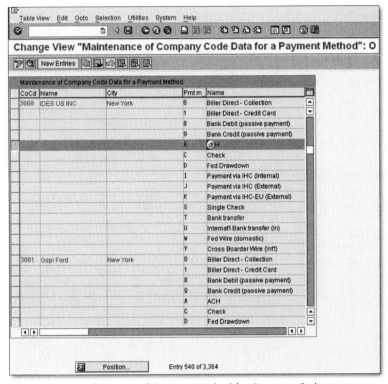

Figure 4.34 Configuration of Payment Method for Company Code

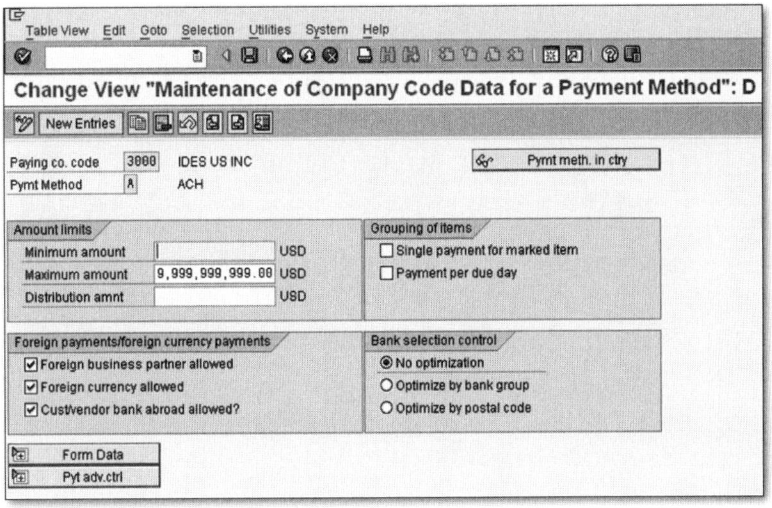

Figure 4.35 Company Code Parameters

Enter the maximum and minimum amounts, and select whether you want to allow foreign business partners, foreign currencies, and customers and vendors abroad. Then click on the Form Data button (Figure 4.36).

In the first section of the Form Data area, the example shows the two standard SAPscripts; in practice, you will have to replace the standard ones with the ones specific to your country and bank. Now click on the Pyt. Adv. Ctrl button. The screen shown in Figure 4.37 appears.

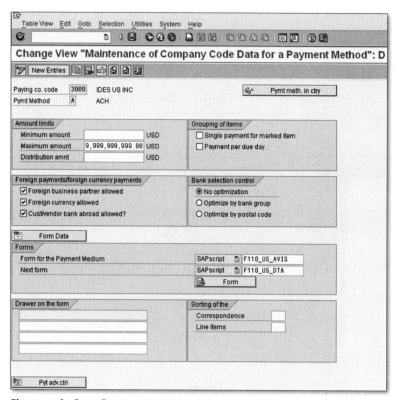

Figure 4.36 Form Data

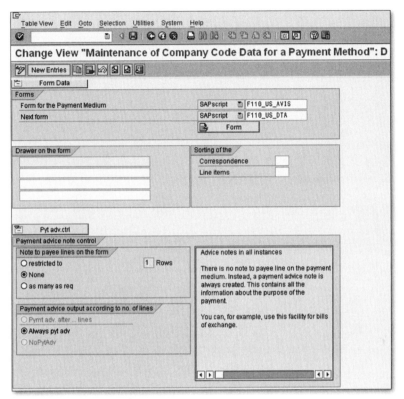

Figure 4.37 Payment Advice Data

Enter the details for the number of lines on the form, or indicate whether or not to send a payment advice with no lines. Click on Pymt. Meth in Ctry (refer back to Figure 4.36). The screen shown in Figure 4.38 appears.

On this screen, select the payment method for outgoing payments, and select Bank Transf in the Payment Method Classification area. Then select the Bank Details indicator so that the system requires that you enter bank details on the vendor master record when ACH is used. Depending on the region and payment method used, check IBAN and SWIFT. Finally, enter the document types for payment and for the clearing document. The system assigns separate document types and number ranges for clearing and payment documents, which is why you need to enter two separate types here. The document type determines the number range.

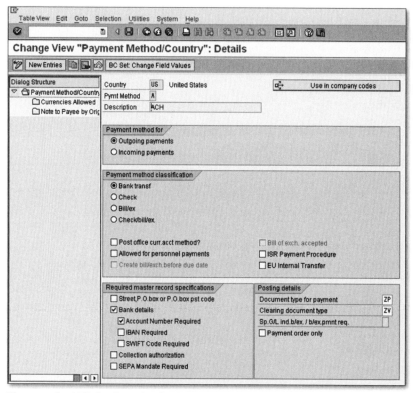

Figure 4.38 ACH Configuration for Country

Save, go back to the main payment program configuration in Transaction FBZP, and then click on Paymnt Methods in Company Code. The screen shown in Figure 4.39 appears.

Click on the Position button at the bottom, and enter your paying company code. Select the Check Payment method; if it doesn't exist, create it. The screen shown in Figure 4.40 appears.

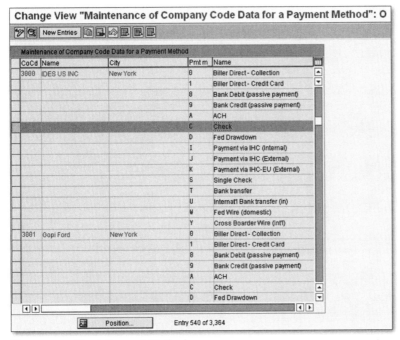

Figure 4.39 Check Payment Method

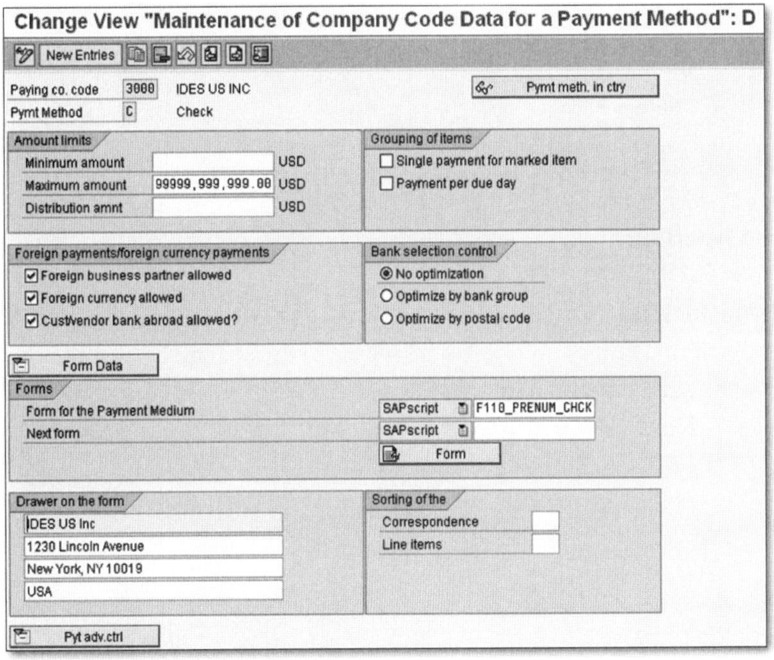

Figure 4.40 Check Payment Method Details

Configure the top part of the screen similar to the way you configured ACH in Figure 4.36. On the form, enter the text you want to be printed on the check. Click on the Pymt Meth. in Ctry button. This brings you to the screen shown in Figure 4.41.

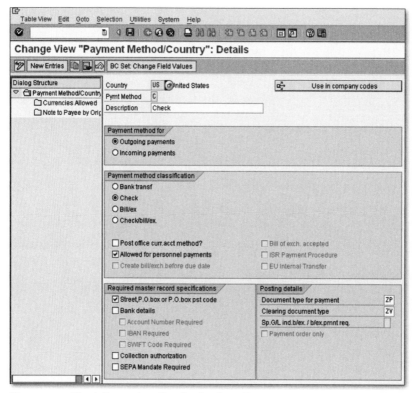

Figure 4.41 Check Payment — Country Configuration

Select whether the method is for outgoing or incoming payments, and then select the Check classification. Enter the document types for the payment and for the clearing document. Then scroll down to the Payment Medium section, shown in Figure 4.42.

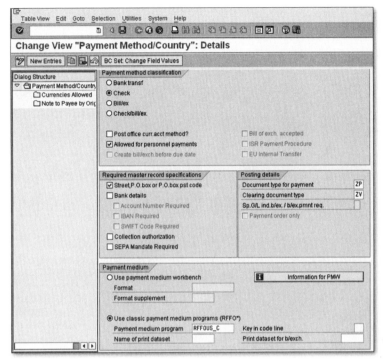

Figure 4.42 Payment Medium for Check

Note that we selected the standard printing program for checks, RFFOUS_C. If necessary, you can replace this with your own printing program. Now save, exit, and then execute Transaction F110, which is shown in Figure 4.43.

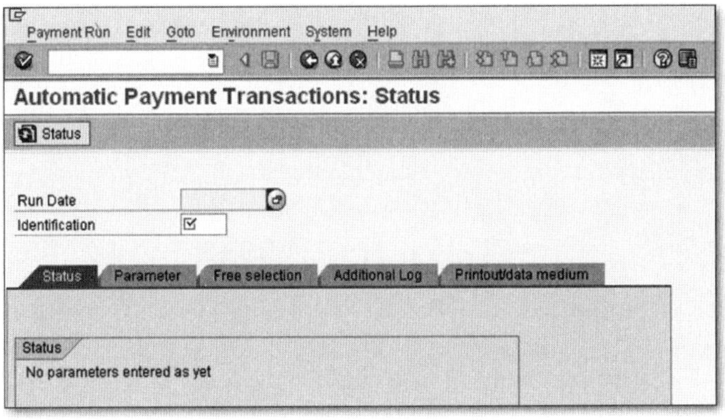

Figure 4.43 Payment Program Initial Screen

Follow the menu path shown in Figure 4.44, and the screen shown in Figure 4.45 appears.

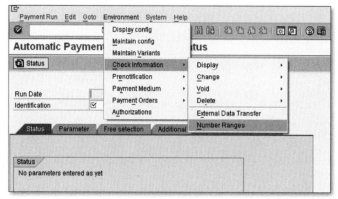

Figure 4.44 Access to Check Lot Configuration

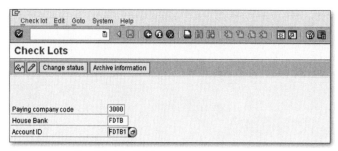

Figure 4.45 Check Lot Initial Screen

Enter your paying company code, house bank, and account ID, and click on the pencil icon. The screen shown in Figure 4.46 appears.

Now click on the Create icon, and the screen shown in Figure 4.47 appears.

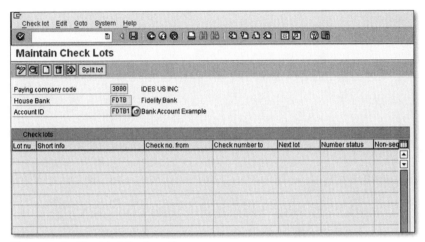

Figure 4.46 Check Lot Configuration

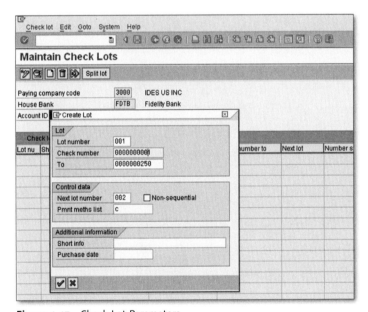

Figure 4.47 Check Lot Parameters

Enter the check lot number, the number range for the lot, the next lot number, and the payment method for which the lot is valid. Select Enter. This brings you to the screen shown in Figure 4.48.

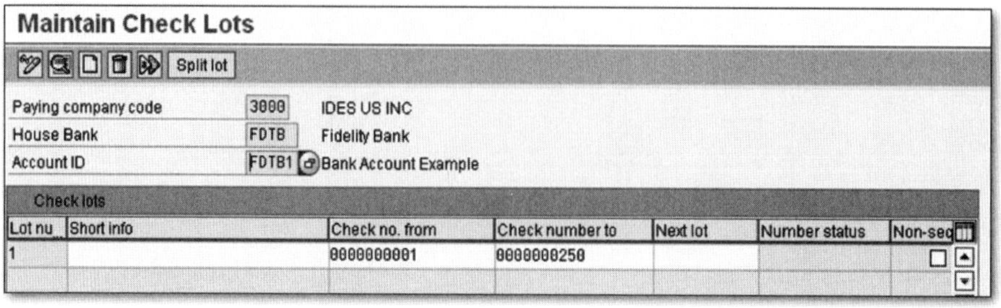

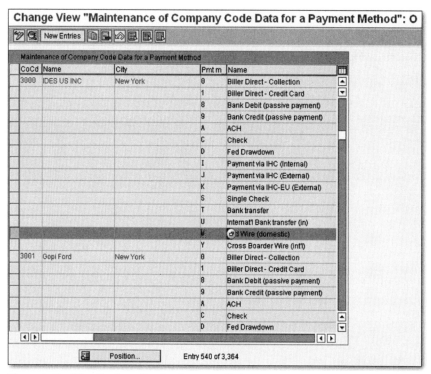

Figure 4.48 Check Lot Configured

Save and go back to Transaction FBZP, the main Payment Program configuration screen. Click on Payment Method Configuration for Company Code; the resulting screen is shown in Figure 4.49.

Figure 4.49 Wire Configuration for Company Code

Select the Fed Wire (Domestic) row, and then click the magnifying glass icon. The screen shown in Figure 4.50 appears.

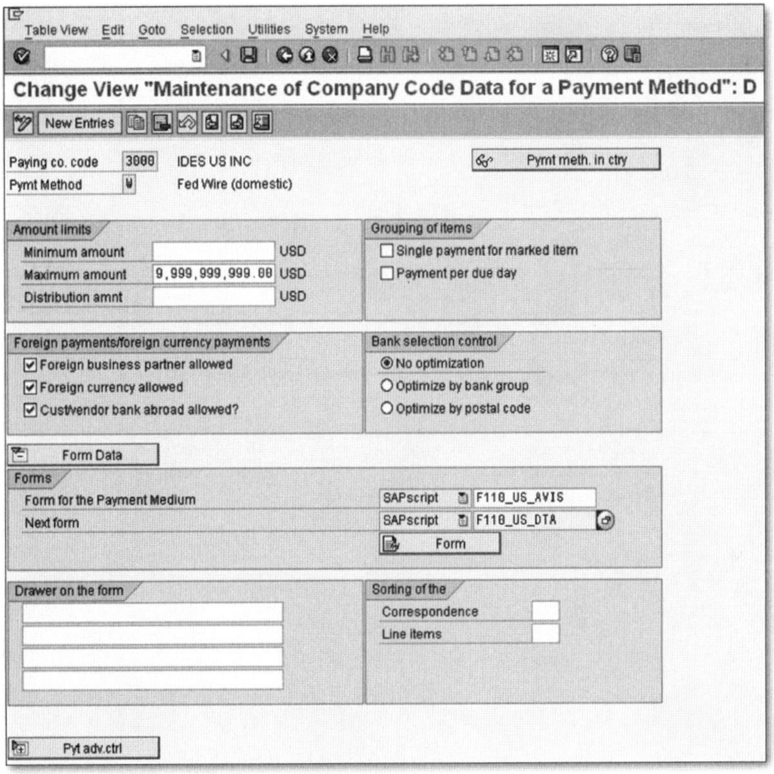

Figure 4.50 Wire Company Code Configuration Screen

Enter the payment details and the form data, as we did in the other payment methods, but use the SAPscripts that correspond to wire transfers. If you select Payment Optimization by Bank Group, the system tries to select banks for you and the vendors that are in the same group. (Bank groups are configured in Transaction FI01, when you create the bank master data.) If you select Payment Optimization by Postal Code, the system selects banks for you and the vendors that are in the same, or nearby, postal codes.

After you complete this step, click on Pymt Meth. in Ctry, which brings you to the screen shown in Figure 4.51.

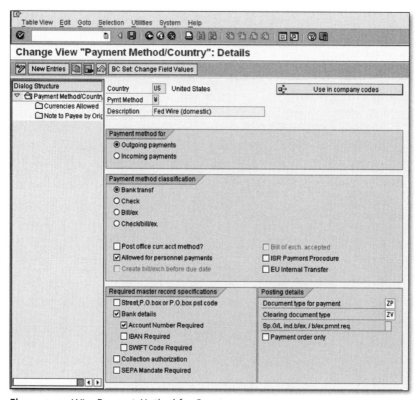

Figure 4.51 Wire Payment Method for Country

In this case, the parameters are similar to those for the ACH shown earlier in Figure 4.38. Save and go back to the screen shown in Figure 4.52.

Figure 4.52 International Wire Transfer Company Code Data

Select the Cross Boarder Wire (Int'l) row as your payment method, double-click it, and then click on the Payment Method in Country button. This brings you to the screen shown in Figure 4.53.

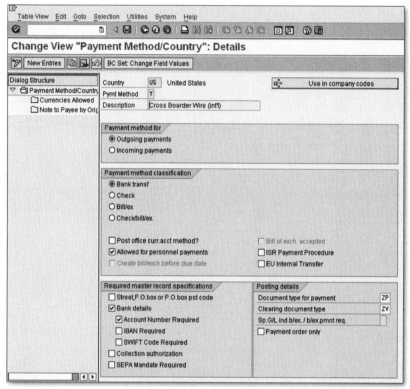

Figure 4.53 International Wire Transfer Country Parameters

In this screen, select details similar to the domestic wire. The only differences here are that the IBAN and SWIFT are required, and, depending on the country, the SEPA Mandate and the EU Internal Transfer could also be required. Fill out the company code parameters as we did for the other payment methods, except that the form and the SAPscripts here will be the ones that correspond to the international wire transfer. After that, go to the Payment Program configuration main screen using Transaction FBZP (Figure 4.54).

Click on the Bank Determination button, which brings you to the screen shown in Figure 4.55.

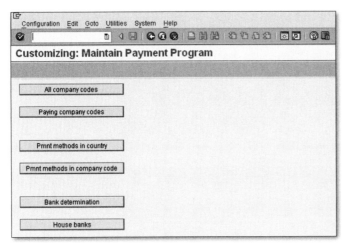

Figure 4.54 Payment Program Configuration Screen

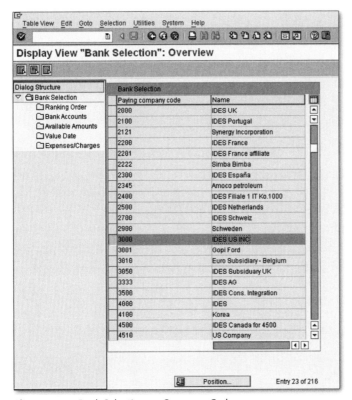

Figure 4.55 Bank Selection — Company Code

Select your company code, and then click on Ranking Order on the left menu (see Figure 4.56).

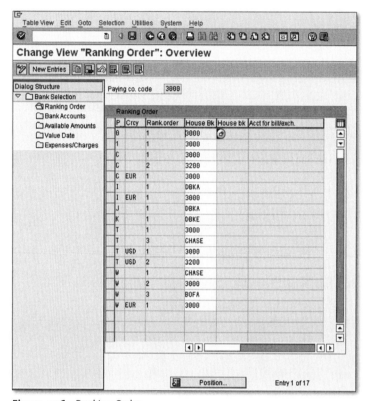

Figure 4.56 Ranking Order

Here you enter the method, the ranking order, and the house bank from which to pull the funds. The ranking order determines which bank and bank account should be used for each payment method, and what the alternative should be if the first one runs out of funds. Now click on Bank Accounts, which brings you to the screen shown in Figure 4.57.

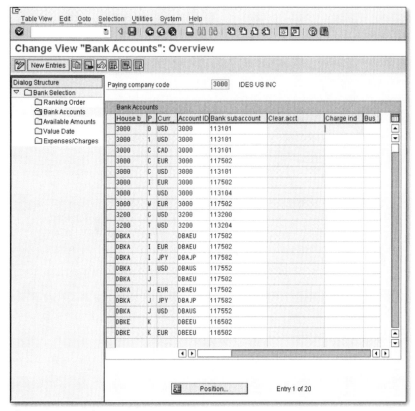

Figure 4.57 Bank Accounts

On this screen, select the house bank, method, currency, account ID, and general ledger clearing account that corresponds to each payment method. Click on Available Amounts, which brings you to the screen shown in Figure 4.58.

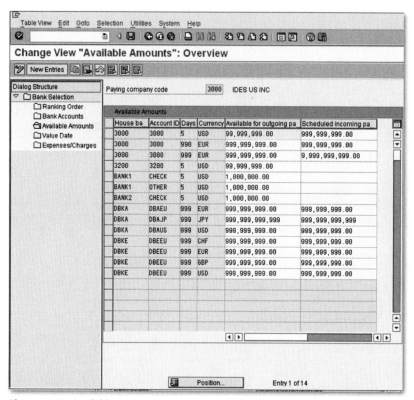

Figure 4.58 Available Amounts

Now enter the available amounts for the combination of house bank, account ID, and currency.

4.2.3 Cash Concentration Configuration

In terms of configuration required for cash concentration, you can access it in the IMG using this menu path: Financial Supply Chain Management • Cash and Liquidity Management • Cash Management • Business Transactions • Cash Concentration • Define Intermediate Account, Clearing Accounts and Amounts.

Access the path, and the screen shown in Figure 4.59 appears.

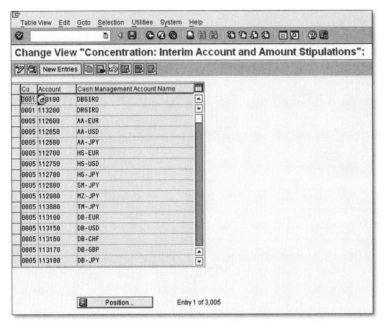

Figure 4.59 Cash Concentration Program Configuration Access Screen

Select the row that contains the company code, general ledger account, and cash management account that you want to configure, and click on the magnifying glass. The screen shown in Figure 4.60 appears.

If you populate the Intermediate Account Company and Account fields, the system moves the funds from the account configured to the account entered here. If you leave it blank, the funds are moved to the target account entered in the main screen of the Cash Concentration program.

The Planner Balance field ensures that if the balance at the end of the day is above the amount entered here, the system moves the cash to the target account. The Minimum Balance field ensures that if the balance at the end of the day is below the amount entered here, the system moves cash into this account.

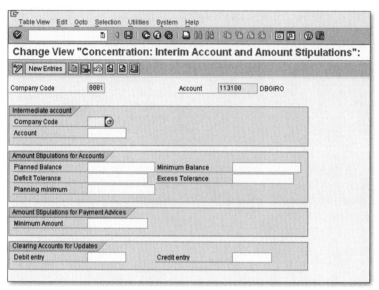

Figure 4.60 Cash Concentration Configuration Detail

The tolerances for deficit and excess determine the amount of the allowed deviations from the planned and minimum amounts.

Finally, the payment advice minimum ensures that the system avoids transfers for amounts that are too small, and the clearing accounts determine the accounts to be posted for debits and credits.

4.3 Business Process Examples

In this section, we provide a walkthrough of both the payment process and the cash concentration process.

> **Note**
>
> We will not repeat all of the payment program steps for each payment method, as they are mostly the same. The only exception is the last step, which involves the payment media and the transmission or printing.

4.3.1 Payment Process

The payment process is the result of the invoice verification process. Note, however, that we do not discuss the invoice verification process here because it is not directly related to cash management. Similarly, although the process of creating a vendor master record has a number of fields that are important from a Purchasing and Logistics perspective, we also won't discuss those here. Because the focus of the book is cash management, we focus only on those fields that are relevant for our discussion.

To create a vendor master record in the Accounts Payable component, access the following menu path: SAP MENU • ACCOUNTING • FINANCIAL ACCOUNTING • ACCOUNTS PAYABLE • MASTER RECORDS • FK01 – CREATE. The screen shown in Figure 4.61 appears.

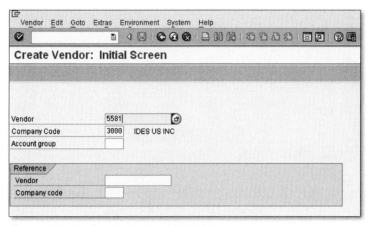

Figure 4.61 Vendor Master Record Initial Screen

On this screen, enter the company code and account group. If the vendor number is external, enter this number as well. Then press Enter, which brings you to the screen shown in Figure 4.62.

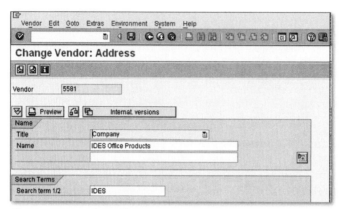

Figure 4.62 Vendor Address

On this screen, enter the vendor address and contact information. Then press Enter, which brings you to the screen shown in Figure 4.63.

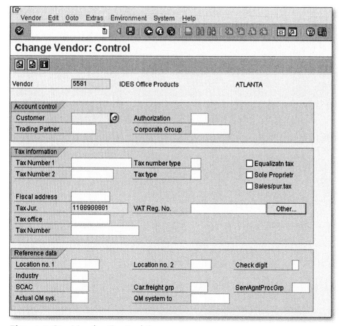

Figure 4.63 Vendor Control Screen

On this screen, enter tax-related information according to your jurisdiction requirements. Then press Enter, which brings you to the screen shown in Figure 4.64.

On this screen, enter the bank account to pay the vendor. Recall that when we did the country configuration of the wire transfer and ACH payment methods in Figure 4.38 of this section, we selected a Bank Details indicator — this is the screen of the vendor master record that the indicator referred to. For those payment methods, it is necessary to populate this information here. Press Enter, which brings you to Figure 4.65.

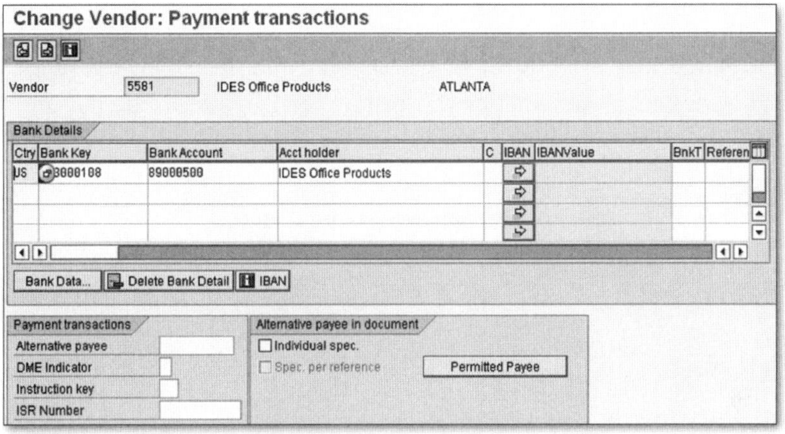

Figure 4.64 Bank Account Information

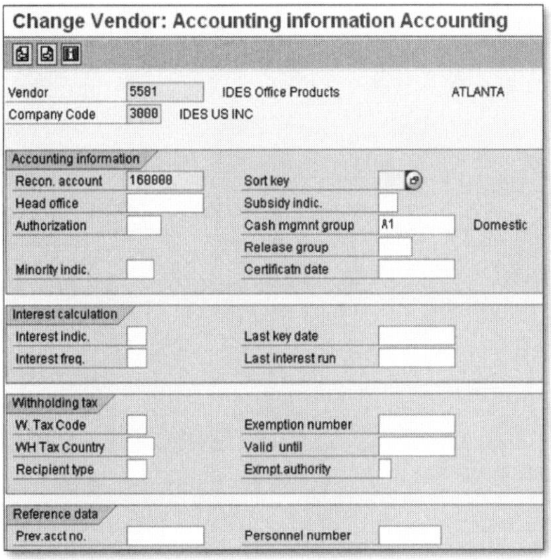

Figure 4.65 Accounting and Cash Management Information

In the Recon. Account field, enter the general ledger account where all of the vendor subledger transactions should be posted. In the Cash Mgmnt Group field, provide the group that represents how you want to see the transactions related to this vendor in the cash position report. (We discuss this in more detail in Chapter 8, Integration with Procure-to-Pay, Order-to-Cash, and Other Financial Processes.) Then press Enter, which brings you to the screen shown in Figure 4.66.)

Enter the payment terms, and select the Chk Double Inv. Indicator. This causes the system to give you a warning when the system recognizes the same reference number on the same vendor twice. Optionally, you can also enter the payment method, the house bank from which you will pay this vendor, and an alternative payee.

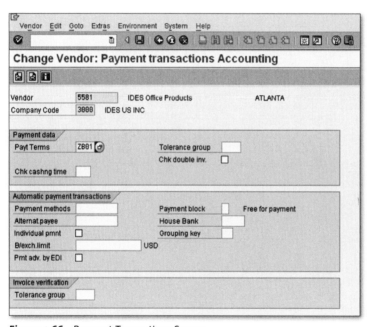

Figure 4.66 Payment Transactions Screen

Now execute Transaction FB60 to access the screen shown in Figure 4.67. (There is a different transaction code for entering an invoice from Logistics, but, again, we are focusing on cash management here.)

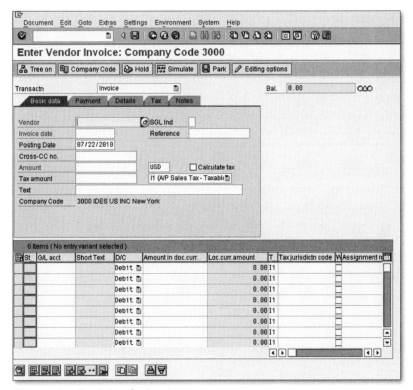

Figure 4.67 Create Vendor Invoice

In addition to the date, the offset general ledger account, and the vendor information, this screen contains the very important payment terms and baseline date fields, which, when combined, produce the due date. (We discuss this process in more detail in Chapter 8.)

Now execute Transaction F110, which is shown in Figure 4.68.

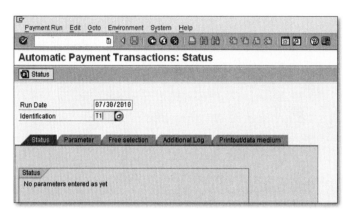

Figure 4.68 Payment Program Initial Screen

Enter the run date and an identifier for your proposal. The run date is the date in which you are running the program, and the identifier is a code that can be recognized by the user (the latter is important if the same user runs multiple proposals on the same day). Then click the Parameter tab (Figure 4.69).

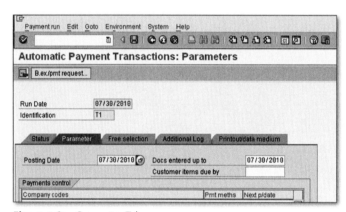

Figure 4.69 Parameter Tab

In the Parameter tab, enter the date for the Docs Entered Up To field. This field determines the last due date to be included in the payment run, the company codes to include in the proposal, and the payment method. Combined with the

Docs Entered Up To field, the Next P/Date field determines the range of dates for open items that will be included in the proposal. It is advisable to separate payment runs for each payment method to give the proper attention to the payment media and communications aspects of each method. Finally, on this screen, you can indicate a vendor number as a filter. Several other fields are also available to restrict the number of items the system selects.

Now click on the Additional Log tab, shown in Figure 4.70.

On this screen, indicate the kind of situations in which you want additional log information and also the customers or vendors for which you want it. Click on the Printout/Data Medium tab, shown in Figure 4.71.

On this screen, indicate the print program for checks and the variants that you want to use. After that, save and go back. Then click on the Proposal button to run the program. After you have run the proposal, if there are no errors, you should be able to click on the Proposal button (with the glasses icon), and look at the payments included on it, as shown In Figure 4.72.

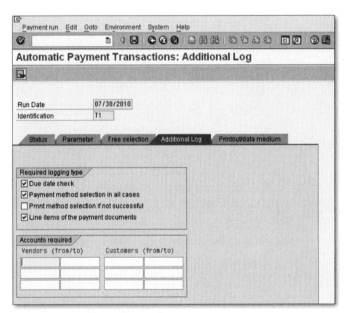

Figure 4.70 Additional Log Tab

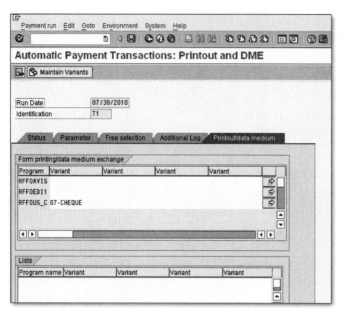

Figure 4.71 Printout/Data Medium Screen

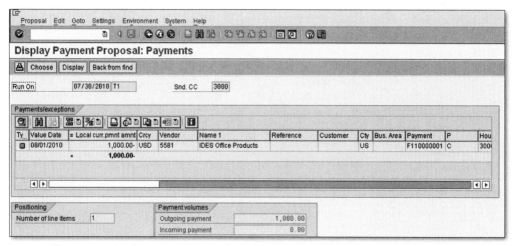

Figure 4.72 Display Payment Proposal

If the proposal was successful, go back and click on Payment Run.

Figure 4.73 shows the outcome after the payment run has taken place successfully. The next step is to print the checks.

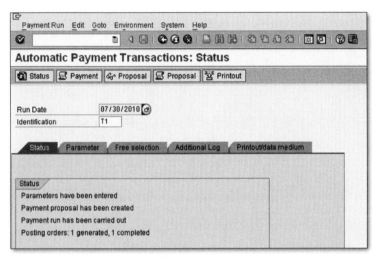

Figure 4.73 Payment Proposal Posted

Using the menu path shown in Figure 4.74, you can review the list of payments issued as a result. The payment list report looks like the screen shown in Figure 4.75.

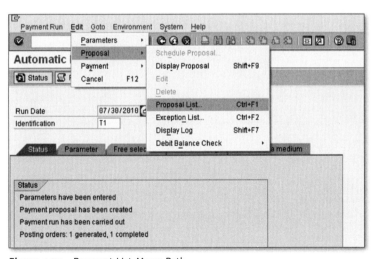

Figure 4.74 Payment List Menu Path

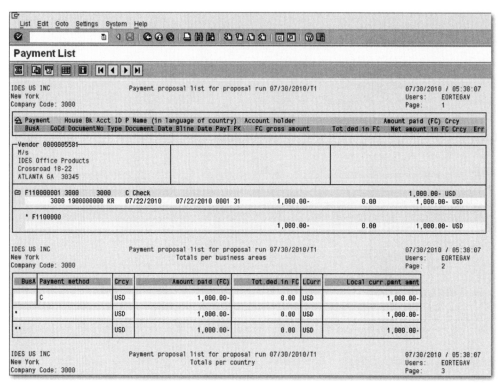

Figure 4.75 Payment List Report

Go back and click on the Printout button, and the screen shown in Figure 4.76 appears. Select the job name and the Start Immediately indicator. Remember, check printers and printer stock should always be handled in a secured place.

The last step for the check payment method is the creation of the positive pay file. Execute Transaction FCHX, which is shown in Figure 4.77.

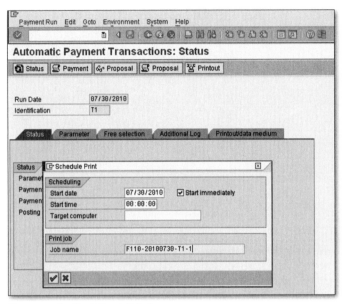

Figure 4.76 Start Check Printing

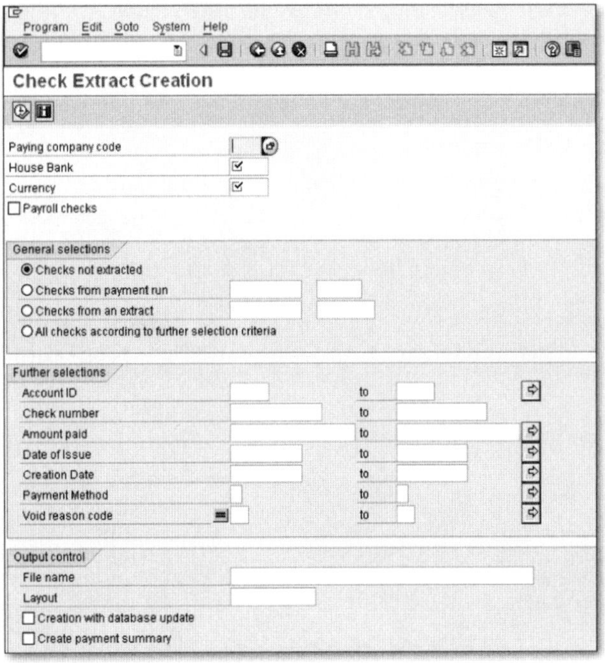

Figure 4.77 Positive Pay File Creation

Transaction FCHX produces a sample of the information contained on the check register. Check whether any of the existing layouts match the format required by the bank (unfortunately, each bank has its own format; there is no standard). If not, you can copy an existing layout into a custom program, and have an ABAP programmer write code to produce the specific format you need.

Figure 4.78 shows the differences between the process just explained and the process using ACHs and wires.

Check	Wire and ACH
▶ Check payment method in vendor master record	▶ Wire or ACH payment method in vendor master record
▶ Bank account information not required in vendor master record	▶ Bank account information required in vendor master record
▶ In payment proposal, select Print/Data Medium Programs to Advices	▶ In payment proposal select Print/Data Medium Programs to create Wire or ACH file and remittance advice
▶ SAP BCM can be used to send positive pay file to the bank	▶ SAP BCM can be used to group payments in batches
▶ Payment media transmission to the bank is not mandatory unless your country uses positive pay	▶ Payment media transmission to the bank is mandatory

Figure 4.78 Payment Media Parameters in Payment Program for Wire Transfers and ACH

For wires transfers and ACHs, the main differences in the payment programs are as follows:

▶ In the vendor master record, the payment program has to be either ACH or wire transfer (or both).

▶ In the vendor master record, bank account information is mandatory.

▶ In the payment proposal, the Printout/Data Medium tab has to be populated with specific programs and variants for wire transfers or ACH file production (Figure 4.79).

▶ You can use SAP BCM to group payments in batches and approve them using the Batch and Payment Monitor. We discuss this topic in more detail in the next chapter.

▶ The transmission of the payment media to the bank is mandatory because the payment cannot take place without it. The details on how this transmission takes place are covered in the next chapter.

As you can see in Figure 4.79, you don't have the check printing program for ACH and wire transfers; rather, you have a program that creates the payment file and the payment advice.

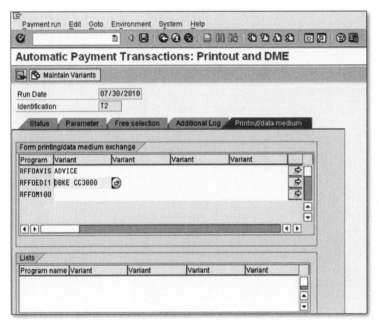

Figure 4.79 Printout/Data Medium Tab on Payment Proposal

4.3.2 Cash Concentration

Cash concentration is the result of the cash management process, which we discuss in more detail in Chapter 9, Global Cash Position Reporting and Management. For now, you should know that after reviewing the existing cash balances and the cash requirements for each bank account, you then need to move cash around to ensure that each account has what it needs and that cash surpluses get invested at the best possible rate. Here we show the SAP ERP steps for this process.

To access the Cash Concentration program, use the following menu path: SAP MENU • ACCOUNTING • FINANCIAL SUPPLY CHAIN MANAGEMENT • CASH AND LIQUIDITY MANAGEMENT • CASH MANAGEMENT • PLANNING • CASH CONCENTRATION • FF73 – CREATE. When you access this menu path, the screen shown in Figure 4.80 appears.

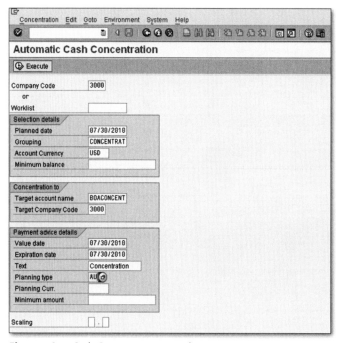

Figure 4.80 Cash Concentration Initial Screen

Enter the origin and destination company codes, the planned date, and the grouping to use (a grouping is a group of general ledger accounts, planning groups, and planning levels configured in the Cash Management functionality — we explain this more in Chapter 9). Also enter the value date, planning level type to use, and the minimum balance that you want to leave in each account.

Click on Execute, and the screen shown in Figure 4.81 appears.

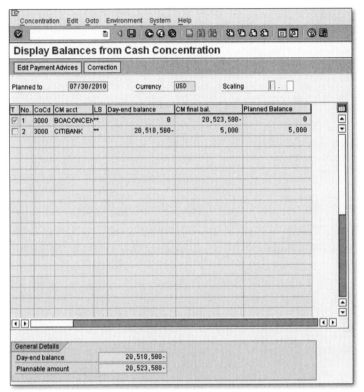

Figure 4.81 Cash Concentration Proposal

On this screen, you can review the movements of cash that will take place, and the payment advices that the system will create. If you click on the Edit Payment Advices button, the screen shown in Figure 4.82 appears.

On this screen, you can edit the payment advices for the amount, date, or account. After that, save the payment advices. Now access the program to post the payment advices using the following menu path: SAP MENU • ACCOUNTING • FINANCIAL SUPPLY CHAIN MANAGEMENT • CASH AND LIQUIDITY MANAGEMENT • CASH MANAGEMENT • PLANNING • CASH CONCENTRATION • FF.9 – POST. This transforms them into payment requests.

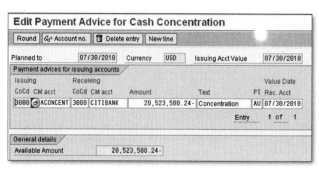

Figure 4.82 Edit Payment Advices

Using the screen shown in Figure 4.83, you can select the payment advices created in the previous step and transform them into payment requests. These payment requests can then be paid using the payment program for payment requests to create either wire transfers or ACH files.

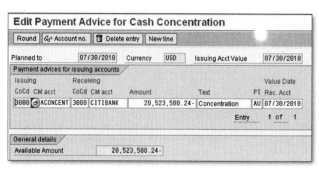

Figure 4.83 Post Payment Advices Program

Now access the payment program for payment requests using Transaction F111 or the following menu path: SAP Menu • Accounting • Financial Supply Chain Management • Cash and Liquidity Management • Cash Management • Planning • Payment Program • F111 – Payment Requests. The screen shown in Figure 4.84 appears.

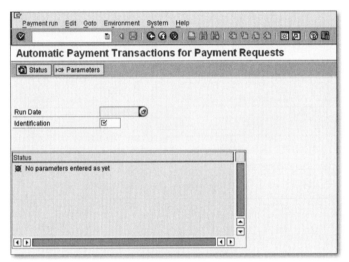

Figure 4.84 Payment Program for Payment Requests

As you can see, the payment program for payment requests is similar to the one for AP. For this reason, we do not provide step-by-step instructions; for more details, review Figure 4.68.

Finally, the last part of the cash concentration process is sending the payment media to the bank. We cover this in the next chapter.

4.4 Summary

In this chapter, we reviewed the outbound business processes for check processing, ACHs, and wire transfers. We also discussed the different formats and how to produce them in SAP ERP. In addition, we explained the configuration required for bank master data, house banks, account IDs, ALE configuration, and the payment program. Finally, in the last section, we provided examples of the outbound processes in SAP ERP, specifically for checks, and explained the differences for ACH and wire transfers. We then provided a step-by-step example of cash concentration. In the next chapter, we cover the use and configuration of the Bank Communications functionality.

SAP Bank Communication Management is available with SAP ERP 6.0 enhancement pack 2.0 onward, and facilitates and optimizes the financial information flows between a company and its business partners through leveraging the SAP NetWeaver Process Integration (SAP NetWeaver PI) infrastructure.

5   Overview of SAP Bank Communication Management

This chapter covers the functionality that is available with SAP Bank Communication Management, especially with respect to payment processing through the Batch and Payment Monitor and for bank statement processing through the Bank Statement Monitor. It also covers SAP Integration Package for SWIFT (a separate component available as an add-on) that provides direct access to the international payment network called SWIFTNet. (SWIFTNet provides access to more than 7,800 financial institutions worldwide.) This chapter also explains the functionality available for the support and processing of international payments.

In Section 5.1, Evolution of Bank Communications and Introduction to the SWIFT-Net Service, we review the evolution of bank communications in the past 15 years and the current trends, including SWIFT offerings. In Section 5.2, SAP Bank Communication Management Functionality Overview, we provide an overview of the functionalities contained in SAP Bank Communication Management (SAP BCM). In Section 5.3, SAP Bank Communication Management Configuration, we provide configuration instructions for each of the SAP BCM components. Finally, in Section 5.4, SAP Bank Communication Management in Action, we provide a demonstration of the main functionalities.

5.1 Evolution of Bank Communications and Introduction to the SWIFTNet Service

Until the mid-1990s, SAP was an isolated box that had no connections to the outside world; back in 1996, the system didn't even have connectivity to the Internet (this came with the mySAP version in the late 1990s). Thus, in the earlier days of SAP cash management (circa 1996), communication to and from the bank consisted primarily of accessing a bank terminal to download an electronic bank statement, and printing and faxing wire transfer letters.

As companies and banks became more sophisticated, however, other methods of communication came into existence:

▶ Receiving electronic bank statements via EDI or value added network

▶ Creating ACH and wire files from SAP and sending them to the bank via EDI

▶ Creating ACH files and uploading them to a bank website

Today some of the main methods of communication with banks include the following:

▶ **Consolidator bank**

A *consolidator bank* provides you with a secure source of aggregated account data from multiple institutions. This service saves you time by consolidating all of your trust, custody, and cash account information across institutions. One important feature of this type of service is that you don't need to disclose user and password information for each of your accounts, which can cause security concerns and also pose questions about data integrity. Instead, the consolidator obtains authorized information feeds directly from the banks, which means the data quality and security are much improved.

HSBC (Hongkong and Shanghai Banking Corporation Limited) offers this type of services for companies that have bank accounts in multiple countries. Other large banks do it as well.

▶ **Value added network**

A *value added network* is a communications network that provides services beyond normal transmission, such as automatic error detection and correction, protocol conversion, and message storing and forwarding.

▶ **Direct connection**

There are many ways to create a *direct connection*, from the old bank terminal that initiates a dial-up connection, to the bank server, to Internet- and VPN-based connections. The specific connection type depends on the volume of transactions, available infrastructure, and budget.

Companies that implemented SAP Accounts Receivable, Accounts Payable, and Cash Management needed to use one of the methods shown in Figure 5.1.

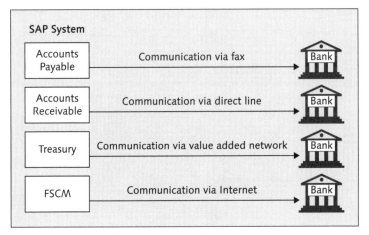

Figure 5.1 Traditional Bank Communication Methods

Connecting to a bank was usually a long, tedious, and expensive process. In many cases, individual interfaces had to be built for each bank to facilitate file mapping and conversion, encryption, and secure transmission of data. This kind of investment in a connection meant that switching to a different bank was a laborious process; thus, selecting a bank meant a long-term commitment. This allowed banks to increase their fees after a couple of years of being connected to a client because they knew it would be hard for the client to move their business to a different bank.

One of the leading companies specializing in communications between banks is SWIFT, as we discussed in Chapter 2, Global Banking and Payment Systems and Practices. In the past few years, SWIFT started offering one of its latest products, SWIFTNet, a global system for communicating with banks. At the time of this writing, it is estimated that about 7800 banks and 500 corporations are connected to it — and the number grows by the day. Using SWIFTNet allows companies to build a single connection to SWIFTNet and use it to communicate with thousands of banks around the globe, which results in a reduction of the effort required to connect to a new bank and therefore more opportunity to obtain better prices for banking services.

In the past few years, SAP has developed functionality to facilitate file mapping and conversion, encryption, and secure transmission of data to integrate SAP with SWIFTNet. The platform in which this was developed was SAP NetWeaver Process Integration (SAP NetWeaver PI). SAP is no longer an isolated box; NetWeaver acts as the gate to the outside world, and SWIFTNet acts as the highway that connects a corporation to the banking community. As a result, companies around the world are starting to communicate with banks using SAP and SWIFTNet.

As you can see in Figure 5.2, several pieces need to be connected for the process to work. The first one is the SAP system, which contains the applications that typically send or receive files from the bank. There is also a new component called SAP Bank Communication Management (SAP BCM), which facilitates the monitoring and approval of those files. Next, SAP Bank Communication Management sends the payment media file to SAP NetWeaver PI, specifically the integration package for SWIFT, which maps, formats, and encrypts the file. After that, the file is sent to the bank using SWIFTNet.

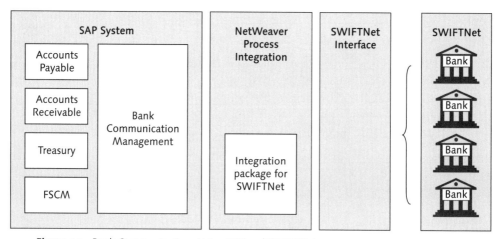

Figure 5.2 Bank Communications Using SAP and SWIFTNet

During this process, you receive status messages that alert you to successes or errors with the files, something that was previously not possible in SAP. Before this new feature, you had to process your payment files in SAP and send them to EDI; then EDI would send them to the bank, and you would simply have to hope that you wouldn't get a call back from the EDI department reporting an error. If there *was* an error, EDI would have to communicate it to you, you would have to decipher it (which sometimes required an in-person visit to the office), and then you would have to fix it and send the file again. Even if there was no error, but you wanted to make sure that your payment made it without a problem, you would need to call either EDI or the payee, and they would then confirm verbally that the transmission was successful. Now, however, SAP can receive those messages and display them in the Batch and Payment Monitor, which also enables a quick reaction in case of an issue.

To connect a corporation to SWIFTNet, SWIFT offers three options, depending on the volume and existing infrastructure:

▶ **Alliance Lite**
This option is used by small and mid-size businesses that issue less than 200 payments per day. It uses the Internet and a web browser to access the service.

▶ **Indirect Connection**
This option requires you to hire a service bureau that has the technical infrastructure to connect your company with SWIFTNet, as well as the staff to support it and resolve any issues. You can access your service bureau server using the Internet. The advantage of this option is that you don't need to have a full department to run the operation; however, many large corporations are concerned about sending confidential banking data to a third party, depending on a vendor to process urgent payments, and the consequences a contractual dispute could bring to the operations of the company.

▶ **Direct Connections**
Most large corporations opt for this model. In many cases, they use some of the staff and infrastructure they already have in place for their EDI department to manage the transition; in other cases, they establish a new department inside IT to manage it.

Direct Connections is the most reliable model because all confidential information is stored in-house, the operations are not dependent on a vendor, and it just has the regular costs associated with equipment, licenses, support, and staff.

Global and multinational companies benefit significantly from a SWIFTNet connection because it enables them to send payments and receive electronic bank statements all over the world, thus enabling global electronic banking and global cash positioning. Companies in the Single Euro Payment Area (SEPA) especially should consider this option because it helps them to fulfill the new payment process requirements.

5.2 SAP Bank Communication Management Functionality Overview

To illustrate the use of SAP Bank Communication Management, the following list provides an example of a standard process:

1. An invoice is paid in the AP department using the payment program.

2. The payment media is produced in SAP BCM, and the wire file goes to SAP NetWeaver PI.

3. The wire file is encrypted and formatted in SAP NetWeaver PI and sent to SWIFTNet using SAP Integration Package for SWIFT.

4. SWIFT confirms receiving the file (acknowledgement) by sending a confirmation message, and the message is imported into SAP BCM, where the payment status is updated.

5. SWIFT sends another message as delivery notification.

6. The new message is imported into SAP BCM, and the payment status is updated again.

7. SWIFT sends the payment file to the bank using SWIFTNet.

8. The bank validates the file and processes the payment.

9. The bank sends a status message to SWIFT.

10. The message is imported from SWIFTNet into SAP BCM.

11. The payment status is updated again in SAP BCM.

12. The bank creates a bank statement the next day.

13. The bank statement is sent to the company using SWIFTNet.

14. SAP BCM receives the bank statement and updates the Bank Statement Monitor.

The following list includes the main features and functions of SAP Bank Communication Management:

▶ Merge Payments

▶ Approve Payments — Batch and Payment Monitor

▶ Bank Statement Monitor

▶ Digital Signature and Release Workflow

▶ Status of Collector Payments

▶ Reservation for Cross-Payment Run Payment Media

▶ Define Alerts

In this section, we focus on the most important of these features: merging payments, approving payments, and the Bank Statement Monitor.

5.2.1 Merge Payments

This feature allows you to group payments from multiple payment runs into a single one and then transfer them to payment media. Functions supported by this are the Accounts Payable and Accounts Receivable payment program (accessed via Transaction F110), the payment program for payment requests (accessed using Transaction F111), and the Data Medium Exchange (DME). To enable this function, it is necessary to configure payment run identifiers for cross-payment run payment media.

5.2.2 Approve Payments — Batch and Payment Monitor

When you are implementing Accounts Payable and Cash Management, one of the most common situations is that the user wants to have two levels of approvals for payments, particularly for wire transfers of large amounts of money. In these cases, companies feel that it is important for at least two sets of eyes to review the amount, payee, banking information, compliance with policies, and so on.

Since the inception of the Sarbanes-Oxley Act (SOX) in 2003, another major requirement is that a segregation of duties exists for any transaction that moves large amounts of cash outside the company. Before the creation of SAP Bank Communication Management, your options to achieve it were limited and cumbersome. You could do one of the following:

▶ **Set up a workflow process.**
However, because cash can go out via invoice payments or payment request payments, a workflow process had to have multiple legs, making it more complicated. In addition, the information about the payment was embedded in the payment proposal, so for the person to drill down was a time-consuming and not very user-friendly task.

▶ **Segregate the functions in the payment proposal to create the proposal, post-proposal, and payment media.**
However, there were no authorization objects to produce such segregation, so custom authorization objects were required. In addition, even with authorization segregation, the information for the review and approval was inside payment proposal reports that contained unnecessary details (i.e., unnecessary for the payment approver), and the relevant information was hard to find.

SAP BCM made the approval process much easier because the Batch and Payment Monitor and the approval processing features of SAP BCM include user-friendly reports that give the approver the necessary information in one screen with easy drilldowns. It also has the segregation of duties for the review, approval, and payment media creation steps, so compliance is now a lot easier, and the risk of sending a wire to the wrong payee is significantly reduced.

Figure 5.3 shows how payments from the payment program flow into the SAP BCM Batch and Payment Monitor and can be subject to approval workflows.

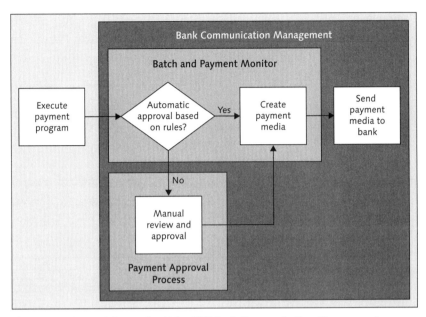

Figure 5.3 Payment Processing Using SAP Bank Communication Management

Multiple levels of approval are possible because you can also set up rules to automatically approve repeat payments for which no additional reviews are desired. For those batches not automatically approved, workflow items are created by the system; those batches can be approved or rejected.

Digital signatures are also used for the approval workflow. If SAP ERP is replacing a bank website for generation of wire and ACH payments, they have token security in place, and most likely the treasurer will want to have token security in place in SAP ERP. With SAP BCM, it is possible to enable third-party software to provide this. If you reject a batch, or part of a batch, the workflow facilitates the reversal of the Financial Accounting document created for the payment.

Another important feature is that batches can be created and tracked in the system. Prior to SAP BCM, if you sent 10 ACH payments to the bank, the bank would group them into a batch, and the bank statement of the next day would have a total amount per batch. Reconciling the batch to each individual outgoing ACH for banking reconciliation was difficult because it was not always easy to know which payments were grouped into which batch. However, because SAP BCM groups the payments in batches and displays them in a worklist that becomes the link between the payment program and payment media creation inside SAP before they are sent to the bank, tracking a batch or researching it for banking reconciliation becomes much easier.

Finally, you can display the batches in several tabs to differentiate which are new, which are in approval, which are completed, and so on.

5.2.3 Bank Statement Monitor

Importing the bank statement into SAP was not always an uneventful job; several aspects of the process needed to be coordinated and often resolved. This often included the following:

▸ Talking with the bank if the file was not received on time

▸ Requesting a new file if the one received was incorrect, or fixing the file if it had a minor error that could be repaired manually

▸ Adding new configuration if a new, not yet configured BAI code was included in the file, or if a new general ledger account was required

▸ Making sure the accounting period was open for posting or asking the accounting department to open it to post the file

▸ Performing configuration every time there was a new bank account

▸ If the bank statement file was processed in a batch, making sure that the batch session ended with no errors and was processed completely

▸ Validating that all records in the file were posted to the general ledger

As you can see, all of these pieces encompass multiple parts of SAP ERP, such as Basis, bank accounting, the general ledger, and so on; they also involve many departments in an organization, such as IT, EDI, treasury, accounting, and more. As a result, making sure all of the pieces come into place harmoniously and produce the desired result is not always easy. Because of the variety of scenarios that can happen, having a single place where you can make sure that everything that needed to happen had actually happened was very challenging.

Fortunately, this is exactly that what the Bank Statement Monitor provides — a single place where you can see the following:

- Whether the file arrived and came in the correct format
- If initial and ending balances match internal records
- If the file that arrived has the correct serial number
- If the required configuration was in place to perform the posting
- If all of the records were processed and posted in the general ledger with no warnings or errors

The importance of this monitoring cannot be overemphasized. To understand it, you should remember that treasury departments need to finish their cash position by noon and that they process several bank statements before that time; a late or unresolved bank statement can result in a delay of the cash position, which is unacceptable by any standard. Any treasurer will tell you that such a delay can be the cause of high bank fees and penalties if payments are not funded properly or if urgent wire payments are not sent successfully; it can also result in much higher fees for loans if you have to negotiate with the banks during rush hour instead of at noon (banks generally charge much higher rates for urgent loans). It could also mean that you get very low nightly money market rates for excess cash that was not invested in the instruments that are more profitable at noon.

Figure 5.4 shows the steps for processing bank statements using SAP Bank Communication Management.

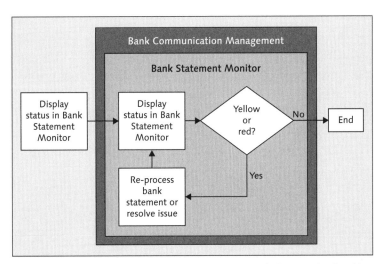

Figure 5.4 Bank Statement Processing Using SAP Bank Communication Management

The Bank Statement Monitor offers several statuses:

- **Processing status**

    - Red: If the configuration in the system indicates that the statement should have been received, but it is not available.

    - Yellow: If not all records were successfully posted.

    - Green: If the statement was received and posted correctly.

- **Difference status**

    - Red: If the difference between the bank statement balance and the internal bank account balance is larger than the tolerance.

    - Yellow: If the difference is within the tolerance.

    - Green: If there are no differences.

- **Serial number status**

    - Red: If the sequence of the last five bank statements are incomplete.

    - Green: If the bank statements have the complete sequence.

- **Reconciliation status**

    - Red: If open items are still present.

    - Yellow: If unposted items still exist.

    - Green: If all items have been posted.

5.3   SAP Bank Communication Management Configuration

In this section, we explain the steps required to enable the SAP Bank Communication Management functionality. The steps can be separated into the following sections:

- Basic settings

- Payment grouping

- Payment status management

▸ Bank Statement Monitor

▸ Release strategies

5.3.1   Basic Settings

To get to the configuration of the basic settings, access the following menu path: SAP Customizing Implementation Guide • Financial Supply Chain Management • Bank Communication Management • Basic Settings • Basic Settings for Approval. The screen shown in Figure 5.5 appears.

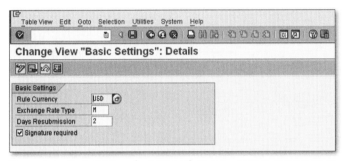

Figure 5.5   Basic Settings for SAP Bank Communication Management

Enter the currency in which the majority of the rules are supposed to occur, the exchange rate type for foreign currencies, the days for resubmission, and whether or not an electronic signature will be required. Then save.

5.3.2   Payment Grouping

The following is the path to the configuration of the grouping rule maintenance: SAP Customizing Implementation Guide • Financial Supply Chain Management • Bank Communication Management • Payment Grouping • Rule Maintenance. If you access this path, the screen shown in Figure 5.6 appears.

On this screen, you can see the list of the rules configured so far, the priority of each, and a description. In this example, the first rule is about merging batches under a certain ID and that fall within a certain value. If you double-click on a rule, you will go to the detail screen, which is shown in Figure 5.7.

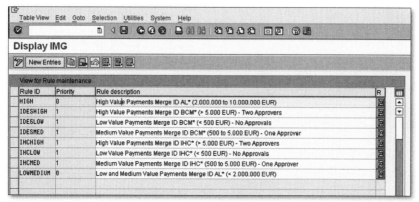

Figure 5.6 Rule Maintenance Screen

Figure 5.7 Detailed Rule Maintenance

On this screen, enter any operator that applies (AND, OR, etc.) on the left. Then enter the sequence for each step in the second column. In this example, the rule says to merge payments under an ID starting with AL with values going from 000 to ZZZ whose value is between 2,000,000 and 99,999,999.99 (or the same negative values).

Now access the following path: SAP Customizing Implementation Guide • Financial Supply Chain Management • Bank Communication Management • Payment Grouping • Additional Criteria for Payment Grouping. The screen shown in Figure 5.8 appears.

On this screen, you can select two additional fields to be used as criteria for grouping your existing rules.

The next step is to access payment media configuration. To this, use the following menu path: SAP Customizing Implementation Guide • Financial Supply Chain

MANAGEMENT • BANK COMMUNICATION MANAGEMENT • PAYMENT GROUPING • PAYMENT MEDIUM CREATE/ASSIGN SELECTION VARIANTS. The screen shown in Figure 5.9 appears.

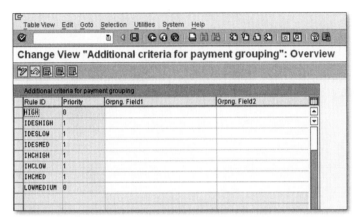

Figure 5.8 Additional Criteria for Grouping

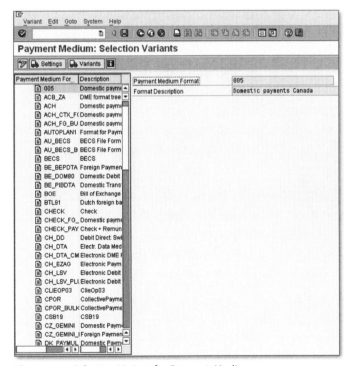

Figure 5.9 Selection Variant for Payment Medium

In this example, we selected the payment medium format for CTX wires in the United States. Now click on Settings, and the screen shown in Figure 5.10 appears.

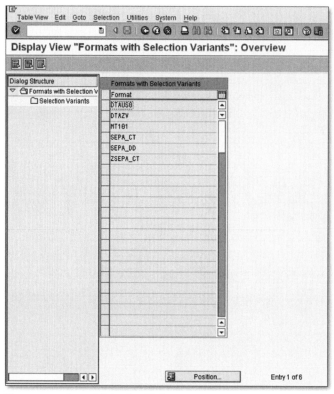

Figure 5.10 Format Selection Variant

On this screen, select a format for your selection variant. As you can see, the NACHA format for CTX ACH payments is not available here, which means it has to be created in the Payment Media Workbench. A detailed discussion of the Payment Media Workbench configuration is beyond the scope of this book, but you can consult online documentation if you need more information.

After the required format is created in the Payment Media Workbench, select it, and then click on Selection Variants on the left. After you access that screen, you link your format to a paying company code. As you complete this configuration, it will be added into a transport request.

This configuration step is necessary because if you're not using SAP BCM when you select your payment method, the payment method is configured to use a certain DME format, and you enter the variant for the program linked to that DME format when you enter the parameters for the payment run. In SAP Bank Communication Management, however, you don't necessarily create the payment media for each payment run; instead, you can group it by the criteria we discussed in the previous two steps (see Figure 5.7): merge ID and amount (in the preceding example). The batches are then created according to those grouping rules. As a result, the system doesn't determine the payment media format based on the payment run parameters, and instead uses this configuration to determine the proper format.

One of the disadvantages of using the Payment Media Workbench instead of the IDoc is that some banks were set up to receive IDoc formats from the old payment media standard programs, so you didn't have to write a functional spec for the mapping and translation of the IDoc into either the Fedwire, the NACHA formats, or SWIFT. Unfortunately, when using SAP Bank Communication Management, you cannot use IDocs; instead, you must produce the SWIFT, Fedwire, or NACHA directly from SAP ERP and link it here to your payment media configuration in SAP BCM. As a result, you will need to create any unavailable formats using the Payment Media Workbench before performing the configuration. That being said, the inconvenience of this one extra configuration step is very small compared to all of the benefits that result from the SAP BCM functionality.

5.3.3 Payment Status Management

To configure Payment Status Management, access the following menu path: SAP Customizing Implementation Guide • Financial Supply Chain Management • Bank Communication Management • Payment Status Management • Map External Status to Internal Status. The screen shown in Figure 5.11 appears.

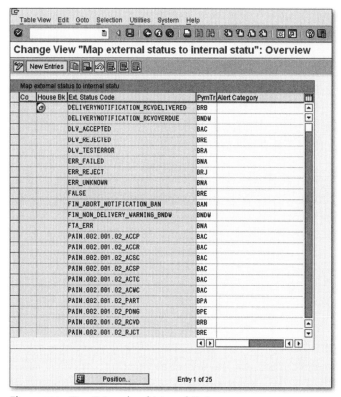

Figure 5.11 Map External and Internal Status

As we explained in Section 5.1, Evolution of Bank Communications and Introduction to the SWIFTNet Service, one of the value-added features of SAP BCM is that it can receive and display status messages. This is important because wire transactions often involve urgent payments, and this allows you to find out about any potential problems as early as possible.

In this configuration step, you map the most commonly received status messages to an internal three-digit status code for display in the SAP BCM screens. Figure 5.12 shows some of the available three-digit codes.

If the message you want to map is not available, click on the New Entries button and add it to the table. Then select the internal three-digit code that corresponds to it, and save.

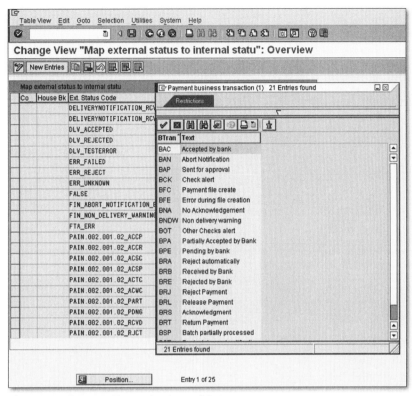

Figure 5.12 Payment Transaction Internal Status

In addition, you can determine if a specific message needs to trigger an alert by entering it in the Alert Category field. To configure the alerts, use Transaction ALRTCATDEF.

5.3.4 Bank Statement Monitor

Use the following path to access Bank Statement Monitor configuration: SAP CUS-TOMIZING IMPLEMENTATION GUIDE • FINANCIAL SUPPLY CHAIN MANAGEMENT • BANK COMMUNICATION MANAGEMENT • BANK STATEMENT MONITOR • SETTINGS FOR BANK STATEMENT MONITOR. The screen shown in Figure 5.13 appears.

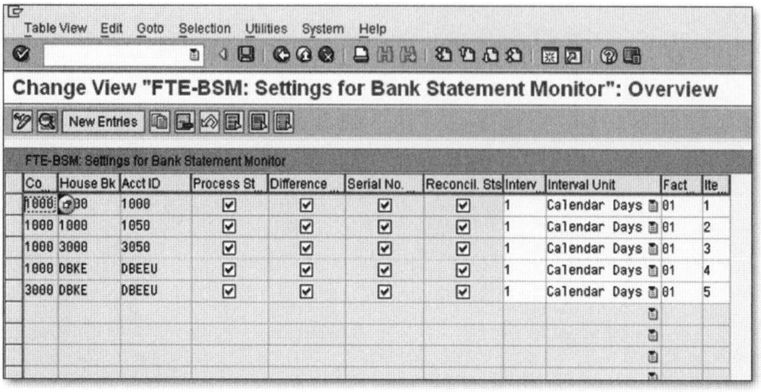

Figure 5.13 Settings for Bank Statement Monitor

In Section 5.2.3, Bank Statement Monitor, of this chapter, we explained the different types of statuses that the Bank Statement Monitor can report, and what they mean. In the screen shown in Figure 5.13, for each of the bank statements that you want to monitor, you configure the company code, house bank, and account ID. Then indicate whether you want to monitor process statuses, difference statuses, serial number statuses, or reconciliation statuses, how often you want to monitor them, and the interval and the factory calendar to use.

Now, if — for example — a bank statement file doesn't arrive in the system, and your settings indicate that it should, the system reports a red status. This is likely to trigger either a call to the bank or some other action.

5.3.5 Release Strategy

The following is the menu path for release strategy configuration: SAP CUSTOMIZING IMPLEMENTATION GUIDE • FINANCIAL SUPPLY CHAIN MANAGEMENT • BANK COMMUNICATION MANAGEMENT • RELEASE STRATEGY. Access this path, and the screen shown in Figure 5.14 appears.

In this screen, enter a rule ID and the rule priority. (In Figure 5.6 earlier, we showed how to maintain the settings for a rule.) After this is complete, select whether or not the rule results in an automatic approval and whether or not drill-down is required.

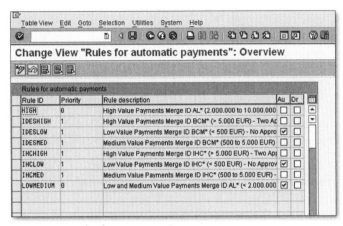

Figure 5.14 Rules for Automatic Payments

The next step is to assign rules to release strategies. Similar to release strategies in Purchasing, whenever cash is sent outside of the company, several parties will likely have to approve it. At the same time, however, you don't want to burden a very high-level executive with the job of reviewing hundreds of payments that are repetitive in nature (e.g., local city and county tax payments), that were formulated by an expert department (e.g., the tax department), and for which it is extremely unlikely that high-level management will have a comment or a reason to stop it. Thus, to differentiate those payments that require little oversight from those that require one, two, or more levels of approval, you create *release strategies*.

To do this, access the following menu path: SAP CUSTOMIZING IMPLEMENTATION GUIDE • FINANCIAL SUPPLY CHAIN MANAGEMENT • BANK COMMUNICATION MANAGEMENT • RELEASE STRATEGY • CHANGE AND RELEASE • ASSIGN RULE TO RELEASE STEPS. The screen shown in Figure 5.15 appears.

On this screen, enter the workflow release object, the step, and the rule. Then, using the Create Rule button, define the rule.

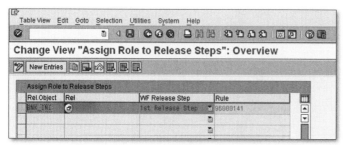

Figure 5.15 Assign Rules to Release Steps Configuration

On the screen shown in Figure 5.16, click the Create button, and then enter the workflow object from the previous screen. Add those individuals that need to approve it. You can also give a certain validity period to the rule; it is useful to do periodic updates to make sure the structure is kept current and to ensure segregation of duties.

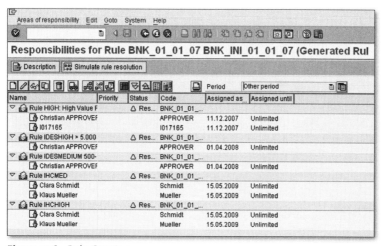

Figure 5.16 Rule Creation

Now test your configuration with the Simulate Rule Resolution button (Figure 5.17).

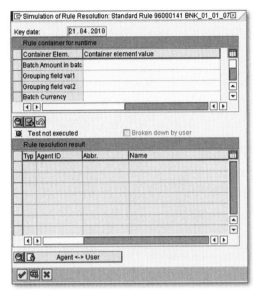

Figure 5.17 Rule Simulation Screen

In this screen, enter the batch amount, grouping fields, and the currency. Now click on the Continue button, and the screen shown in Figure 5.18 appears.

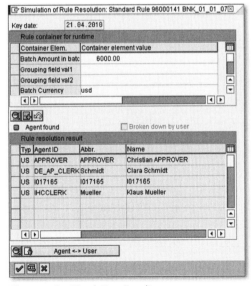

Figure 5.18 Simulation Results

In our example, we entered $6,000 USD as the amount, and the simulation shows the approvers required. This way you can validate whether the rule is producing the results you intended.

The next step is to define release procedures. To do this, access the following menu path: SAP CUSTOMIZING IMPLEMENTATION GUIDE • FINANCIAL SUPPLY CHAIN MANAGEMENT • BANK COMMUNICATION MANAGEMENT • RELEASE STRATEGY • ADDITIONAL RELEASE STEPS • DEFINE RELEASE PROCEDURE. The screen shown in Figure 5.19 appears.

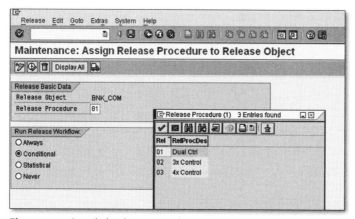

Figure 5.19 Detailed Release Procedure Screen

On this screen, select the same release object used in previous steps, and then enter a number for the release procedure. (The release procedure determines how many approvers you need for the payment.) Then determine under which circumstances you run the release workflow (Always, Conditional, etc.).

The next step is to configure additional release steps. To do this, access the following menu path: SAP CUSTOMIZING IMPLEMENTATION GUIDE • FINANCIAL SUPPLY CHAIN MANAGEMENT • BANK COMMUNICATION MANAGEMENT • RELEASE STRATEGY • ADDITIONAL RELEASE STEPS • ASSIGN WORKFLOW TEMPLATE TO RELEASE PROCEDURE. The screen shown in Figure 5.20 appears.

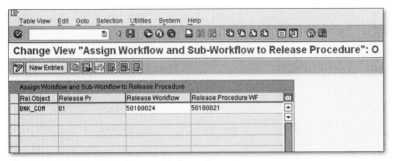

Figure 5.20 Assign Workflow to Release Procedure

In the previous step, we created a release procedure. In this step, we assign it to a workflow procedure and subprocedure, if needed.

The following path is used to configure digital signatures: SAP Customizing Implementation Guide • Financial Supply Chain Management • Bank Communication Management • Release Strategy • Digital Signatures. A digital signature is an SAP BCM feature that adds extra security to the payment process: a user approves a payment, and then has to enter his digital signature, which is usually an additional password (but could be something like a token number, provided you installed third-party add-on software to enable it). When you access this path, the screen shown in Figure 5.21 appears.

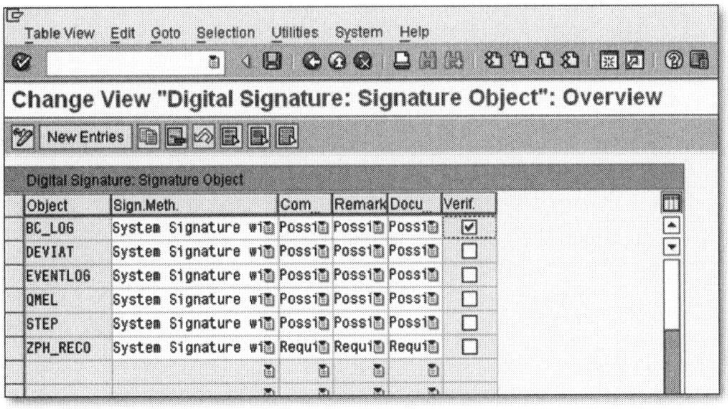

Figure 5.21 Digital Signature Configuration Screen

On this screen, enter your signature object, the signature method, and whether document display, remarks, verification, and comments are possible, required, or forbidden. In the last column, define whether verification is needed. You should select this in most cases, unless you only intend to use the rule for testing purposes. You should also select it if you are using a third-party software product such as Secude, or other digital signature software.

5.4 SAP Bank Communication Management in Action

This section demonstrates two parts of SAP Bank Communication Management: the Bank Statement Monitor, and the Batch and Payment Monitor.

5.4.1 Bank Statement Monitor

To open the Bank Statement Monitor, access the following menu path: SAP Customizing Implementation Guide • Financial Supply Chain Management • Bank Relationship Management • Status Management • FTI_BSM – Bank Statement Monitor. The screen shown in Figure 5.22 appears.

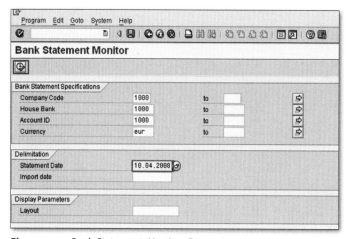

Figure 5.22 Bank Statement Monitor Parameters

On this screen, enter your company code, house bank, account ID, currency (you can enter ranges), and the statement date to be monitored. Then click Execute. If the statement file has not yet arrived, the status is shown is red (Figure 5.23).

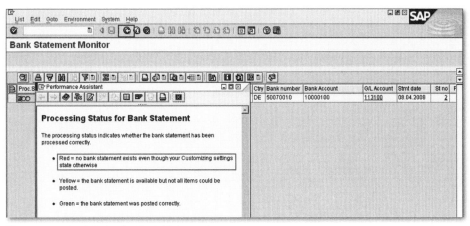

Figure 5.23 Red Status for Bank Statement

Now let's assume that the person in charge called the bank and received the file later, making it necessary to import it into the system. To do this, access the following menu path: SAP MENU • ACCOUNTING • FINANCIAL ACCOUNTING • BANKS • INCOMINGS • BANK STATEMENT • FF_5 – IMPORT. The screen shown in Figure 5.24 appears.

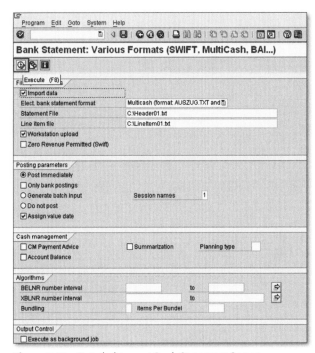

Figure 5.24 Detailed Import Bank Statement Screen

Because we covered this process in Chapter 3, Advanced Inbound Electronic Banking in SAP ERP, we won't go into detail here. Enter the proper parameters and continue. Now, access the following menu path: SAP MENU • FINANCIAL SUPPLY CHAIN MANAGEMENT • BANK RELATIONSHIP MANAGEMENT • STATUS MANAGEMENT • FTI_BSM – BANK STATEMENT MONITOR.

> **Note**
>
> Depending on the version you are working with, the menu may say Bank Relationship Management or Bank Communication Management.

The screen shown in Figure 5.25 appears.

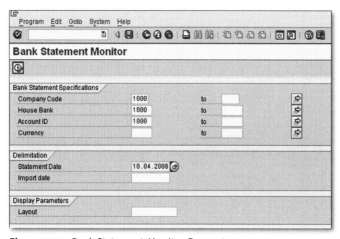

Figure 5.25 Bank Statement Monitor Parameters

In this screen, enter the same parameters shown in Figure 5.22, and click Execute. This brings you to the screen shown in Figure 5.26.

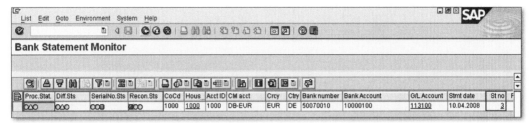

Figure 5.26 Bank Statement Monitor Showing Status

On this screen, you can see the different statuses. The processing status is yellow, which means that the file was received but not all items were successfully processed. The difference status is also yellow, which means that there are differences between the statement balance and the internal account balance, but the difference is within the tolerance. The serial number status is green because the imported file serial number corresponds to the correct sequence. Finally, the reconciliation status is red because some transactions have not yet been properly cleared.

From here, you can branch to bank statement postprocessing, as shown in Figure 5.27.

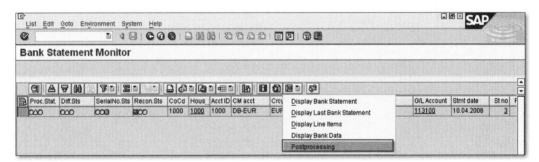

Figure 5.27 Postprocessing a Bank Statement from Bank Statement Monitor

In Figure 5.28, you can see what the problem is, resolve it, and then select Post, using the menu shown in Figure 5.28.

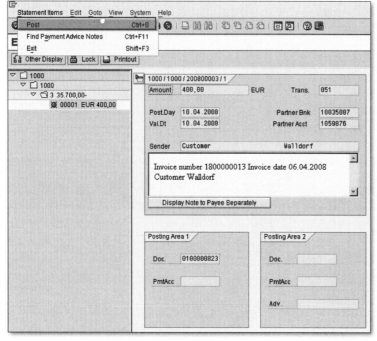

Figure 5.28 Bank Statement Post Processing

After the statement is postprocessed and posted, return to the Bank Statement Monitor. Now you can see that, with the exception of the difference status (which is yellow and won't change because the statement amounts should not be tampered with), all of the statuses are green (Figure 5.29).

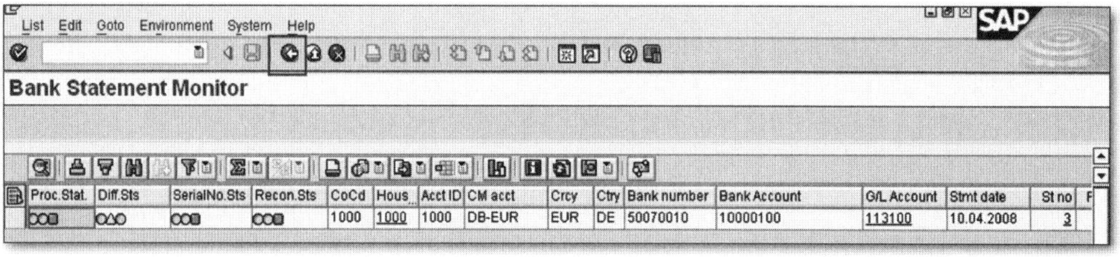

Figure 5.29 Bank Statement Monitor with New Statuses

5.4.2 Batch and Payment Monitor

Figure 5.30 shows the payment program, this is where the traditional Accounts Payable functionality produces the payment approvals and payment media. From here, we will go to the SAP BCM functionality, which is where you create the payment media.

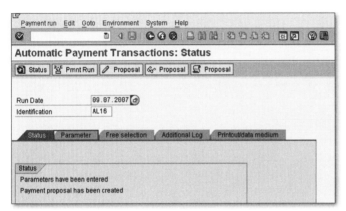

Figure 5.30 Payment Program Screen after Proposal Creation

In this step, you enter the parameters for a payment proposal and execute it (as we explained in Section 4.3.1, Payment Process, in the previous chapter). After this is completed, you can review the proposal. If it is correct, click on the Payment Run button, and the proposal is posted (Figure 5.31).

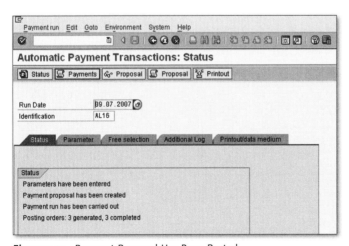

Figure 5.31 Payment Proposal Has Been Posted

As you can see from Figure 5.31, the proposal was executed, and three payments were posted. If you click on the rightmost Proposal button, you can see more details (Figure 5.32).

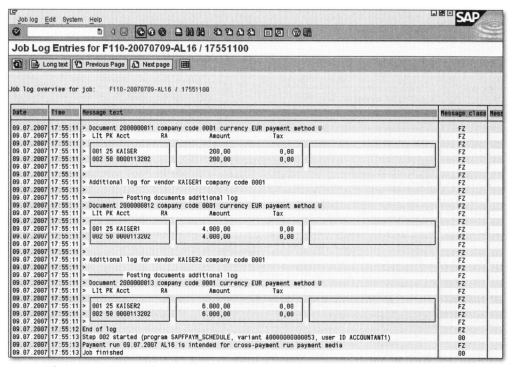

Figure 5.32 Payment Run Log

On this screen, you can see that SAP ERP produced three payment documents for three different invoices. Now follow the path shown in Figure 5.33, which shows you how to access the payment media creation function of SAP BCM from the payment program. Note that this is different from what you would do if you weren't using SAP BCM. (We covered this in Chapter 4, Section 4.3.1, Payment Process.)

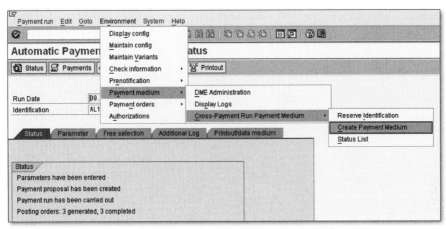

Figure 5.33 Accessing Payment Media Creation for SAP BCM from the Payment Program

The screen shown in Figure 5.34 appears.

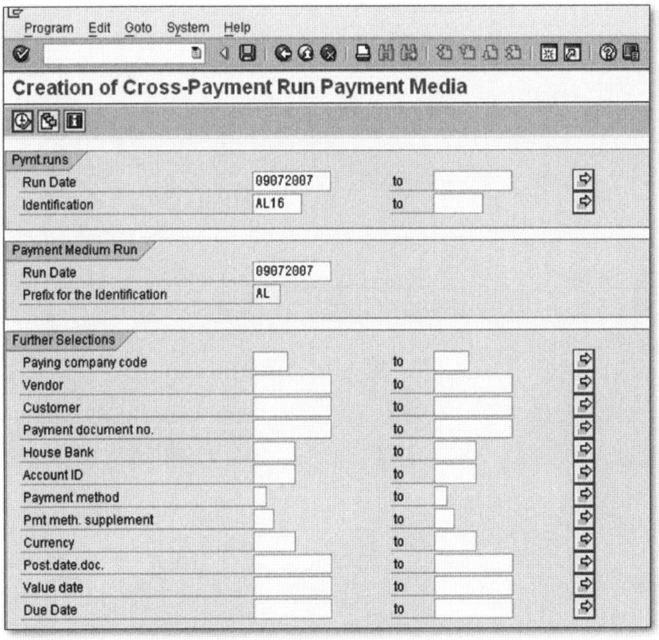

Figure 5.34 Payment Creation Parameters

On this screen, enter your payment run date and ID, and click Execute. The screen shown in Figure 5.35 appears.

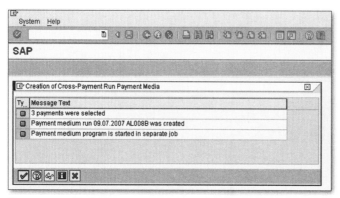

Figure 5.35 Media Program Was Executed

The screen in Figure 5.35 indicates that the payment media was executed for the parameters indicated. As you will see, this doesn't mean that all payment media was created — only the media of those payments that were automatically approved. To see the results of the payment media creation program, access the following menu path: SAP MENU • FINANCIAL SUPPLY CHAIN MANAGEMENT • BANK RELATIONSHIP MANAGEMENT • ENVIRONMENT • BNK_MONIP - STATUS OF COLLECTOR PAYMENTS (Figure 5.36).

Note: Depending on the version you are working on, the menu will say Bank Relationships Management or Bank Communication Management.

Enter your run date, your ID, and, if you merged payments, your merger date. (In this case, it is the same as the run date.) Merge takes place automatically if you configured rules to group payments. Click Execute, and the screen shown in Figure 5.37 appears.

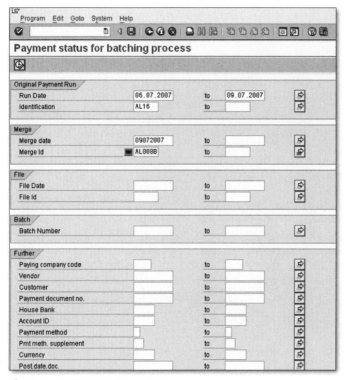

Figure 5.36 Program Parameters

Co...	Payment	Year	Stat	Run Date	ID	Merge date	Mrgld	File Date	File Id	Batch_No	P	Acct ID	Hous	Paym Amount	Crcy
0001	2000000811	2007		09.07.2007	AL16	09.07.2007	AL008B	09.07.2007	00013B	283	U	GIRO	DRE	200,00-	EUR
0001	2000000812	2007		09.07.2007	AL16	09.07.2007	AL008B	09.07.2007	00014B	284	U	GIRO	DRE	4.000,00-	EUR
0001	2000000813	2007		09.07.2007	AL16	09.07.2007	AL008B			282	U	GIRO	DRE	6.000,00-	EUR

Figure 5.37 Payment Status for Batching

As you can see in Figure 5.37, there are file dates and IDs for two of the payments but not for the third; this is because this one payment requires additional approval.

At this point, return to the Batch and Payment Monitor (Figure 5.38).

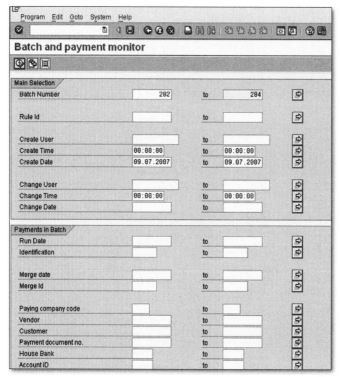

Figure 5.38 Batch and Payment Monitor Parameters

Indicate the batch numbers shown in the previous step — in this example, 282 to 284 — and click Execute. This brings you to the screen shown in Figure 5.39.

	BatNo	#Pay	Rule description	Status	Btch Amt	Curr	House Bk	Acct ID	Create User	Create Date	CrtTm	File Date	File Id
	282	1	Payments > 5.000	Payment batch created	6.000,00	EUR	DRE	GIRO	ACCOUNTANT1	09.07.2007	17:56:16		
	283	1	Payments < 500	Payment medium created	200,00	EUR	DRE	GIRO	ACCOUNTANT1	09.07.2007	17:56:16	09.07.2007	00013B
	284	1	Payments 500 to 5.000	Payment medium created	4.000,00	EUR	DRE	GIRO	ACCOUNTANT1	09.07.2007	17:56:16	09.07.2007	00014B

Figure 5.39 Batch and Payment Monitor

On this screen, you can see that, once again, there is one batch with no file created for the payment media. Select the batch with no payment file, and click on the icon with two human-like figures to see who the approvers are (Figure 5.40).

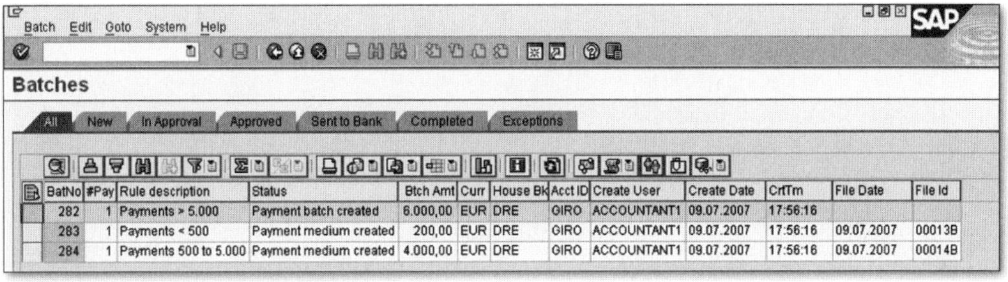

Figure 5.40 Select Batch with No Media

After you select this icon, the screen shown in Figure 5.41 appears.

Figure 5.41 Required Approvers

To move to the approval process, access the following menu path: SAP MENU • ACCOUNTING • FINANCIAL SUPPLY CHAIN MANAGEMENT • BANK RELATIONSHIP MANAGEMENT • PROCESSING • BNK_APP APPROVE PAYMENTS. The screen shown in Figure 5.42 appears.

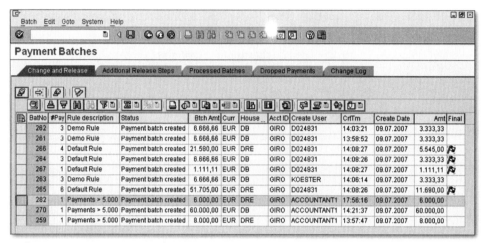

Figure 5.42 Payment Approval Screen

Select the batch you intend to approve, and click on the Approve button in the top-left corner. The message shown in Figure 5.43 appears.

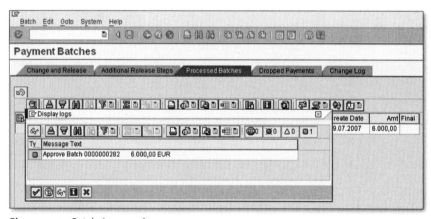

Figure 5.43 Batch Approved

If you required a digital signature during configuration, the screen shown in Figure 5.44 appears.

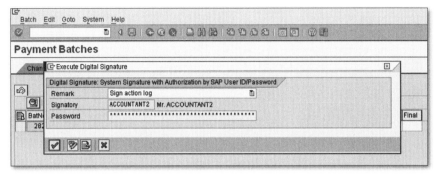

Figure 5.44 Digital Signature

Enter your digital signature. If you configured the system for validation, the system validates it. After this, the batch is approved, and the payment media is created. Now, just to be sure, let's double-check the Batch and Payment Monitor to ensure that the payment media was created after the approval (Figure 5.45).

Batch Edit Goto System Help												
Batches												

	BatNo	#Pay	Rule description	Status	Btch Amt	Curr	House Bk	Acct ID	Create User	Create Date	CrtTm	File Date	File Id
	282	1	Payments > 5.000	Payment medium created	6.000,00	EUR	DRE	GIRO	ACCOUNTANT1	09.07.2007	17:56:16	09.07.2007	00015B
	283	1	Payments < 500	Payment medium created	200,00	EUR	DRE	GIRO	ACCOUNTANT1	09.07.2007	17:56:16	09.07.2007	00013B
	284	1	Payments 500 to 5.000	Payment medium created	4.000,00	EUR	DRE	GIRO	ACCOUNTANT1	09.07.2007	17:56:16	09.07.2007	00014B

Figure 5.45 Batch and Payment Monitor Results

As you can see, after the approvals were done, the system created the payment media. The Batch and Payment Monitor now shows that all of the batches have a file date and ID.

5.5   Summary

In this chapter, we explained how SAP BCM enhances bank communication, specifically with regard to SWIFTNet. We then provided an overview of the different functionalities offered by SAP Bank Communication Management and how they are applied in a real-world business environment, followed by step-by-step configuration instructions for the functionality. Finally, we provided a demonstration of how the functionality works; specifically, we demonstrated the Bank Statement Monitor and the Batch and Payment Monitor. In the next chapter, we explain how to use and configure the In-House Cash functionality.

This chapter uses examples of business scenarios to explain how companies can leverage the SAP ERP Financials In-House Cash component to automate and manage intergroup and intragroup payments, as well as integrate with SAP ERP Financials and Cash Management.

6   In-House Banking with SAP ERP

This chapter reviews most aspects of the SAP In-House Cash functionality. In Section 6.1, Overview of SAP In-House Cash, we provide an overview of the functionality. In Section 6.2, Master Data, we go into more specifics by describing the main master data objects involved in the functionality. In Section 6.3, System Configuration, we provide step-by-step configuration instructions. In Section 6.4, Periodic Tasks, we list the main periodic tasks. In Section 6.5, Reporting, we list and explain the main reports available. Finally, in Section 6.6, Examples of SAP In-House Cash in Action, we provide a walkthrough of the functionality.

6.1   Overview of SAP In-House Cash

In this section, we describe what SAP In-House Cash is, why you should implement it, how to determine whether it's a good fit for your company, and what the cost implications are.

SAP In-House Cash is used to perform what is known as *in-house banking*, which provides you with some services that are usually provided by external banks, for example, intercompany cash transfers, loan services, investment services, and netting services.

The best way to understand the SAP In-House Cash functionality is to see how companies work with and without it, so let's analyze some examples. Figure 6.1 shows a typical decentralized treasury process that does not use SAP In-House Cash, with payments to vendors and collections from customers being processed at each subsidiary, and in which headquarters only gets a copy of each subsidiary's bank statement and reports on cash.

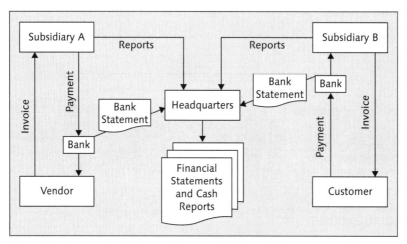

Figure 6.1 Decentralized Treasury Processing Without SAP In-House Cash

Although this is the easiest process to set up, there is some inefficiency associated with it because you are processing the same functions for each company and having to keep a headcount for that purpose. For example, if you have 100 subsidiaries that pay the same vendor, you may also have to maintain 100 AP departments, receive and review 100 invoices, cut 100 checks, and reconcile 100 outstanding checks. In this case, even though the setup is very easy, the ongoing cost is very high.

Figure 6.2 shows a *centralized* treasury process that also does not use SAP In-House Cash. (Although it is a common misconception that you need SAP In-House Cash to centralize treasury processes, this is not true.) In this example, payable invoices are forwarded to a shared services department at headquarters, where they are validated and paid. In addition, payments from customers are forwarded to a headquarters bank account via cash concentration.

The resulting debits and credits between subsidiaries and headquarters are resolved through automated intercompany postings.

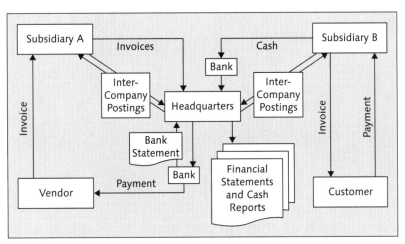

Figure 6.2 Centralized Treasury Processing Without SAP In-House Cash

In the specific example shown in Figure 6.2, if 100 subsidiaries get invoices from the same vendor, you need maintain only 1 AP department, cut only 1 check, and reconcile the clearing for only that check. The setup is more complicated because you have to configure the automatic intercompany postings, but the ongoing costs are much lower.

What's inconvenient about this schema is that if you want to determine how much cash belongs to each subsidiary at any moment in time, you must read the line items of the intercompany account, which can be tedious and time-consuming. It is a bit like managing fixed assets using general ledger accounts instead of the Assets component: It's possible, but time-consuming and not user-friendly.

In Figure 6.3, payments and collections are processed centrally; however, instead of using the intercompany account to reconcile how much cash belongs to each subsidiary, you use SAP In-House Cash. This component keeps track of cash at all times, produces bank statements for each subsidiary, and provides reports of how much cash belongs to each subsidiary at any moment in time. The system also allows you to put together surpluses of cash from all subsidiaries and use those surpluses to lend money to the subsidiaries that need it. While doing this, SAP In-House Cash can charge interest to those subsidiaries that borrow and pay interest to those subsidiaries that lend.

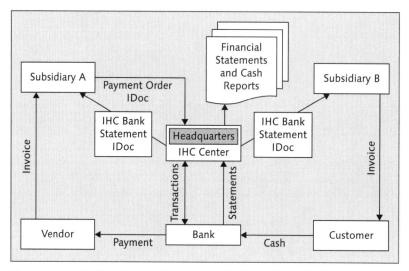

Figure 6.3 Centralized Treasury Processing with SAP In-House Cash

In this section, we provide an overview of SAP In-House Cash, specifically focusing on the key drivers for implementing the component, business scenarios supported for it, and cost-benefit considerations associated with it.

6.1.1 Key Drivers for Implementing SAP In-House Cash

Your company might consider investing in SAP In-House Cash for a number of reasons, including the following:

▶ **To optimize your capital structure.**
Instead of having to keep a large number of bank accounts and loans with multiple institutions, incurring multiple fees, SAP In-House Cash allows you to use virtual bank accounts for many of your needs and only use external banks for those things that cannot be resolved internally.

▶ **To save in interest and banking fees.**
By using your own system to provide financial services, you avoid paying contract fees, wire transfer fees, interest on external loans, and so on.

▶ **To solve some financial needs internally instead of using a bank.**
Instead of processing an international wire transfer to send money from one company to another, you can do a payment order in SAP In-House Cash and avoid the fee. This can also be done with loans and other features.

▶ **To use cash surpluses to finance other companies within the group.**
Instead of investing cash surpluses at 1%, you can lend them to another of your companies for a little more. This will still be cheaper for that company than if it were to borrow the money from a bank.

▶ **To increase interest revenue.**
By lending money within your group, you gain interest revenue.

▶ **To have a better control of your cash.**
The system allows you to monitor where your cash goes and how much belongs to each company within your group.

▶ **To gain the ability to net and combine payments for multiple subsidiaries.**
Instead of cutting multiple checks for the same vendor, you combine and produce only one check.

▶ **To comply with statutory cash reporting requirements.**
Several requirements for regulated industries and for international companies can only be fulfilled with SAP In-House Cash.

6.1.2 Business Scenarios Supported by SAP In-House Cash

Three main scenarios are supported by SAP In-House Cash:

▶ Central payments

▶ Intercompany payments

▶ Central collections

In Figure 6.4, we show an example of a central payment in which a subsidiary receives an invoice from a vendor, reviews and approves it, and then runs the payment program at the subsidiary level. This generates an IDoc with a payment order.

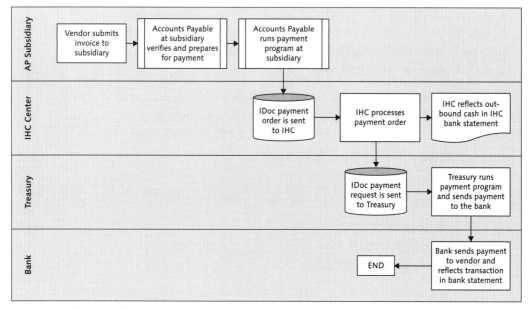

Figure 6.4 Central Payments

The payment order is approved in the SAP In-House Cash component, and, when this is done, the cash balance of the subsidiary is updated (lowered), and a payment request is created. The treasury department then uses the payment program for payment requests to issue a wire payment to the vendor. The bank receives the wire instructions and sends the cash to the vendor, which is reflected in the electronic bank statement the next day.

In Figure 6.5, we show an example of an intercompany payment where one subsidiary submits an invoice to another, and the receiving subsidiary reviews/approves it and runs the payment program. This produces an IDoc with a payment order.

The treasury department approves the payment order within SAP In-House Cash, which lowers the cash balance of the paying subsidiary and increases the cash balance of the receiving subsidiary. SAP In-House Cash then issues updated internal bank statements to each subsidiary; each subsidiary receives the internal bank statement and automatically updates its general ledger.

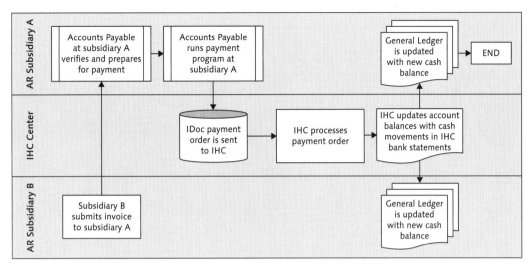

Figure 6.5 Intercompany Payments

At this point, the cash balance in the general ledger matches the cash balance in SAP In-House Cash. The transfer is completed without having to issue an external payment or talk to an external bank; virtual cash is moved, but real cash stays in the same place. This may be hard to grasp the first time you hear the process explained, but hundreds of companies do this around the world every day.

Figure 6.6 shows an example of central collections, in which a subsidiary sends an invoice to a customer, and the customer reviews it and sends the payment to the bank. The bank then processes the payment and sends an updated electronic bank statement to headquarters, and then headquarters processes all of the bank statements for all of the subsidiaries. After this is completed, SAP In-House Cash determines which deposits belong to which subsidiaries, and sends updated electronic internal bank statements to each subsidiary. Each subsidiary receives the internal bank statement and automatically updates the accounting to reflect the new cash balance.

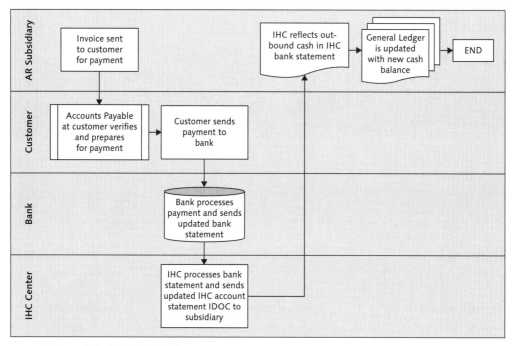

Figure 6.6 Central Collections

6.1.3 Cost Benefit Considerations

SAP In-House Cash is not suitable for all companies because it has significant process implications and costs. It's important to make sure it fits the needs of your organization, or your return on investment won't justify its implementation.

Some of the costs and implications associated with SAP In-House Cash are as follows:

▶ The AP process gains two extra steps, which makes the process more complex.

▶ The new process requires the extensive use of IDocs, so the AP and treasury teams must be trained on how to handle them.

▶ At least one individual is needed to run and follow up on end-of-day processes.

▶ There is tighter integration among AP, treasury, and accounting, which requires coordination.

▶ Some custom reports and enhancements may be needed to fulfill some specific requirements.

Following are some guidelines that might indicate that your company needs SAP In-House Cash:

▶ **You have more than one company in your group.**
SAP In-House Cash requires more than one company in your group to work.

▶ **You incur very high costs on banking fees.**
If you send a lot of international wire transfers between companies, and pay fees to invest excess cash in some companies and set up loans in others, you may have a good business case to implement SAP In-House Cash.

▶ **You operate in more than one country.**
Most countries require detailed cash reporting. Even if the cash is deposited in bank accounts in a different country, cross-border payments are closely monitored by authorities (even more so after 9/11).

▶ **Your company is part of a regulated industry that requires detailed reporting on cash.**
Certain industries, such as utilities, cannot be allowed to go bankrupt. To avoid that from happening, they have their cash balances and liabilities closely monitored by authorities. In most cases, the required reports can be accommodated by SAP In-House Cash.

▶ **You pool cash between companies.**
If you are already used to lending cash between companies, SAP In-House Cash can make this task easier. Instead of having to use the intercompany account to track the balance of these loans, SAP In-House Cash keeps track for you.

If several of these points apply to your company, you should consider an SAP In-House Cash implementation.

6.2 Master Data

This section lists and describes the main master data objects associated with SAP In-House Cash.

▶ **Business partners**
In this component, business partners are primarily banks, brokerage firms, other subsidiaries in your group, and, in some instances, customers or vendors. If you have more than one bank area, you must set up each bank area as a business partner too.

▶ **Conditions**
If you charge interest to subsidiaries who borrow from the SAP In-House Cash center and pay interest to those who invest on it, or if you charge fees to the subsidiaries, you must set up *conditions* that detail interest rates, value dates, and so on.

▶ **Limits**
In some instances, particularly in regulated industries, there are some limits to how much you can borrow from the SAP In-House Cash center (commonly referred to as the *money pool*). Sometimes, companies can borrow up to a certain percentage of the pool assets; other times, there are restrictions known as *limits*. If the particular condition you want to implement is not supported with standard limit functionality, you may have to do some development.

▶ **Product definition**
SAP In-House Cash uses products in a similar way to the Transaction Manager, in the sense that the conditions you use, the transaction types associated with them, and several other functions are determined by which product you configure and use.

▶ **Accounts**
In SAP In-House Cash, you must create an account for each of your subsidiaries (possibly more); the account controls a number of management and administration functions, which we discuss in more detail in Section 6.3, System Configuration.

6.3   System Configuration

To make the explanations easier to understand, this section is divided into six different subsections:

- Bank key terms

- Virtual bank creation

- ALE configuration

- SAP In-House Cash general configuration

- SAP In-House Cash payments configuration

- SAP In-House Cash collections configuration

6.3.1   Bank Key Terms

Before we get into bank configuration details, let's look at the definitions for some of the most important bank terms:

- **Bank master data**
  Refers to all existing banks in the world, regardless of whether or not your company has a bank account there.

- **House bank**
  Refers to only those banks in which your company has accounts.

- **Account ID**
  Refers to those bank accounts owned by your company.

- **Bank ALE partner**
  Refers to the settings in ALE needed to send/receive IDocs to/from a specific bank.

- **Bank area**
  Refers to the highest organizational structure within SAP In-House Cash and is usually the entity where SAP In-House Cash processes are centralized and performed. It is also known as the *SAP In-House Cash center*.

6.3.2 Virtual Bank Creation

Even though the SAP In-House Cash center is a virtual bank, it has to exist in the SAP system to be used. To create the bank, execute Transaction F101 (Figure 6.7).

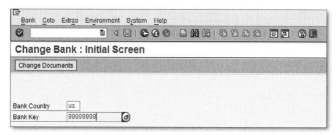

Figure 6.7 Create Bank: Initial Screen

On the screen shown in Figure 6.7, enter the country and the numbers 99999999, which don't belong to any real bank, and thus can be used for a virtual bank. Select Enter.

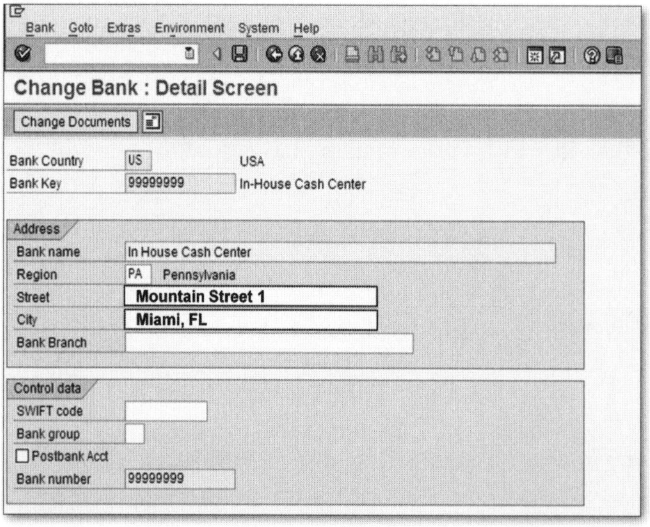

Figure 6.8 Change Bank: Detail Screen

The screen shown in Figure 6.8 contains specific bank information. Enter "In-House Cash Center" in the Bank Name field, and then enter the state and street address. Because this is a virtual bank, you don't need to enter additional address details.

6.3.3 ALE Configuration

Application Link Enabling (ALE) is the SAP functionality used to connect two separate systems. This communication occurs via IDocs (*intermediate documents*), which are files that have a specific layout definition and are sent to a specific destination (port). IDocs are frequently used when customers have multiple instances of SAP and decide to set up SAP In-House Cash in more than one of them. For this to work, you need IDocs to send and receive the information between systems.

Figure 6.9 shows the technical architecture options for SAP In-House Cash. As you can see, SAP In-House Cash can be set up on the same system as SAP ERP, or it can be set up in a different system (which is common when you have different subsidiaries in different instances of SAP) — but it's important to understand that, in either case, ALE has to be fully configured. This is the way the system is designed.

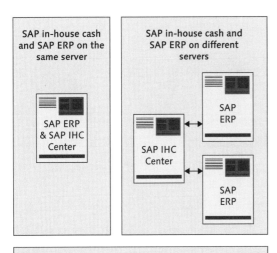

Figure 6.9 Technical Architecture Options for SAP In-House Cash

Figure 6.10 shows the required ALE settings, a screen that is accessed via Transaction WE21. The purpose of the transactions is to create a port, which is the destination of an IDoc.

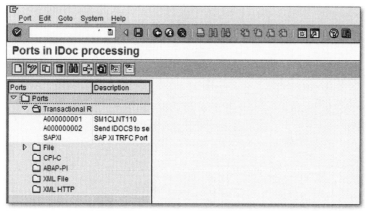

Figure 6.10 ALE Port Creation Initial Screen

Click on the Create icon in the top-left corner, and the prompt shown in Figure 6.11 appears.

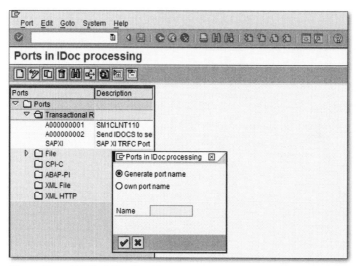

Figure 6.11 ALE Port Creation Prompt

The system asks if you want it to create the port name, or if you will assign it yourself. In general, we recommend letting the system assign it. Click the Enter button, and the screen shows in Figure 6.12 appears.

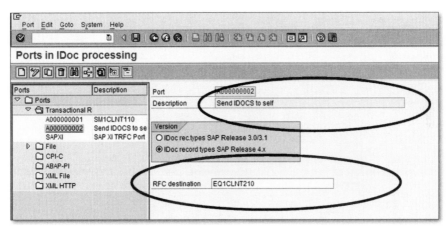

Figure 6.12 Create ALE Port Details

Enter a description in the Description field; if your SAP In-House Cash system is on the same server as SAP ERP, enter "Send IDocs to self." Then, in the RFC Destination field, enter the technical name of the SAP instance and client to which you will be sending the IDocs.

Now execute Transaction WE20, which is the screen shown in Figure 6.13. Create bank partner 99999999, which, you will recall, is the bank we previously created in Transaction FI01. The bank needs to exist in the system for ALE to recognize it.

Create the ALE partner for the bank as partner type B (Bank), and then link it to a message type. In our example, we use message type PAYEXT, which is the message typically used for payment transactions. In the Message Code field, enter "IHC" for SAP In-House Cash. Enter "F1" in the Message Function field.

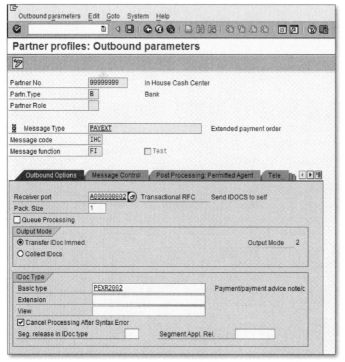

Figure 6.13 Bank ALE Partner Profile Definition

In the Outbound Parameters tab, enter the receiver port that you created in the preceding step, select Transfer IDoc Immed., and enter "PEXR2002" in the Basic Type field (this is the IDoc used for sending payment files to banks).

6.3.4 SAP In-House Cash General Configuration

In this subsection, we discuss settings that are not specific to either payments or collections but that are needed for the system to operate. The first step is to create the bank area. This is the top organizational entity in SAP In-House Cash; you usually create it either in the company that holds your headquarters or the one that holds your Shared Services Center. If you have multiple Shared Services Centers around the globe, you can create multiple bank areas, but, remember, the more you have, the more complex your process will be.

To access the configuration of a bank area, use the following menu path: SAP Customizing Implementation Guide • Financial Supply Chain Management • In-
House Cash • Basic Settings • Bank Area • Define Bank Area.

On the screen shown in Figure 6.14, enter a description, the country, the bank key
(usually, 99999999), the language and currency, a calendar, a time for post cut off
(this is the time at which you close postings for the day), an exchange rate type (M
is the default), the company code where the bank area will reside, and the general
ledger variant.

You will probably need to create your own general ledger variant; to do this, go
to the IMG, and use the following menu path: SAP Customizing Implementation Guide • Financial Supply Chain Management • In-House Cash • Periodic
Tasks • General Ledger Transfer • Maintain GL Variants. In that screen, enter
your variant name and description, the chart of accounts used, the clearing account
for transactions, the document type, and the posting keys to use for IHC postings.
Activate the log and the IHC area.

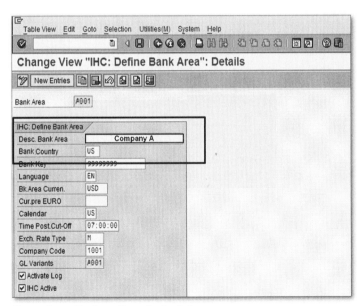

Figure 6.14 Configuration of a Bank Area

The next step is to assign products to a bank area; to do this, use the following menu path: SAP Customizing Implementation Guide • Financial Supply Chain Management • In-House Cash • Master Data • Product Definition • Product • Assign Products to Bank Areas. This takes you to the screen shown in Figure 6.15.

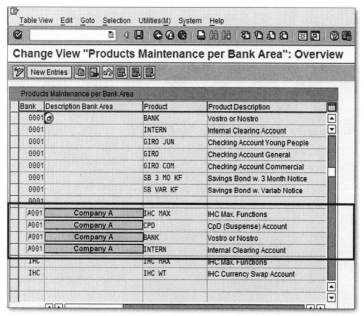

Figure 6.15 Assign Products to Bank Area

In the screen shown in Figure 6.15, assign SAP In-House Cash product types to your newly created bank area. You can copy the ones assigned to 0001 to your own bank area.

The next step is to define transaction types. To do this, use the following menu path: SAP Customizing Implementation Guide • Financial Supply Chain Management • In-House Cash • Account Management • Payment Processes in In-House Cash • Define Transaction Types. This takes you to the screen shown in Figure 6.16.

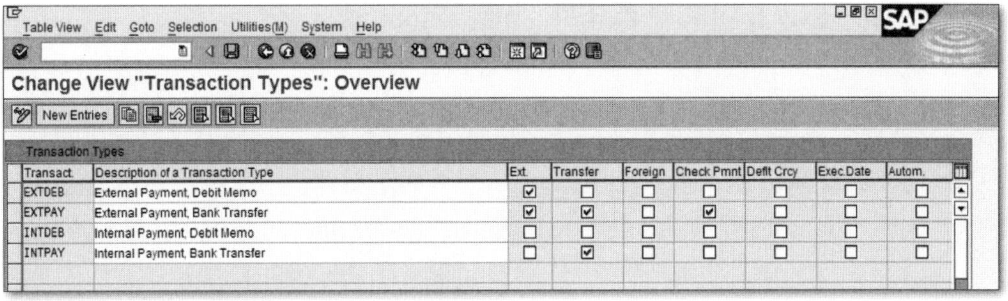

Figure 6.16 SAP In-House Cash Transaction Types

There are two types of transaction, debits and credits, and for each of those, there are both external and internal transactions. In the screen shown in Figure 6.16, you configure the settings specific to each, specifying information such as which requires a check, which requires a transfer, which is external, and so on. If you are not sure, you can probably copy the settings in this example.

The next step is to define a clearing partner, which you can think of as the clearing house used by the banks to settle interbank transactions. Use the following menu path: SAP CUSTOMIZING IMPLEMENTATION GUIDE • FINANCIAL SUPPLY CHAIN MANAGEMENT • IN-HOUSE CASH • ACCOUNT MANAGEMENT • PAYMENT PROCESSES IN IN-HOUSE CASH • DEFINE CLEARING PARTNER. This takes you to the screen shown in Figure 6.17.

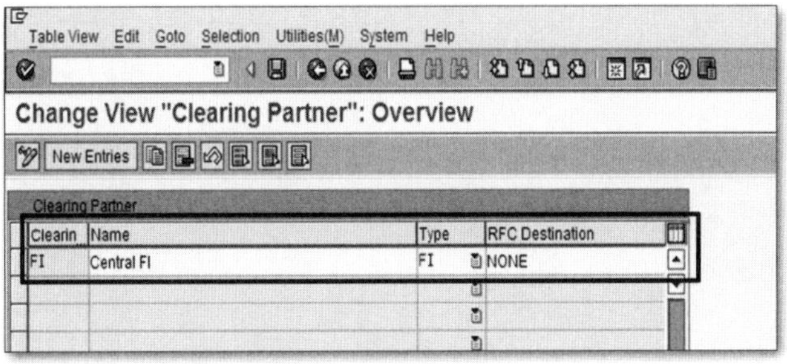

Figure 6.17 Clearing Partner Definition

In the preceding example, the clearing partner is called FI, which is the default setting. We explain how this works later in Figure 6.21.

6.3.5 SAP In-House Cash Payments Configuration

Let's now discuss the settings that are necessary for payment transactions to work properly. Use the following menu path: SAP CUSTOMIZING IMPLEMENTATION GUIDE • FINANCIAL SUPPLY CHAIN MANAGEMENT • IN-HOUSE CASH • ACCOUNT MANAGEMENT • PAYMENT PROCESSES IN IN-HOUSE CASH • MAKE BASIC SETTINGS FOR PAYMENT PROCESSES. In the resulting screen, select your bank area, and then click on Processing Transaction on the left menu. The screen shown in Figure 6.18 appears.

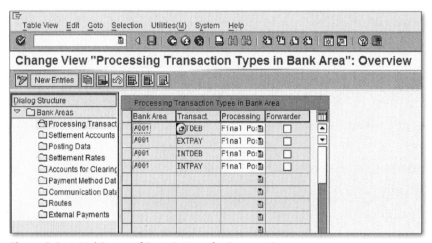

Figure 6.18 Initial Screen of Basic Settings for Payment Processes

Figure 6.18 is the initial screen for processing payment transactions. In this screen, you must link your bank area and each of the transaction types to a processing method, which can be provisional or final. If you select Provisional, you must run another process to make the final posting; if you select Final, the extra process is unnecessary. We recommend selecting Final.

If you select the Forwarder indicator for a provisional processing method, the system sends IDocs with the payment to the clearing partner; if you don't check it, the IDoc is only created when you run the additional process to make the final posting.

Now click on Settlement Accounts, and the screen shown in Figure 6.19 appears.

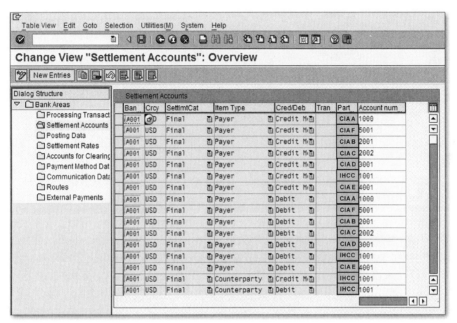

Figure 6.19 Configuration of Settlement Accounts

Enter your bank area in the Bank column, enter your main currency in the Crcy column, enter "Final" in the SettlmtCat column (unless you selected Provisional in the previous section), and enter each of your SAP In-House Cash accounts (each of your subsidiaries) as Payer in the Item Type column. The only exception to this last option is the company where your bank area sits; in this case, enter the Item Type as Counterparty. In the Cred/Deb column, you need an entry for Debit and an entry for Credit for each of your subsidiaries. Leave the Tran column blank. Enter the business partner that you created for each subsidiary in the Part column. Enter the SAP In-House Cash account that you created for each subsidiary in the Account Num column.

Click on Posting Data, and the screen shown in Figure 6.20 appears.

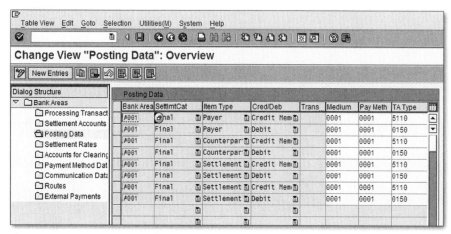

Figure 6.20 Posting Data Configuration

Enter your bank area in the Bank Area column, enter "Final" (unless you previously entered Provisional) in the SettlmtCat column. Add one entry for Debit and another for Credit Memo. Leave the Transaction column blank. In the Medium and Pay Meth columns, enter "0001"; in the TA Type column, enter "5110" for credit and "0150" for debit. You can think of these numbers as the equivalent of 40 and 50 for the posting keys in the general ledger.

Click on Accounts for Clearing, and the screen shown in Figure 6.21 appears.

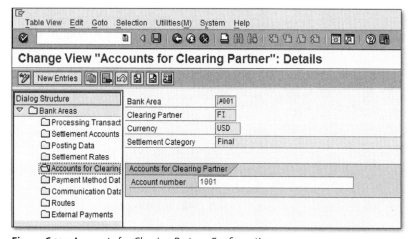

Figure 6.21 Accounts for Clearing Partner Configuration

Enter your bank area, the clearing partner created previously (FI, in our example), your currency, and the settlement category you're using (most likely Final). In the Account Number field, enter the SAP In-House Cash account of the subsidiary (or headquarters) where the bank area sits.

Click on Payment Method Data, and the screen shown in Figure 6.22 appears.

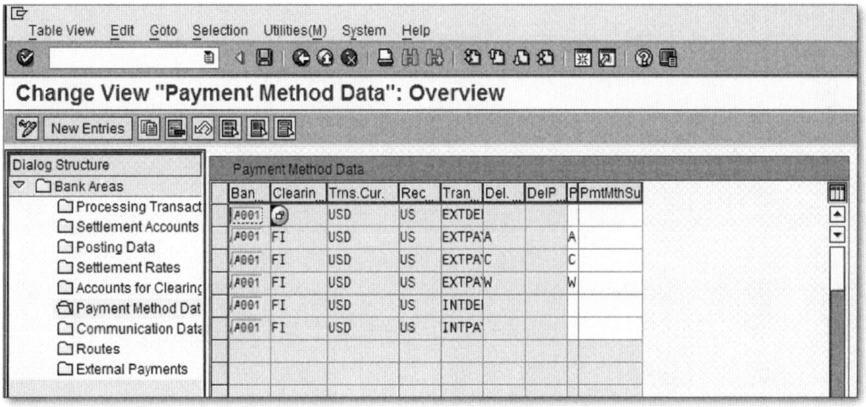

Figure 6.22 Payment Method Data

In the screen shown in Figure 6.22, enter your bank area, clearing partner, and currency in the appropriate columns. In the Transaction column, create an entry for each transaction type (EXTDEB, EXTPAY, INTDEB, and INTPAY). For EXTPAY, instead of one entry, enter one for each payment method that you will use. In the example in Figure 6.22, our payment methods were Wire, Check, and ACH — hence the A, C, and W. However, don't confuse these letters with the names of the payment methods used in the payment program; we map these to the payment methods used in the payment program later.

Click on Communication Data, and the screen shown in Figure 6.23 appears.

It is important that you configure this screen correctly, or the IDocs won't work. Enter your bank area, clearing partner, and currency in the appropriate columns. In the Rec. Partn. Type, enter "B" for the bank partner type. In the Partn. No. column, enter the bank key for your SAP In-House Cash center (the one we configured in Section 6.3.2, Virtual Bank Creation). In the Msg. Var. column, enter "IHC"; in Msg, Funct., enter "FI"; in the Account column, enter the account of the subsidiary where your SAP In-House Cash center sits. (You may remember that these are the same values we configured in Section 6.3.3, ALE Configuration.)

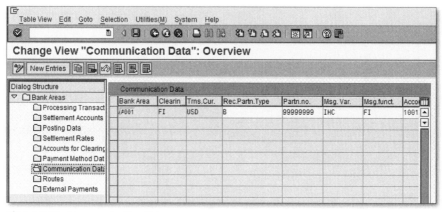

Figure 6.23 Communication Data

Click on Routes, and the screen shown in Figure 6.24 appears.

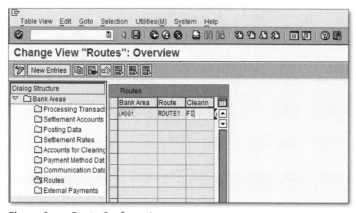

Figure 6.24 Route Configuration

Enter your bank area, "Route1" in the Route column, and your clearing partner (most likely "FI").

Click on External Payments, and the screen shown in Figure 6.25 appears.

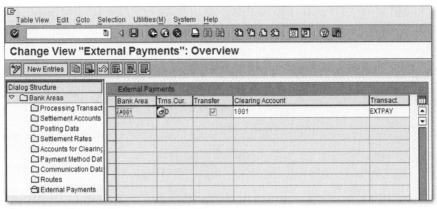

Figure 6.25 External Payment Configuration

In this screen, you configure the clearing account and transaction type used for external payments. Enter your bank area and currency, check the Transfer indicator, and enter the account of the company where your bank area sits in the Clearing Account column. Enter "EXTPAY" in the last column. (This is another configuration that affects the IDoc, and it may become relevant if you have to troubleshoot the IDoc.)

The next step is to configure the default settings for transaction types. To do this, use the following menu path: SAP CUSTOMIZING IMPLEMENTATION GUIDE • FINANCIAL SUPPLY CHAIN MANAGEMENT • IN-HOUSE CASH • ACCOUNT MANAGEMENT • PAYMENT PROCESSES IN IN-HOUSE CASH • DEFINE DEFAULT SETTING FOR TRANSACTION TYPE. This brings you to the screen shown in Figure 6.26.

Table View Edit Goto Selection Utilities(M) System Help

Change View "IHC: Default Settings for Transaction Types": Overview

New Entries

Customizable Transactions		User	Transact.	Description of a Transaction Typ
External Debit Memo			EXTDEB	External Payment, Debit Memo
External Transfer			EXTPAY	External Payment, Bank Transfe
Internal Debit Memo			INTDEB	Internal Payment, Debit Memo
Internal Transfer			INTPAY	Internal Payment, Bank Transfe
Expert Mode			EXTPAY	External Payment, Bank Transfe

Figure 6.26 Default Settings for Transaction Types

In this screen, you link the EXTDEB transaction to External Debit Memo, the EXTPAY to External Transfer, the INTDEB to Internal Debit Memo, the INTPAY to Internal Transfer, and the EXTPAY to Expert Mode.

The next step is to define transaction types for automatic payments. To do this, use the following menu path: SAP CUSTOMIZING IMPLEMENTATION GUIDE • FINAN-CIAL SUPPLY CHAIN MANAGEMENT • IN-HOUSE CASH • ACCOUNT MANAGEMENT • PAYMENT PROCESSES IN IN-HOUSE CASH • DEFINE TRANSACTION TYPE FOR AUTOMATIC PAYMENTS. The screen shown in Figure 6.27 appears.

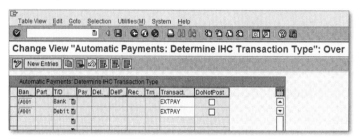

Figure 6.27 Determine SAP In-House Cash Transaction Type

On this screen, copy the settings shown here with your own bank area. This will tell the system that for both credits and debits it should use the EXTPAY IDoc.

In the next step, we set up route processing. Access the following menu path: SAP CUSTOMIZING IMPLEMENTATION GUIDE • FINANCIAL SUPPLY CHAIN MANAGEMENT • IN-HOUSE CASH • ACCOUNT MANAGEMENT • PAYMENT PROCESSES IN IN-HOUSE CASH • SET UP ROUTE PROCESSING. The screen shown in Figure 6.28 appears.

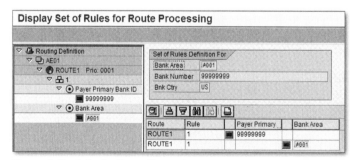

Figure 6.28 Rules for Route Processing

As you will recall, we created Route1 in a previous step. Now is when we tell the system what Route1 means. In this case, all you need to do is tell the system that your payer is always bank 999999999 (your own IHC bank) and what your bank area is.

At this point, it's time to configure the settings for payment orders. To do this, access the following menu path: SAP Customizing Implementation Guide • Financial Supply Chain Management • In-House Cash • Account Management • Payment Processes in In-House Cash • Outgoing Payment Orders • Set Up Creation of Payment Requests for Inbound IDOC in FI. The screen shown in Figure 6.29 appears.

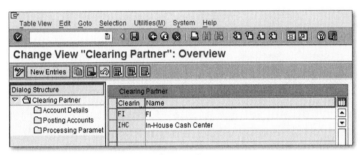

Figure 6.29 Clearing Partner Selection Screen

On this screen, select your clearing partner (most likely FI), and then click on Account Details. The screen shown in Figure 6.30 appears.

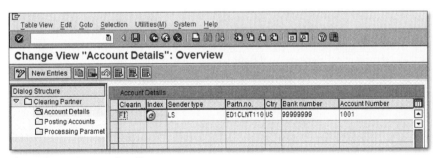

Figure 6.30 Account Details

On this screen, enter your clearing partner, and leave the Index column blank. In the Sender Type column, enter "LS" (logical system); in the Partn. No. Column, enter the name of your SAP server and the client used by Basis; in the Ctry column, enter your country; in the Bank Number column, enter "999999999"; and in the Account Number field, enter the SAP In-House Cash account of your clearing partner.

Click on Posting Accounts, and the screen shown in Figure 6.31 appears.

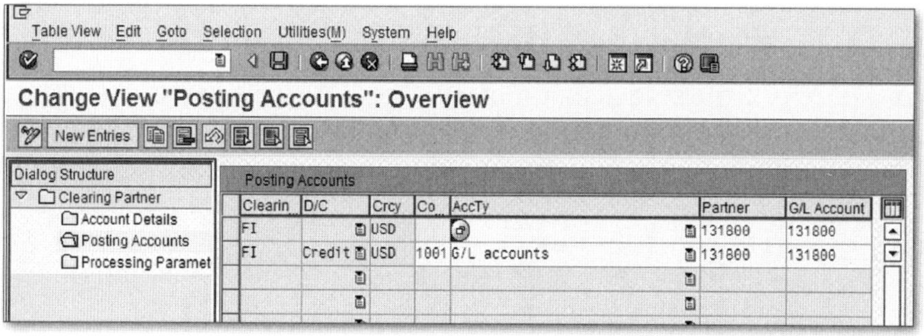

Figure 6.31 Posting Accounts

On this screen, enter your clearing partner, an entry for debit, and an entry for credit (in the D/C column). In the Co column, enter the company where your bank area sits. Enter your currency (Crcy) and the general ledger accounts that you will use forSAP In-House Cash debits andSAP In-House Cash credits (G/L Account column).

Click on Processing Parameters, and the screen shown in Figure 6.32 appears.

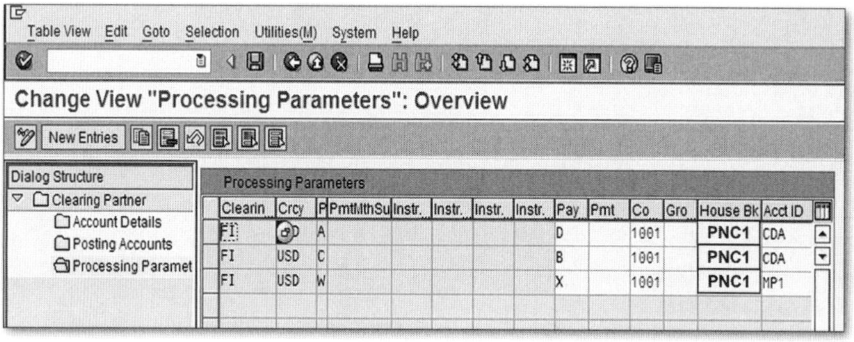

Figure 6.32 Processing Parameters Screen

On this screen, map your clearing partners and the SAP In-House Cash payment methods configured previously (in Figure 6.22) to the payment methods configured in the payment program, and the bank accounts and account IDs used by the company that issues payments.

6.3.6 SAP In-House Cash Collections Configuration

This configuration ensures that when you upload your bank statement reflecting the cash collected, the system finds the SAP In-House Cash account that corresponds to each bank account and each item in the electronic bank statement. Access the following menu path: SAP CUSTOMIZING IMPLEMENTATION GUIDE • FINANCIAL SUPPLY CHAIN MANAGEMENT • IN-HOUSE CASH • ACCOUNT MANAGEMENT • PAYMENT PROCESSES IN IN-HOUSE CASH • CENTRAL CASH RECEIPT/INCOMING BANK STATEMENTS • IHC ACCOUNT DETERMINATION FROM EXTERNAL BANK ACCOUNT. The screen shown in Figure 6.33 appears.

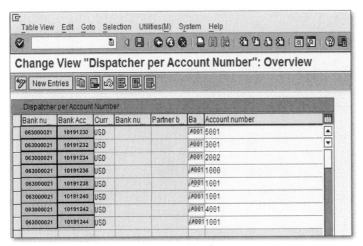

Figure 6.33 Dispatcher per Account Number

Map the real routing numbers and bank accounts to your bank area and SAP In-House Cash accounts.

The next step is to set up the account determination for incoming payments. To do this, access the following menu path: SAP CUSTOMIZING IMPLEMENTATION GUIDE • FINANCIAL SUPPLY CHAIN MANAGEMENT • IN-HOUSE CASH • ACCOUNT MANAGEMENT • PAYMENT PROCESSES IN IN-HOUSE CASH • CENTRAL CASH RECEIPT/INCOMING BANK STATEMENTS • SET UP ACCOUNT DETERMINATION FOR INCOMING PAYMENT. The screen shown in Figure 6.34 appears.

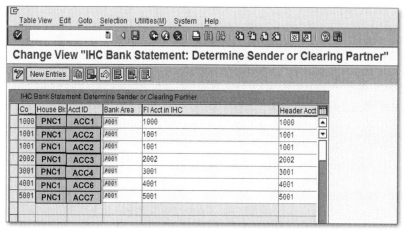

Figure 6.34 SAP In-House Cash Bank Statement Determine Sender

On this screen, map your house banks and account IDs to your bank area and your SAP In-House Cash accounts.

The next step is to define transaction types for incoming payments. To do this, access the following menu path: SAP CUSTOMIZING IMPLEMENTATION GUIDE • FINANCIAL SUPPLY CHAIN MANAGEMENT • IN-HOUSE CASH • ACCOUNT MANAGEMENT • PAYMENT PROCESSES IN IN-HOUSE CASH • CENTRAL CASH RECEIPT/INCOMING BANK STATEMENTS • DEFINE TRANSACTION TYPES FOR INCOMING PAYMENT. The screen shown in Figure 6.35 appears.

On this screen, map your bank area, the transaction type you use in the electronic bank statement (BAI, in this example), and the external bank statement codes to the SAP In-House Cash transaction type that correctly reflects the nature of the transaction.

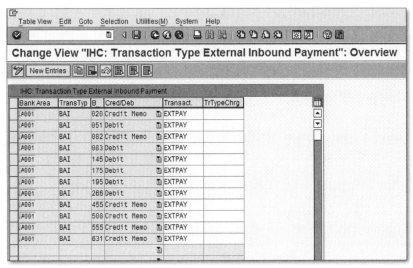

Figure 6.35 Transaction Types for External Inbound Payments

6.4 Periodic Tasks

This section briefly describes several periodic tasks that have to be performed for SAP In-House Cash to be in sync with the general ledger, Cash Management, Transaction Manager, and so on. The following are the most important:

▶ **Posting cut off**
This process ends the transactions for a specific date and sets the date of the next transaction day in the system. This is particularly important regarding reporting and accounting because, in many instances, interests and fees are calculated based on the balances and transactions that occur on a certain day.

▶ **Balancing accounts**
If you configured conditions for interest and fees, these are calculated and posted during the balancing process.

▶ **Generating SAP In-House Cash bank statements**
This process consists of creating statements for individual subsidiary accounts. When you run it, the system creates an IDoc that is then imported into each subsidiary, and automatically updates the general ledger of the subsidiaries

with the correct SAP In-House Cash account transactions and balances. For this to happen, configuration for the electronic bank statement has to be done for the bank, in addition to the configuration already in place for real external bank statements.

▶ **General Ledger integration**
The SAP In-House Cash statements update the transactions and balances in the general ledger of the subsidiaries, but the general ledger transfer updates the transactions and balances in the general ledger of the company code that hosts the SAP In-House Cash center. This is similar to banks, where you have your accounting of the bank in your books, and the bank has its own accounting of your balance and transactions.

6.5   Reporting

This section briefly describes the main reports available in SAP In-House Cash. To access these reports, go to the application menu and access: ACCOUNTING • FINANCIAL SUPPLY CHAIN MANAGEMENT • IN-HOUSE CASH • INFORMATION SYSTEM.

▶ **Condition histories**
If you configured conditions for interest and fee calculation, the auditors will want to verify the integrity of the master data. This report shows you all of the changes done to the master data.

▶ **Balance list**
This gives you an overview of the balances in all your bank areas and SAP In-House Cash accounts.

▶ **Balance List by key date**
This report shows you an overview of the balances but also allows you to filter by key date to review the specifics of a certain period of time.

▶ **Overdraft list**
This gives you a list of those accounts for which the limit has been exceeded.

▶ **Display account locks**
This shows you locked and inactive accounts.

▶ **Interest scale**
This report displays the interest scales used for a certain combination of bank area, account number, product, business partner category, and calculation period.

▶ **Limit overview**
This report displays the internal and external limits of the selected accounts.

▶ **Display individual conditions**
With this report, you can see which conditions are still valid and which are expired.

6.6 Examples of SAP In-House Cash in Action

In this section, we explore an example that shows how a large corporation uses SAP In-House Cash, which will help you better understand the typical use of the functionality. This particular company (names and actual account numbers are changed to protect confidential information) concentrates the cash of all its subsidiaries into a central account and then allows subsidiaries to invest or borrow money from it. Vendor invoices are approved for payment at the subsidiary level, but the Shared Services Center processes the payments, netting as many payments as possible into one payment (as due date and other restrictions allow).

Figure 6.36 shows one of the available reports, which displays all of the accounts associated with a bank area, as well as the balance and limit of each. Note that the SAP In-House Cash center balance is zero; this is usually the case because the SAP In-House Cash center acts as a Shared Services Center that processes transactions but has no business of its own, other than supporting the operational companies. Therefore, all of the money held by the SAP In-House Cash bank is really owned by different subsidiaries.

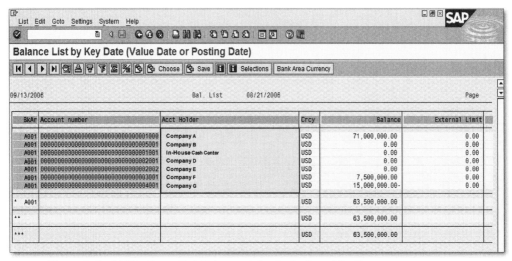

Figure 6.36 SAP In-House Cash Balances at the Beginning of the Day

Figure 6.37 shows the screen where you manually change the next posting date. After you do this, every transaction in the system has the new posting date. You can create a batch job to run this transaction.

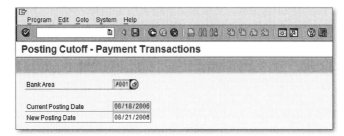

Figure 6.37 Posting Cutoff

Figure 6.38 shows an invoice for $1,000,000 USD being entered for Company A. The way the process works, the payment program (Transaction F110) is executed to pay the invoice at the subsidiary level, but instead of cutting a check or issuing an electronic payment, the system creates an IDoc that contains an SAP In-House Cash payment order.

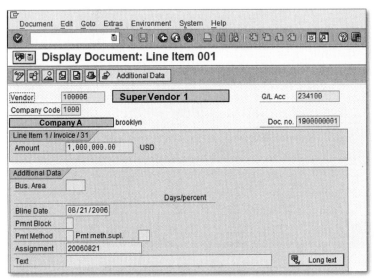

Figure 6.38 Enter Vendor Invoice for Company A

Figure 6.39 shows another invoice for $500,000 USD being processed for Company F. As with the previous example, the payment process begins by running the payment program at the subsidiary level, which triggers an IDoc with an SAP In-House Cash payment order.

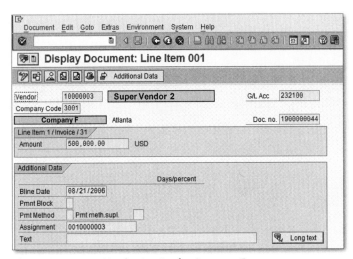

Figure 6.39 Enter Vendor Invoice for Company F

The payment orders created by the IDocs just mentioned are shown in Figure 6.40. Also on this screen, you can drill down, sort, add totals and subtotals, and — most importantly — approve the payment order.

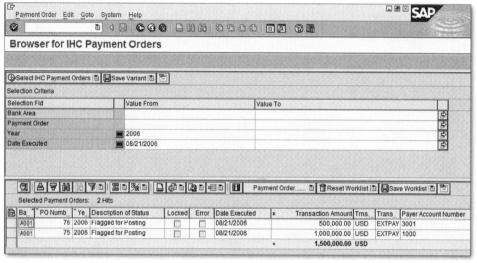

Figure 6.40 Browser for IHC Payment Orders

When you approve the order, several things happen:

▸ An IDoc with a payment request is created.

▸ The SAP In-House Cash account balance for the subsidiary where the vendor payment was originated decreases.

▸ The SAP In-House Cash account balance for the subsidiary where the SAP In-House Cash center sits (either headquarters or the Shared Services Center) increases.

In a subsequent step, you can pay that payment request using a payment program for payment requests (Transaction F111). One of the advantages of this process is the ability to net multiple payment requests (i.e., when the same vendor sends invoices to multiple subsidiaries) into a single wire or check, saving on wire fees and making the payment process easier.

Figure 6.41 shows how the SAP In-House Cash balance of Company A was reduced by $1,000,000 USD, and the balance for Company F was reduced by $500,000 USD, while the balance for the SAP In-House Cash center was increased by $1,500,000 USD. As we explained previously, whenever the balance in the SAP In-House Cash center increases, it should be temporary; the balance should usually be $0. In this example, the balance will be $0 again when the payment requests are paid to the external vendors.

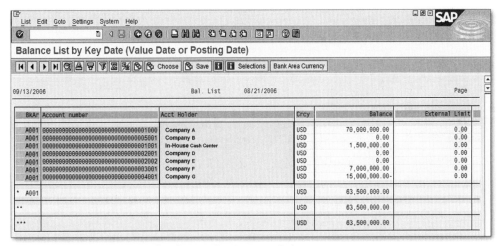

Figure 6.41 SAP In-House Cash Balances after Payment Orders

Figure 6.42 shows an internal transfer from Company A to the SAP In-House Cash center. This can be done to invest money, to process an adjustment, and so on.

Figure 6.43 shows the SAP In-House Cash balance increased for the $2,000,000 USD that were transferred to it, and Company A's balance decreased by the same amount.

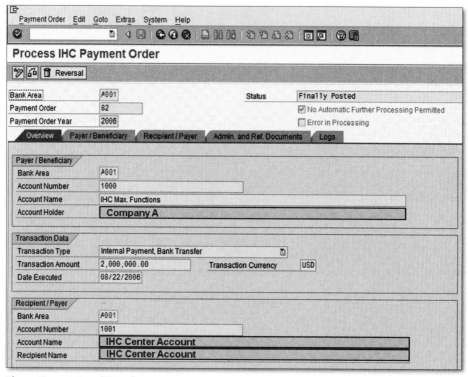

Figure 6.42 Internal Transfer

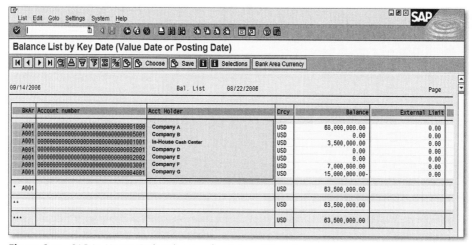

Figure 6.43 SAP In-House Cash Balances after Internal Transfer

Figure 6.44 shows an internal payment order reversing $1,500,000 USD of the $2,000,000; this could be due to a mistake in the original amount, or some other adjustment being processed.

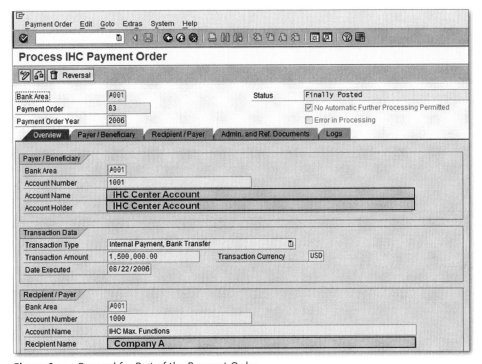

Figure 6.44 Reversal for Part of the Payment Order

Figure 6.45 shows the updated balances of the SAP In-House Cash center down by $1,500,000 USD, and Company A up by the same amount.

Figure 6.46 shows the parameter entry screen for the payment program for payment requests (Transaction F111); this is different from the payment program for vendors (Transaction F110) because it's specifically designed to be used by treasury department processes. This payment program would be used to send the

$2,000,000 USD that sit in the SAP In-House Cash center to a vendor or to a bro-kerage firm for investment.

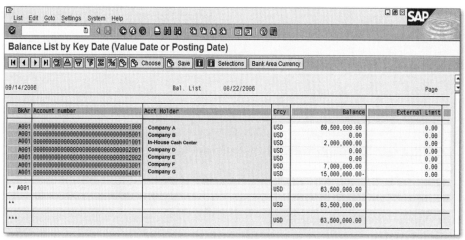

Figure 6.45 SAP In-House Cash Balances after Reversal for $1,500,000 USD

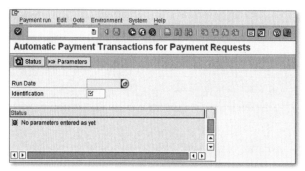

Figure 6.46 Payment Program for Payment Requests

Finally, Figure 6.47 shows the balances at the end of the day. The SAP In-House Cash center balance is again $0, and the individual balances are updated with the amount that accurately reflects their transactions during the day.

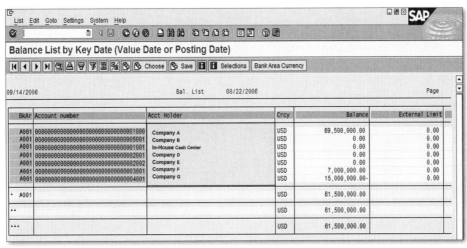

Figure 6.47 SAP In-House Cash Balances at the End of the Day

6.7   Summary

In this chapter, we reviewed the SAP In-House Cash functionality, starting with an overview of what it is and how it works, and then continued with an explanation of the criteria you should use to decide when it is a good idea to implement it. We also explained the main business scenarios covered by the functionality and provided business process diagrams for them.

We then provided an explanation of the master data associated with the functionality, as well as the configuration required for banking, ALE, and the SAP In-House Cash functionality. To conclude the chapter, we explained the main periodic processes and reports, and provided an example of the functionality being used.

Although there are many areas of SAP In-House Cash that cannot be covered in a single chapter, we expect that the information contained here will allow users, consultants, and project managers to resolve some of their questions and make the correct decisions about this important functionality. In the next chapter, we review the use and configuration of the Liquidity Planner functionality.

Liquidity Planner addresses the medium- to long-term liquidity require-ments of an organization and enables tracking of actual cash flows as com-pared to forecasted cash flows.

7 Global Liquidity Forecasting with Liquidity Planner

This chapter covers the Liquidity Planner functionality and explains how all of the components come together to enable reporting and forecasting. In the first section, we provide a basic introduction to the business processes involved in Liquidity Planner. In the second section, we discuss the concept of liquidity assignment programs. In the third section, we explain the configuration of Cash Accounting, one of the two components in Liquidity Planner. Finally, in the fourth section, we provide a high-level overview of the second component, Liquidity Planning and Reporting. We only cover this at a very high level because SAP has a brand new release of the component for SAP BusinessObjects Planning and Consolidation. For more information on this release, please consult *help.sap.com* or *service.sap.com*.

7.1 Business Process Overview

All treasurers need to be able to perform the following functions:

- Enter a forecasted same-day cash position.
- Track actual cash flows.
- Run a comparative actual versus forecast report.
- Carry out long-term cash forecasting.
- Tie each inflow or outflow of cash to an actual expense or revenue item.
- Lock the cash position after it is completed.

Prior to the release of the Liquidity Planner functionality, it was possible to accomplish most of these tasks using workarounds, but the result was never exactly what the client wanted. For example, consider the following:

▸ To enter a cash position forecast for the same day, you could create several memo record types (i.e., planning types); however, memo records either expire or have to be archived to avoid duplication with actual values.

▸ To track actual cash flows, you could leverage the electronic bank statement and the General Ledger postings it creates; however, in most cases these postings and the booking of expenses and revenues don't happen on the same document or at the same time.

▸ To create an actual versus forecast cash report and to lock the position, you could export the information to SAP NetWeaver BW and then create another key figure for the forecast; however, the standard extractors cannot handle the two key figures (actual versus forecast), and the Cash Management cube updates the entire position for a day every time you import it into SAP NetWeaver BW.

▸ For long-term planning, you could use Excel to import memo records, which are planning documents that are entered into the liquidity forecast report to reflect expected inflows or outflows of cash; however, this report has a limited time horizon display and no version control.

▸ To tie inflows and outflows of cash to revenues and expenses, you could use the liquidity forecast report and assign each vendor and customer to an expense or revenue item using the Cash Management Group field; however, when the actual payment took place, the item disappeared from the liquidity forecast report.

All of these examples show the result of trying to use an application for purposes beyond its original design. The good news is that a few years ago, SAP created an application specifically to fulfill these requirements: Liquidity Planner.

Liquidity Planner has two main components:

▸ **Cash Accounting**
The purpose of this component is to calculate and track actual cash flow movements and classify them by their source or use (revenue or expense) using the concept of liquidity items.

▶ **Liquidity Planning and Reporting**

The purpose of this component is to create a cash flow forecast by source or use. The creation of such forecasts takes place in SAP NetWeaver BW and leverages the use of formulas and algorithms known as planning functions, which can start with a given input (the previous year forecast or the sales forecast) and calculate the desired output by copying, revaluating, deriving, extrapolating, and using formulas with the final result of achieving the new forecast. Manual entries and Excel uploads are possible too. After that, the creation and execution of actual versus forecast reports is possible, as well as multiple analytics, slices, and views of the data.

Figure 7.1, created by SAP, compares Cash Management and Liquidity Planner.

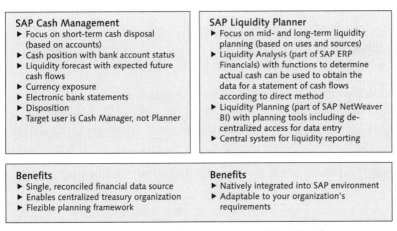

SAP Cash Management
▶ Focus on short-term cash disposal (based on accounts)
▶ Cash position with bank account status
▶ Liquidity forecast with expected future cash flows
▶ Currency exposure
▶ Electronic bank statements
▶ Disposition
▶ Target user is Cash Manager, not Planner

SAP Liquidity Planner
▶ Focus on mid- and long-term liquidity planning (based on uses and sources)
▶ Liquidity Analysis (part of SAP ERP Financials) with functions to determine actual cash can be used to obtain the data for a statement of cash flows according to direct method
▶ Liquidity Planning (part of SAP NetWeaver BI) with planning tools including decentralized access for data entry
▶ Central system for liquidity reporting

Benefits
▶ Single, reconciled financial data source
▶ Enables centralized treasury organization
▶ Flezible planning framework

Benefits
▶ Natively integrated into SAP environment
▶ Adaptable to your organization's requirements

Figure 7.1 Comparison Between Cash Management and Liquidity Planner

Now let's go into a bit more detail about each of the two components of Liquidity Planner.

7.1.1 Cash Accounting

Knowing the sources, uses, and amount of actual cash flow is fundamental to refining a cash position forecast. If you can see how far your forecasted numbers were from your actual numbers, you will understand the reasons and factors that made the difference and be able to correct the forecast for next time. Figure 7.2 shows the process for calculating and tracking actual cash flows in Liquidity Planner.

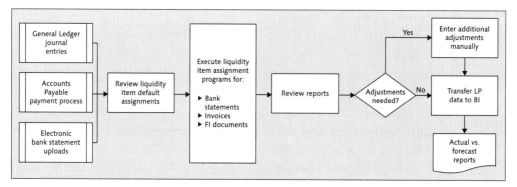

Figure 7.2 Liquidity Planner Cash Accounting Process

In essence, there are postings in the system that are going to affect cash, and the system assigns a default liquidity item for each of them. (You can assign different defaults for debits and credits.) After you calculate the default, you run three programs to replace the default item with the correct one. These programs are the following:

▶ **Calculation of liquidity items based on bank statements**
Assuming you have configured the appropriate queries and query sequences, this program reads all of the postings created by the electronic bank statement and then uses the corresponding fields to derive the liquidity item. After this, it determines the correct item and replaces the default with it (Figure 7.3).

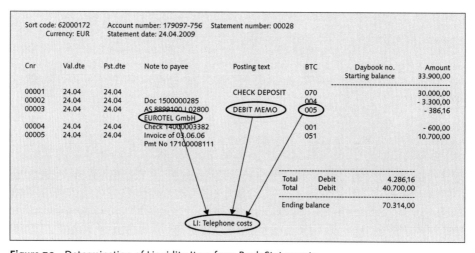

Figure 7.3 Determination of Liquidity Item from Bank Statements

In the example in Figure 7.3, the program reads the note to payee, the posting text, and the bank code, and determines the liquidity item based on it.

▶ **Calculation of liquidity item based on Financial Accounting documents**
If you're familiar with the Controlling component, it may be helpful to understand that this program works in a similar way to the program that derives profit centers and business areas. In this case, you can configure queries that link certain general ledger accounts to certain liquidity items. When you run the program, the system reviews which offset accounts the cash accounts had in the cash postings and determines the liquidity item of the cash based on those.

▶ **Calculation of liquidity item based on Accounts Payable invoices**
In this case, the system issued payments, and you want to determine the correct liquidity item for the payment. To do this, you assign certain general ledger accounts to certain liquidity items, and, then, when you want to determine the liquidity item for a payment, the system reads the paid invoice, finds the original invoice document, and determines the liquidity item based on the offset accounts on the invoice (Figure 7.4)

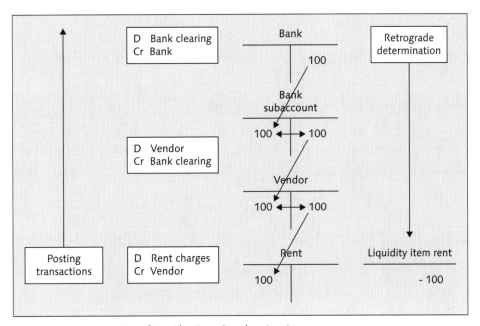

Figure 7.4 Determination of Liquidity Item Based on Invoices

As you can see from Figure 7.4, the bank statement affects the bank subaccount and the cash accounts (the first and second T accounts from top to bottom in the example above), neither of which are revenue or expense accounts. Thus, the system checks the payment document (second and third T accounts from top to bottom in the example above), where the accounts are vendor versus cash clearing accounts — again, not revenues or expenses. Next, the systems checks the previous document up the stream, the invoice (third and fourth T accounts from top to bottom in the example above); in this case, the offset account is for rent, an expense — so the system determines that the rent liquidity item is the correct one.

> **Note**
>
> You can also assign liquidity items manually.

After you have run the programs to calculate the correct liquidity items, you can run cash accounting reports in SAP ERP. If you are using Liquidity Planning and Reporting, you then export the Cash Accounting information into SAP NetWeaver BW and run comparative reports between forecasted and actual cash flows.

If you are not using the Liquidity Planning and Reporting part of Liquidity Planner, you still can export your data to SAP NetWeaver BW; there is business content for Liquidity Planner there.

7.1.2 Liquidity Planning and Reporting

In Chapter 8, Integration with Procure-to-Pay, Order-to-Cash, and Other Financial Processes, we discuss the liquidity forecast functionality of Cash Management. However, this functionality has been in use for more than 15 years and has multiple limitations, such as:

- An inability to forecast out longer than 12 or 14 weeks
- Questionable accuracy of data (because it is dependent on multiple factors)
- No functionality to run formulas, copy data, or revaluate data
- No functionality to derive cash flow plans from the sales budget

As you can see, SAP needed a product that could be used to produce a mid- and long-term cash forecast — and now it has it.

This functionality runs entirely on a BI platform. The first version was available in SEM-Business Planning and Simulation (BPS), the second version was released in Integrated Planning (IP), and the latest version is available in SAP BusinessObjects Planning and Consolidation. Figure 7.5 compares the functionality in SEM-BPS to the functionality in IP.

BW BPS
- Not all BEx and OLAP functions are available for planning applications
- More objects and tools are required
- Configuration or modeling is GUI based
- Restricted to predefined layouts
- Separate variables are required

BI Integrated Planning
- Most of the BEx and OLAP analysis functions are available
- Fewer variables are required
  - Same variables in analysis and planning
  - The only tools required are Query Designer and Web Application Designer
- Modeling and designing are more presentable than BPS
- Switching to BI-IP is easy

Figure 7.5 Comparison Between Liquidity Planner in BPS and IP

More recently, SAP released the chart shown in Figure 7.6, which compares the functionality in IP to the functionality newly available in SAP BusinessObjects Planning and Consolidation.

A detailed explanation of the reasons behind the move from BPS to IP to SAP BusinessObjects Planning and Consolidation is beyond the scope of this book. The point we want to make here is simply that you have at least three different platforms from which to choose. Naturally, SAP recommends the most recent, SAP BusinessObjects Planning and Consolidation, because this application is designed to be driven, managed, and owned by treasury users instead of by IT. This gives treasurers control over the system, something they like and appreciate.

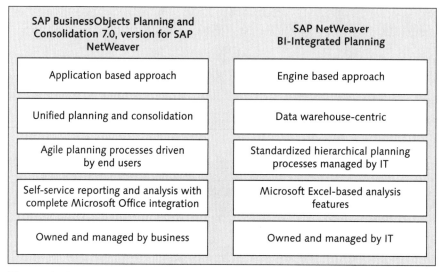

Figure 7.6 Comparison Between Liquidity Planner in IP and in SAP BusinessObjects Planning and Consolidation

Figure 7.7 shows the process for creating a cash forecast in Liquidity Planner.

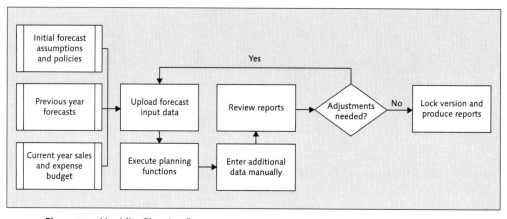

Figure 7.7 Liquidity Planning Process

As you can see, there are at least three main sources of information that are entered into a cash forecast: the current year sales budget, the previous year cash forecast, and the current year assumptions and policies. These are uploaded into SAP NetWeaver BW, planning functions are executed (planning functions are generally formulas and algorithms that copy, revaluate, or apply mathematical functions to the data), and additional adjustments are made manually.

When all of these steps are completed, you can produce a report and see the results. If the result is not optimal, you can run through the cycle again and again, as needed. After the majority of the involved parties approve the forecast, it can be locked and distributed.

The forecast can be created by month, week, or day. Obviously, the more detailed the forecast, the more difficult it is to make it accurate; however, as you do your actual versus forecast analysis over the years, and you make adjustments to them, your forecasts will become more and more accurate.

7.2   Liquidity Item Assignment Programs

To access the Liquidity Planner Cash Accounting assignment programs, use the following menu path: SAP MENU • ACCOUNTING • FINANCIAL SUPPLY CHAIN MANAGEMENT • CASH AND LIQUIDITY MANAGEMENT • LIQUIDITY PLANNER • ASSIGNMENT. The system assigns a default liquidity item to all of the postings to general ledger accounts that are considered relevant for Liquidity Planner, which are the ones used in Table T012 (House Bank and Account ID Configuration) and the ones selected in the Liquidity Planner configuration (which we discuss later in this section).

After those postings and default assignments take place, you can access this functionality and execute the programs to replace the default liquidity items with specific ones from bank statements, Financial Accounting documents, and AP invoices, or you can assign a liquidity item manually.

Two important concepts to understand are the following:

▶ **Query**
  A *query* is a condition or group of conditions that have to be fulfilled for the assignment of a liquidity item to take place. For example, you could specify that if a customer number is between 100001 and 100999, and a company code is between 1000 and 3000, then the system should assign liquidity item MERCH_SALES.

▶ **Query Sequence**

After you have configured your queries, you have to tell the system in which sequence you want it to execute these queries. For example, you may want to make an assignment based on customer number — unless that fails, in which case it should be made based on the document number. In this case, your sequence is customer number and then document number.

We cover the configuration of both queries and query sequences later in this section. In the meantime, let's look at the different programs you can use to assign liquidity items.

7.2.1 Assigning Liquidity Items from Bank Statements

Figure 7.8 shows the initial screen for the program you use to assign liquidity items from bank statements. This can be accessed using Transaction FLQAB.

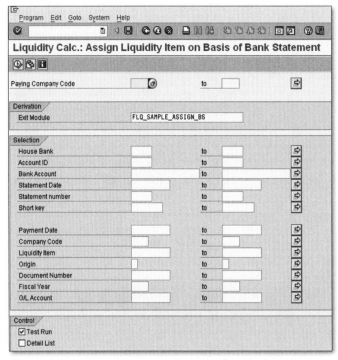

Figure 7.8 Program to Assign Liquidity Items from Bank Statements

Enter the necessary parameters, which are usually the house bank, account ID, and statement date. Then, if you want to see a report of the results of the program first (before doing an actual run), select the Test Run and Detail List indicators.

7.2.2   Assigning Liquidity Items from Financial Accounting Documents

Figure 7.9 shows the initial screen for the program to assign liquidity items from Financial Accounting documents. It can be accessed using Transaction FLQAC.

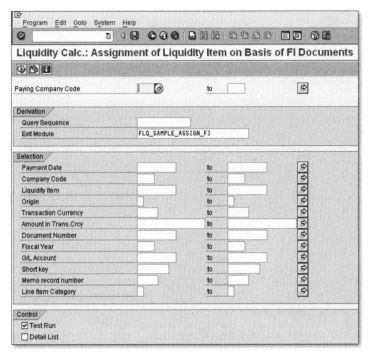

Figure 7.9   Assign Liquidity Items from Financial Accounting Documents

Enter the program parameters and the query sequence (again, we discuss this in more detail later in this section), and decide whether you want a detailed list and test run.

7.2.3 Assigning Liquidity Items from Accounts Payable Invoices

Figure 7.10 shows the initial screen of the program to assign liquidity items from invoices. It can be accessed using Transaction FLQAD.

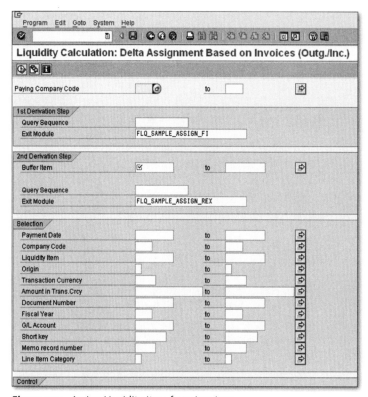

Figure 7.10 Assign Liquidity Item from Invoices

Enter the query sequence. In this case, you may have a two-step process in which you use different query sequences for each step. As with the other programs, enter your parameters and decide whether you want a detailed list and test run.

7.2.4 Assigning Liquidity Items Manually

Figure 7.11 shows the screen for manually assigning liquidity items. It can be accessed using Transaction FLQAM.

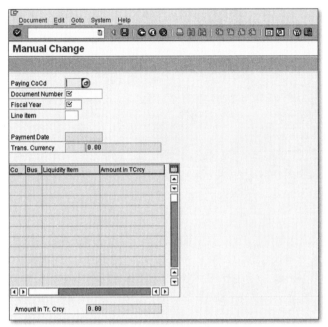

Figure 7.11 Manual Assignment of Liquidity Items

Select the relevant Financial Accounting document by entering the corresponding company code, document number, fiscal year, and item. Then enter the liquidity item and amount. You can also enter the business area, if you are using it.

7.3 Configuration of Cash Accounting

To configure the Cash Accounting component of Liquidity Planner, access the following menu path: IMG • FINANCIAL SUPPLY CHAIN MANAGEMENT • CASH AND LIQUIDITY MANAGEMENT • LIQUIDITY PLANNER • BASIC SETTINGS LIQUIDITY CALCULATION.

7.3.1 Basic Settings Liquidity Calculations

Under Basic Settings Liquidity Calculations, there are four activities: Edit Liquidity Items, Define Global Data, Define Other Actual Nodes, and Activate Company Code. We explain each of these in the following subsections.

Edit Liquidity Items

The first step is to select Edit Liquidity Items from the preceding menu path. The screen shown in Figure 7.12 appears.

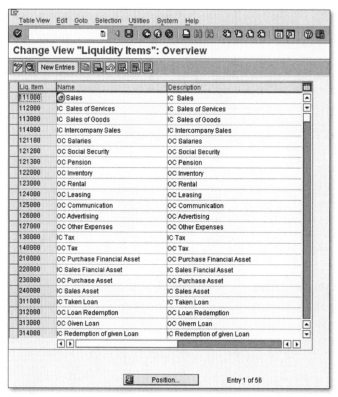

Figure 7.12 Liquidity Item Setup

On this screen, define the liquidity item number, name, and description.

Define Global Data

The next step is to assign the default liquidity items by selecting Define Global Data from the menu path given earlier (IMG • FINANCIAL SUPPLY CHAIN MANAGE-MENT • CASH AND LIQUIDITY MANAGEMENT • LIQUIDITY PLANNER • BASIC SETTINGS: LIQUIDITY CALCULATION • DEFINE GLOBAL DATA). This screen is shown in Figure 7.13.

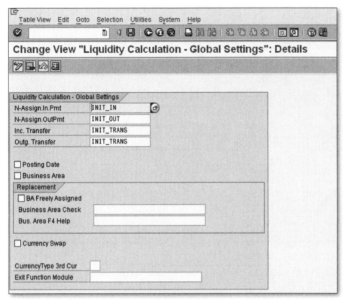

Figure 7.13 Assign Default Liquidity Items

In this step, assign defaults for the following fields: N-Assign.InPmt, N-Assign. OutPmt, Inc. Transfer, and Outg. Transfer. As we mentioned earlier, these items are replaced with the liquidity items calculated by the programs we discussed previously.

Define Other Actual Nodes

The next step is to determine the general ledger accounts relevant for Liquidity Planner selecting Define Other Actual Nodes from the menu path given earlier (IMG • FINANCIAL SUPPLY CHAIN MANAGEMENT • CASH AND LIQUIDITY MANAGEMENT • LIQUIDITY PLANNER • BASIC SETTINGS: LIQUIDITY CALCULATION • DEFINE OTHER ACTUAL NODES). This screen is shown in Figure 7.14.

This step is labeled "other" because, by default, the system marks all general ledger accounts entered in Table T012 (House Bank and Account ID Configuration) as relevant for Liquidity Planner. However, there may be other accounts, such as petty cash or in-house cash accounts, which are relevant for Liquidity Planner. Enter those accounts here.

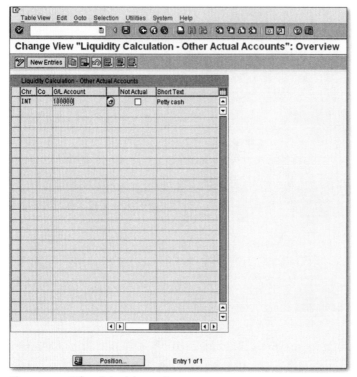

Figure 7.14 Other Actual Accounts

Activate Company Code

The last step is to activate Liquidity Planner by selecting Activate Company Code from the menu path given earlier (Figure 7.15).

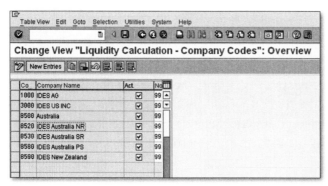

Figure 7.15 Liquidity Planner Activation

As you can see, the Liquidity Planner calculation is activated at the company code level. Enter the company code, click on the checkmark, and save.

7.3.2 Assignment

The next step is to configure the liquidity item assignment via the following menu path: IMG • FINANCIAL SUPPLY CHAIN MANAGEMENT • CASH AND LIQUIDITY MANAGEMENT • LIQUIDITY PLANNER • ASSIGNMENT.

The three activities — From Bank Statement, From FI Information, and From Invoices — are discussed in the following subsections.

From Bank Statement

To begin, click on From Bank Statement in the preceding menu path (Figure 7.16).

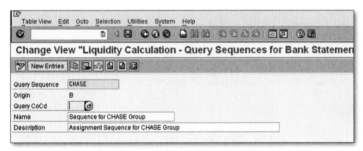

Figure 7.16 Creation of Query Sequences for Bank Statements

On this screen, enter the name of the query sequence, its origin (usually a B, for "bank"), the company code it belongs to, a name, and a description. Now assign those query sequences, as shown in Figure 7.17. You can access this screen using Transaction FLQC6.

Assign the query sequences to a specific company code, house bank, and account ID.

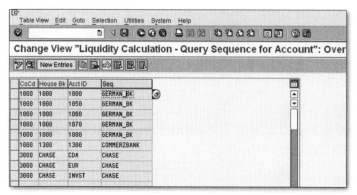

Figure 7.17 Assignment of Query Sequences to Bank Account

From FI Document

Let's now cover the configuration of liquidity item assignments from Financial Accounting documents. To do this, select From FI Document from the menu path provided earlier (Figure 7.18).

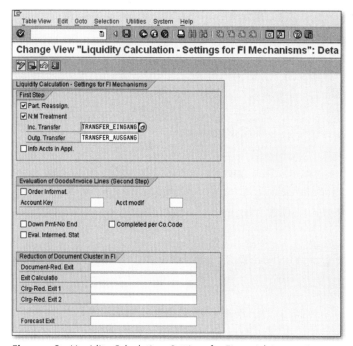

Figure 7.18 Liquidity Calculation, Settings for Financial Accounting

The resulting screen has multiple parameters:

▶ **Part. Reassign.**
Sometimes a customer or vendor invoice is cleared through multiple payment documents. At some points in time, not all of these payment documents will have happened yet. If some of them have happened and others haven't, the document is only partially cleared.

If you check this indicator, the system can assign liquidity items to those portions that have already been cleared and leave pending those that haven't. If you don't use this indicator, the system doesn't make any assignments until all portions of the invoice have been cleared.

▶ **N:M Treatment**
Sometimes the bank statement configuration is done in such a way that it creates general ledger and subledger level documents. In this case, the system tries to assign a liquidity item to each of these.

If you check this indicator, the system won't try to assign a liquidity item to the subledger documents but will carry the liquidity item assigned at the general ledger level and mark the subledger items as nonrelevant for calculation.

▶ **Info Accts in Appl.**
If you check this indicator, the user can maintain which accounts are relevant for Liquidity Planner in the application. If you don't check it, the maintenance is done only as part of configuration and will require a transport to be brought into production.

▶ **Evaluation of Goods/Invoice Lines**
This indicator is relevant only for assignments from invoices.

▶ **Eval. Intermed. Stat.**
Sometimes the assignment process goes through multiple steps and evaluates multiple documents, as was shown earlier, in Figure 7.4. When you define which general ledger accounts are relevant for liquidity calculations, you can mark an account for further calculation; this prompts the system to move into the next step in the query sequence or configuration. Checking the Eval. Intermed. Stat. indicator means that all of the accounts marked as Further Calculation are evaluated even for portions of the document that have not been cleared.

▶ **Reduction of Document Cluster in FI area**
For companies with a large volume of documents and in which payment processes can have multiple stages with hundreds or thousands of payment documents and partial payments, the multi-step calculation of liquidity items can consume a lot of server resources. You can avoid this by writing a user exit that avoids some of the intermediate steps under certain conditions; the exit is entered in this field.

The next step is to define which general ledger accounts are relevant in the screen shown in Figure 7.19. You can access this screen using Transaction FLQC7.

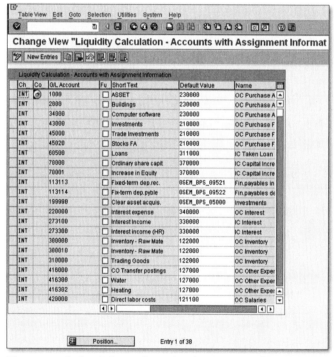

Figure 7.19 Define Relevant General Ledger Accounts for Financial Accounting Assignments

Enter the chart of accounts and, optionally, the company code. Then enter the general ledger account, the default liquidity item, and whether you want this account to be marked for further calculation. (Again, this causes the system to move into the next stage in the query sequence or configuration when you want to replace the default assignment entered here with another value.)

The next step is to define the query sequences, which is done on the screen entered in Figure 7.20. You can access this screen using Transaction FLQC8.

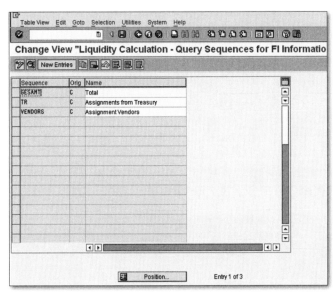

Figure 7.20 Creation of Query Sequences for Financial Accounting Documents and Invoices

Create the query sequences. The fields you need to supply are the same ones we explained for bank statements in Figure 7.16, except that for Financial Accounting documents, the origin is C (clearing documents), and for invoices, it is D (invoices).

From Invoices

The configuration steps we've just explained are the same for assignment from invoices.

7.3.3 Query Definition

Let's now review the steps to configure queries. To begin, access the following menu path: SAP MENU • ACCOUNTING • FINANCIAL SUPPLY CHAIN MANAGEMENT • CASH AND LIQUIDITY MANAGEMENT • LIQUIDITY PLANNER • SETTINGS • ASSIGNMENT FROM BANK STATEMENT • EDIT QUERY. This brings you to the screen shown in Figure 7.21.

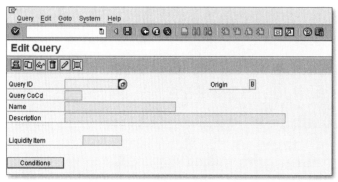

Figure 7.21 Define Query Initial Screen

Enter the query ID, the name, and the liquidity item it points to. Then click on Conditions, and the screen shown in Figure 7.22 appears.

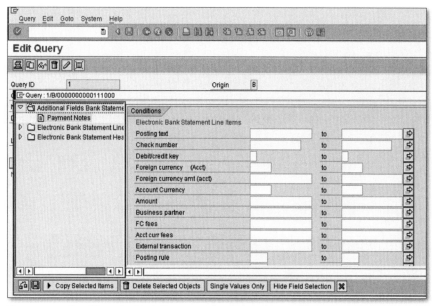

Figure 7.22 Conditions for Bank Statement Query

As you can see, even though the steps to define a query for bank statements, Financial Accounting documents, and invoices are the same, the available fields are different. In the case of bank statements, you have additional fields such as

Payment Notes — which is probably the most commonly used — and then fields for the header and line items as well (on the left side of Figure 7.22).

Let's review the screen where you define queries for Financial Accounting documents by choosing SAP MENU • ACCOUNTING • FINANCIAL SUPPLY CHAIN MANAGEMENT • CASH AND LIQUIDITY MANAGEMENT • LIQUIDITY PLANNER • SETTINGS • ASSIGNMENT FROM FI DOCUMENT • EDIT QUERY. The resulting screen is shown in Figure 7.23.

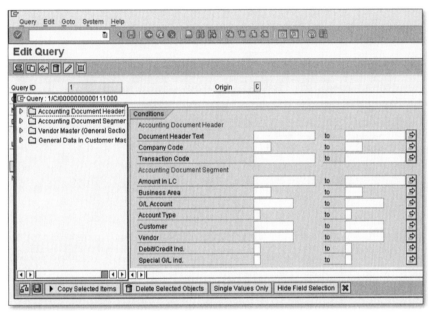

Figure 7.23 Fields for Conditions for Financial Accounting Documents

As you can see, when you create a query for Financial Accounting documents, the available fields come from the document header, the document segments, the vendor master record, or the customer master record.

Finally, let's look at the fields available for assignment from invoices by choosing SAP MENU • ACCOUNTING • FINANCIAL SUPPLY CHAIN MANAGEMENT • CASH AND LIQUIDITY MANAGEMENT • LIQUIDITY PLANNER • SETTINGS • ASSIGNMENT FROM INVOICES • EDIT QUERY (Figure 7.24).

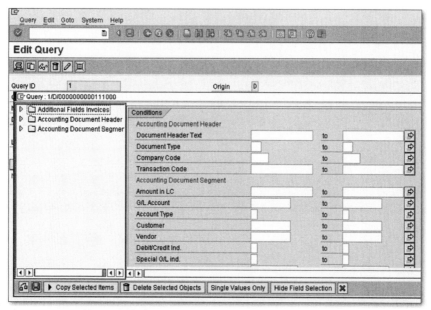

Figure 7.24 Fields Available for Assignment from Invoices

As you can see here, the fields available are specific invoice fields, fields from the document header, and fields from the document segments.

Refer to Figure 7.18, where we explained several fields for the Financial Accounting settings. One of those fields was Info Accts in Appl. indicator. Figure 7.25 is the application screen where you maintain the general ledger accounts relevant for liquidity calculations when you check that indicator in that other configuration screen. This can be accessed from the application using Transaction FLQINFACC.

To conclude our discussion of queries, we provide the following menu path: SAP MENU • ACCOUNTING • FINANCIAL SUPPLY CHAIN MANAGEMENT • CASH AND LIQUIDITY MANAGEMENT • LIQUIDITY PLANNER • SETTINGS • UPLOAD/DOWNLOAD. Here you will find certain upload and download tools that allow you to transfer settings from one system to another (such as QA to production), as well as upload queries, query sequences, or general ledger accounts from a text file into the SAP ERP system.

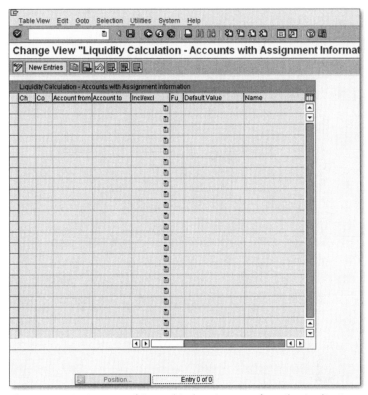

Figure 7.25 Assignment of General Ledger Accounts from the Application

7.3.4 Information System

Information System is a functionality in the Cash Accounting component of Liquidity Planner. To access it, use the following menu path: SAP MENU • ACCOUNTING • FINANCIAL SUPPLY CHAIN MANAGEMENT • CASH AND LIQUIDITY MANAGEMENT • LIQUIDITY PLANNER • INFORMATION SYSTEM.

> **Note**
>
> There are also some standard business content extractors, cubes, and reports for the Cash Accounting part of Liquidity Planner in SAP NetWeaver BW.

Let's take a brief look at the main reports available. Figure 7.26 shows the initial screen to execute a report that shows all of the payments that are linked to a specific liquidity item.

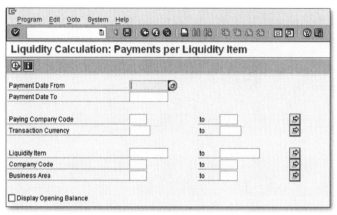

Figure 7.26 Payments per Liquidity Item

Figure 7.27 shows the parameter screen of a report that can provide totals for the available filters: Paying Company Code, Payment Date, Liquidity Item, Company Code, Business Area, and Transaction Currency. You can also access this report with Transaction FLQLS.

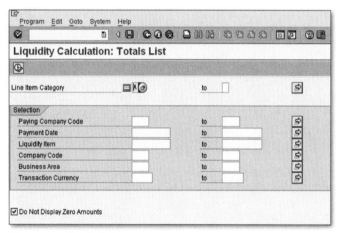

Figure 7.27 Totals List

Figure 7.28 is the parameter screen for the line items report. As with any other line item report, it should be used with caution because it can take some time to execute and consumes significant server resources. It can be filtered by all of the parameters shown on the screen. You can also access this report using Transaction FLQLI.

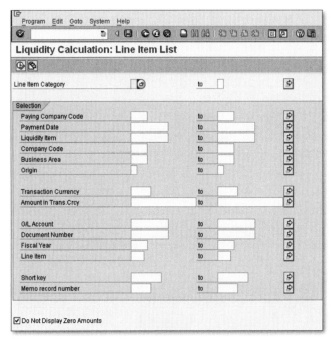

Figure 7.28 Line Item List

Figure 7.29 is the parameter screen for the line item history report. Here you can see the different stages of the liquidity item assignment that a document goes through. You can access this report using Transaction FLQHIST.

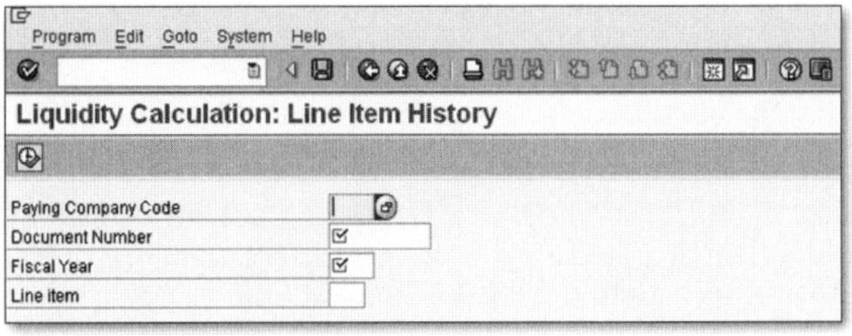

Figure 7.29 Line Item History

Figure 7.30 is the parameter screen for the query sequences report, which shows all of the query sequences in the system and the queries they contain. You can access it using Transaction FLQLGRP.

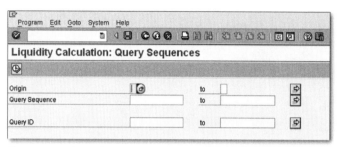

Figure 7.30 Query Sequences Report

Figure 7.31 is the parameter screen for a list of general ledger accounts relevant for liquidity calculations; it can be filtered by company code. You can access it using Transaction FLQLACC.

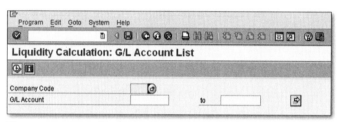

Figure 7.31 General Ledger Account List

7.3.5   Additional Liquidity Planner Tools

Finally, there are three other relevant Liquidity Planner tools that you should know about. These are accessed via the following menu path: IMG • FINANCIAL SUPPLY CHAIN MANAGEMENT • CASH AND LIQUIDITY MANAGEMENT • LIQUIDITY PLANNER • TOOLS.

▶ **Delete flow data**
Eliminates historic data from the system during testing.

▶ **Regenerate data**
Regenerates data after certain modifications in the settings have taken place.

▶ **FI assignment analysis**
Validates query sequences and configuration.

7.4   Liquidity Planner in Action

In this section, we offer a high-level picture of Liquidity Planner in action.

7.4.1   Cash Accounting: Calculation of Actual Cash Flows

Let's begin by taking a look at the Cash Accounting part of Liquidity Planner, where actual cash flows are calculated in SAP ERP. To see a line item report on this subject, use the following menu path: SAP MENU • ACCOUNTING • CORPORATE FINANCE MANAGEMENT • LIQUIDITY CALCULATION • INFORMATION SYSTEM • LINE ITEMS. This report lists the conditions of the liquidity item assignments. The parameter screen for this report is shown in Figure 7.32. Enter the parameters, and execute.

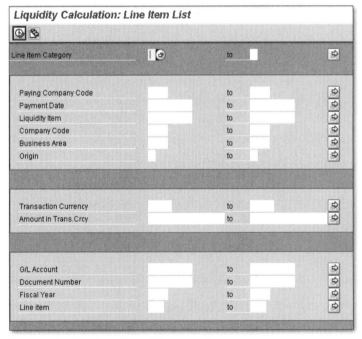

Figure 7.32   Line Items Report Parameter Screen

Figure 7.33 shows the results of the assignment so far. As you can see, all of the cash items are assigned to the default liquidity items, which means that the assignment programs have not been executed.

Liquidity Calculation: Line Item List

CoCd	DocumentNo	Year	Itm	C	Pmnt Date	CoCd	BusA	Liquidity Item	Liquidity Item Name	TCurr	Amount in Tr. Crcy
1000	100008682	2003	1	B	05.09.2003	1000		INIT_IN	Incoming Payment	EUR	3.000,00
1000	100008683	2003	1	B	05.09.2003	1000		INIT_IN	Incoming Payment	EUR	3.150,00
1000	100008684	2003	1	B	05.09.2003	1000		INIT_IN	Incoming Payment	EUR	3.300,00
1000	100008685	2003	1	B	05.09.2003	1000		INIT_IN	Incoming Payment	EUR	3.450,00
1000	100008686	2003	1	B	05.09.2003	1000		INIT_IN	Incoming Payment	EUR	3.600,00
1000	100008687	2003	1	B	05.09.2003	1000		INIT_IN	Incoming Payment	EUR	40.000,00
1000	100008689	2003	1	B	05.09.2003	1000		INIT_OUT	Outgoing Payment	EUR	30.000,00-
1000	100008690	2003	1	B	05.09.2003	1000		INIT_OUT	Outgoing Payment	EUR	31.000,00-
1000	100008691	2003	1	B	05.09.2003	1000		INIT_OUT	Outgoing Payment	EUR	32.000,00-
*										EUR	36.500,00-

Figure 7.33 Results of the Line Items report

The screen shown in Figure 7.34 is used to assign the liquidity items from the bank statement. When you click Execute, the screen shown in Figure 7.35 appears.

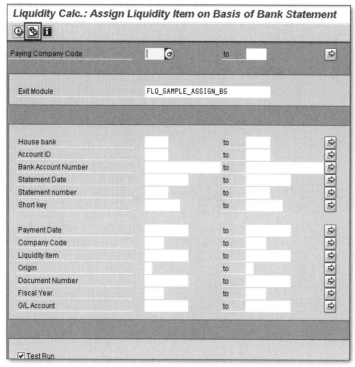

Figure 7.34 Assignment of Liquidity Item from Bank Statement

Liquidity Calc.: Assign Liquidity Item on Basis of Bank Statement

Liquidity Calc.: Assign Liquidity Item on Basis of Bank Statement   Update Run
Number of Documents Edited   9
Number of Documents Changed   5   1

New Item	CoCd	BusA	Query ID	Old Item	C	CoCd	DocumentNo	Year	Itm	TCurr	Amount in Tr. Crcy	Shrt key	MR no
0SEM_BPS_...	1000		CUSTOMER_1000	INIT_IN	X	1000	100008682	2003	1	EUR	3.000,00	49	1
0SEM_BPS_...	1000		CUSTOMER_1000	INIT_IN	X	1000	100008683	2003	1	EUR	3.150,00	49	2
0SEM_BPS_...	1000		CUSTOMER_1000	INIT_IN	X	1000	100008684	2003	1	EUR	3.300,00	49	3
0SEM_BPS_...	1000		CUSTOMER_1000	INIT_IN	X	1000	100008685	2003	1	EUR	3.450,00	49	4
0SEM_BPS_...	1000		CUSTOMER_1000	INIT_IN	X	1000	100008686	2003	1	EUR	3.600,00	49	5
	1000			INIT_IN		1000	100008687	2003	1	EUR	40.000,00	49	9
	1000			INIT_OUT		1000	100008689	2003	1	EUR	30.000,00-	49	6
	1000			INIT_OUT		1000	100008690	2003	1	EUR	31.000,00-	49	7
	1000			INIT_OUT		1000	100008691	2003	1	EUR	32.000,00-	49	8

Figure 7.35   Results of Liquidity Item Assignment from Bank Statement

As you can see in Figure 7.35, there is a New Item column and an Old Item column. The Old Item column shows the default previously assigned by the system, and the New Item column shows the assignments made from the bank statement.

If you filter down the list, you can see an item for $3,150 USD (Figure 7.36). Double-click on this, and the screen shown in Figure 7.37 appears.

Liquidity Calc.: Assign Liquidity Item on Basis of Bank Statement

Liquidity Calc.: Assign Liquidity Item on Basis of Bank Statement   Update Run
Number of Documents Edited   9
Number of Documents Changed   5   1

New Item	CoCd	BusA	Query ID	Old Item	C	CoCd	DocumentNo	Year	Itm	TCurr	Amount in Tr. Crcy	Shrt key	MR no
0SEM_BPS_...	1000		CUSTOMER_1000	INIT_IN	X	1000	100008682	2003	1	EUR	3.000,00	49	1
0SEM_BPS_...	1000		CUSTOMER_1000	INIT_IN	X	1000	100008683	2003	1	EUR	3.150,00	49	2
0SEM_BPS_...	1000		CUSTOMER_1000	INIT_IN	X	1000	100008684	2003	1	EUR	3.300,00	49	3
0SEM_BPS_...	1000		CUSTOMER_1000	INIT_IN	X	1000	100008685	2003	1	EUR	3.450,00	49	4
0SEM_BPS_...	1000		CUSTOMER_1000	INIT_IN	X	1000	100008686	2003	1	EUR	3.600,00	49	5
	1000			INIT_IN		1000	100008687	2003	1	EUR	40.000,00	49	9
	1000			INIT_OUT		1000	100008689	2003	1	EUR	30.000,00-	49	6
	1000			INIT_OUT		1000	100008690	2003	1	EUR	31.000,00-	49	7
	1000			INIT_OUT		1000	100008691	2003	1	EUR	32.000,00-	49	8

Figure 7.36   Filtered List

On this screen, the system shows the specific fields from the $3,150 item from which the system derived the liquidity item within the bank statement. In the blue square within the picture, you can see that the system used the note to payee to find the liquidity item.

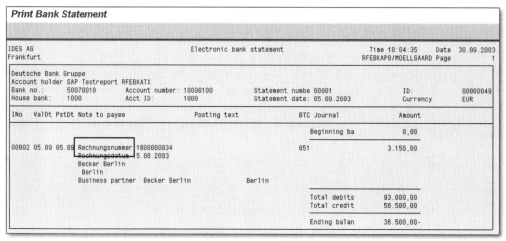

Figure 7.37 Drilldown into Bank Statement

Next, run the program to assign liquidity items from Financial Accounting documents. This screen is shown in Figure 7.38.

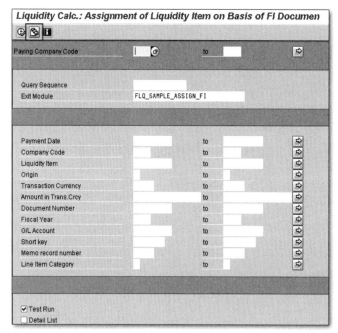

Figure 7.38 Assign Liquidity Items from Financial Accounting Documents

Enter the parameters and execute, and then run the line items report again. The screen shown in Figure 7.39 appears.

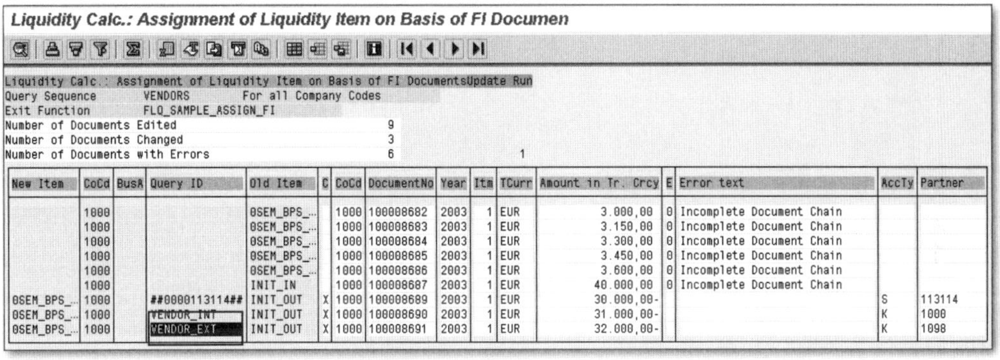

Liquidity Calc.: Assignment of Liquidity Item on Basis of FI Documen

Liquidity Calc.: Assignment of Liquidity Item on Basis of FI DocumentsUpdate Run
Query Sequence VENDORS For all Company Codes
Exit Function FLQ_SAMPLE_ASSIGN_FI
Number of Documents Edited 9
Number of Documents Changed 3
Number of Documents with Errors 6 1

New Item	CoCd	BusA	Query ID	Old Item	C	CoCd	DocumentNo	Year	Itm	TCurr	Amount in Tr. Crcy	E	Error text	AccTy	Partner
	1000			0SEM_BPS_...		1000	100008682	2003	1	EUR	3.000,00	0	Incomplete Document Chain		
	1000			0SEM_BPS_...		1000	100008683	2003	1	EUR	3.150,00	0	Incomplete Document Chain		
	1000			0SEM_BPS_...		1000	100008684	2003	1	EUR	3.300,00	0	Incomplete Document Chain		
	1000			0SEM_BPS_...		1000	100008685	2003	1	EUR	3.450,00	0	Incomplete Document Chain		
	1000			0SEM_BPS_...		1000	100008686	2003	1	EUR	3.600,00	0	Incomplete Document Chain		
	1000			INIT_IN		1000	100008687	2003	1	EUR	40.000,00	0	Incomplete Document Chain		
0SEM_BPS_...	1000		##000011311 4##	INIT_OUT	X	1000	100008689	2003	1	EUR	30.000,00-			S	113114
0SEM_BPS_...	1000		VENDOR_INT	INIT_OUT	X	1000	100008690	2003	1	EUR	31.000,00-			K	1000
0SEM_BPS_...	1000		VENDOR_EXT	INIT_OUT	X	1000	100008691	2003	1	EUR	32.000,00-			K	1098

Figure 7.39 Line Items after Assignment from Financial Accounting Documents

As you can see, there are now other items with data in the New Item column, which got assigned from Financial Accounting documents. After all of the assignment programs have been run, you can run the line items report again; the screen shown in Figure 7.40 appears.

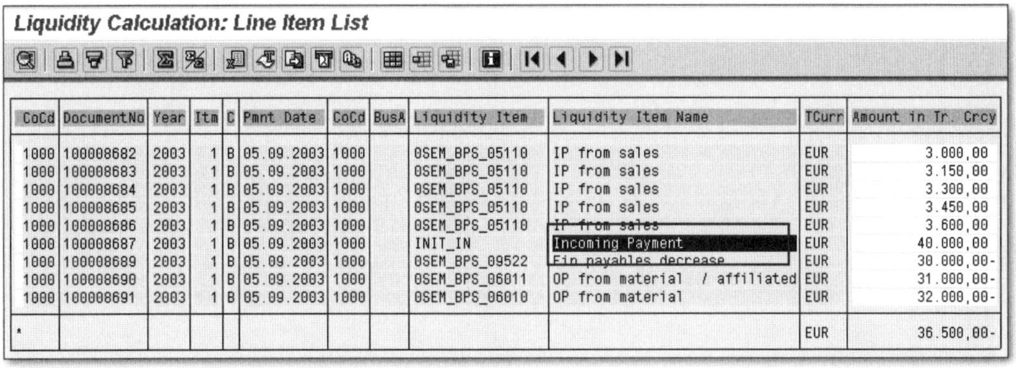

Liquidity Calculation: Line Item List

CoCd	DocumentNo	Year	Itm	C	Pmnt Date	CoCd	BusA	Liquidity Item	Liquidity Item Name	TCurr	Amount in Tr. Crcy
1000	100008682	2003	1	B	05.09.2003	1000		0SEM_BPS_05110	IP from sales	EUR	3.000,00
1000	100008683	2003	1	B	05.09.2003	1000		0SEM_BPS_05110	IP from sales	EUR	3.150,00
1000	100008684	2003	1	B	05.09.2003	1000		0SEM_BPS_05110	IP from sales	EUR	3.300,00
1000	100008685	2003	1	B	05.09.2003	1000		0SEM_BPS_05110	IP from sales	EUR	3.450,00
1000	100008686	2003	1	B	05.09.2003	1000		0SEM_BPS_05110	IP from sales	EUR	3.600,00
1000	100008687	2003	1	B	05.09.2003	1000		INIT_IN	Incoming Payment	EUR	40.000,00
1000	100008689	2003	1	B	05.09.2003	1000		0SEM_BPS_09522	Fin payables decrease	EUR	30.000,00-
1000	100008690	2003	1	B	05.09.2003	1000		0SEM_BPS_06011	OP from material / affiliated	EUR	31.000,00-
1000	100008691	2003	1	B	05.09.2003	1000		0SEM_BPS_06010	OP from material	EUR	32.000,00-
*										EUR	36.500,00-

Figure 7.40 Line Item Report with All Items Assigned

If you click on the item highlighted in Figure 7.40, the screen shown in Figure 7.41 appears.

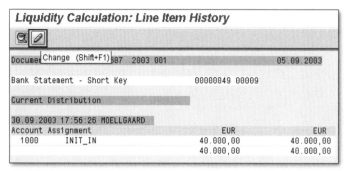

Figure 7.41 Drilldown on Manually Entered Item

As you can see, the $40,000 USD item was entered manually. If you double-click it again, the screen shown in Figure 7.42 appears.

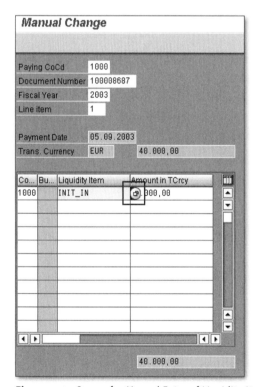

Figure 7.42 Screen for Manual Entry of Liquidity Items

This shows the screen where the item was manually entered.

7.4.2 Data Extraction to SAP NetWeaver BW

In this section, we show you the steps for extracting actual cash flows from SAP ERP into SAP NetWeaver BW. To access the SAP NetWeaver BW system, use the following menu path: SAP MENU • SAP BUSINESS INFORMATION WAREHOUSE • MODELING • ADMINISTRATOR WORKBENCH MODELING (Transaction RSA1). The initial screen of the SAP NetWeaver BW system is shown in Figure 7.43.

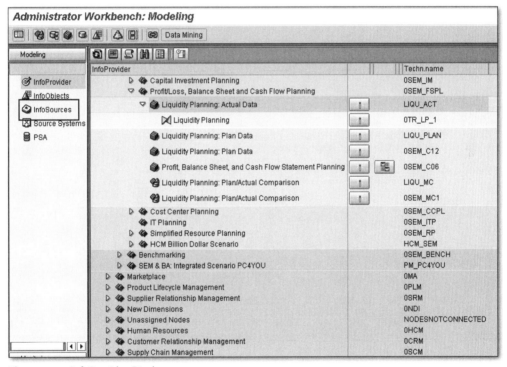

Figure 7.43 InfoProvider Display

This screen displays the Liquidity Planner InfoCubes, or, to use the technical term, InfoProviders. As you can see, there are InfoProviders for actual data and for plan data.

Figure 7.44 shows an InfoPackage, which is the term for the extraction program and the parameters that go with it. Click on Start to initiate the extraction. (In practical usage, most extractions are scheduled in batch using a process chain.)

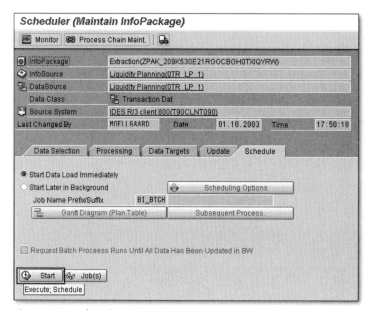

Figure 7.44 InfoPackage to Extract Data

Figure 7.45 shows the screen where the InfoProvider for Liquidity Planner actual data is defined. From here, using the menu shown at the top, you can display the data that is already inside the cube. Because we ran our InfoPackage, the actual records should already be available in this cube. Figure 7.46 shows these records.

If you compare this screen to the screen in Figure 7.40, you can see that the records that we updated in SAP ERP are now available in SAP NetWeaver BW.

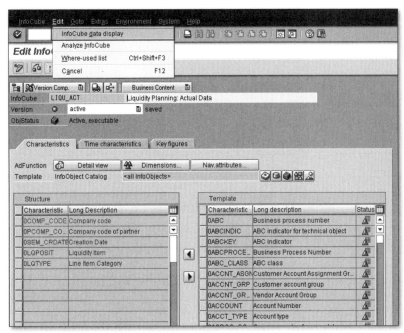

Figure 7.45 Display InfoProvider and Data

0PCOMP_COD	Liquidity Item	0LQTYPE	Creation Date	0CHNGID	Record type	Request ID	0CALDAY	0CALMONTH	0CALWEEK	0CALYEAR	Currency	0AMOUNT_A
1000	0SEM_BPS_03052	B	01.10.2003			REQU_8XGW30I93MVZO7O6FOAX6Q6TB	05.09.2003	200309	200336	2003	EUR	40.000,00
1000	0SEM_BPS_05110	B	01.10.2003			REQU_8XGW30I93MVZO7O6FOAX6Q6TB	05.09.2003	200309	200336	2003	EUR	16.500,00
1000	0SEM_BPS_06010	B	01.10.2003			REQU_8XGW30I93MVZO7O6FOAX6Q6TB	05.09.2003	200309	200336	2003	EUR	32.000,00-
1000	0SEM_BPS_06011	B	01.10.2003			REQU_8XGW30I93MVZO7O6FOAX6Q6TB	05.09.2003	200309	200336	2003	EUR	31.000,00-
1000	0SEM_BPS_09522	B	01.10.2003			REQU_8XGW30I93MVZO7O6FOAX6Q6TB	05.09.2003	200309	200336	2003	EUR	30.000,00-
1000	INIT_IN	B	01.10.2003			REQU_8XGW30I93MVZO7O6FOAX6Q6TB	05.09.2003	200309	200336	2003	EUR	0,00
1000	INIT_OUT	B	01.10.2003			REQU_8XGW30I93MVZO7O6FOAX6Q6TB	05.09.2003	200309	200336	2003	EUR	0,00
3000	0SEM_BPS_03052	F	01.10.2003			REQU_8XGW30I93MVZO7O6FOAX6Q6TB	01.10.2003	200310	200340	2003	USD	50,00
3000	INIT_IN	F	01.10.2003			REQU_8XGW30I93MVZO7O6FOAX6Q6TB	01.10.2003	200310	200340	2003	USD	0,00

Data tgt. browser: "LIQU_ACT", List output

Figure 7.46 Actual Data Display

7.4.3 Planning in Liquidity Planner

This section shows how planning is done in the SEM-BPS application. The Integrated Planning and SAP BusinessObjects Planning and Consolidation versions are slightly different, but the fundamental concepts and logic are the same. To access the Planning Workbench, use the following menu path: SAP MENU • STRATEGIC ENTERPRISE MANAGEMENT/BUSINESS ANALYTICS • STRATEGIC ENTERPRISE MAN-

AGEMENT • BUSINESS PLANNING AND SIMULATION • CROSS-APPLICATION PLANNING •
PLANNING WORKBENCH. This is where most of the SEM configuration for liquidity
planning takes place.

Once inside the Planning Workbench, you can see the different planning areas.
In the example in Figure 7.47, you can see that there are Planning Areas for LP
Corporate, LP Corporate Intercompany, and LP Planning, as well as for IDES US
inside LP Planning.

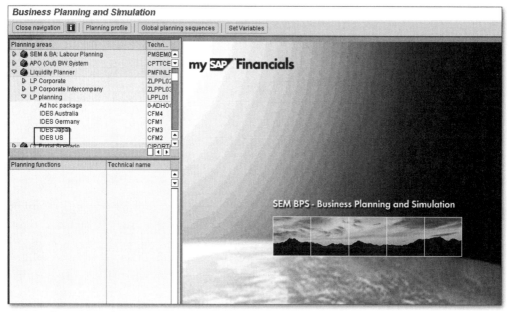

Figure 7.47 Planning Area Display

InfoCubes and planning areas are essentially the same thing, except that from
the SAP NetWeaver BW perspective, a cube is seen as a data repository without
transactional functionality, and from the SEM perspective, a planning area is seen
as a data repository *with* transactional functionality. There is a switch to convert a
nontransactional InfoCube into a transactional one, and vice versa.

In the bottom-left corner of the screen in Figure 7.48, you can see the different *Planning Functions*, which are the pieces of code that perform different tasks.
For example, the copy plan data function copies the plan from a previous year

or another company. There are planning functions for manual planning, which contain planning layouts (i.e., entry screens for planning data that is entered manually).

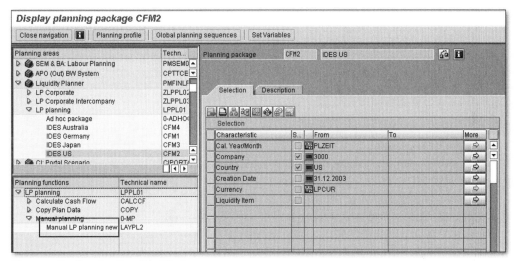

Figure 7.48 Planning Function Display

On the right side of the screen, you can see a Planning Package. After you create a planning function, the values entered as the selection parameters become a planning package.

On the bottom-left side of the screen shown in Figure 7.48, you can see that there is a Manual Planning function. Double-click on it, and on the right side, the system displays the entry screen for this manual plan data (as shown in Figure 7.49). Users can access this screen through the SAP NetWeaver BW menu and enter the data, or they can access it through the Web. We provide an example of the web screen later in this section.

As you can see on the left side of the screen shown in Figure 7.50, there is a highlighted function to calculate cash flow. After executing it, the operating cash flow on the right side of the screen gets populated with the calculation results. This is an example of how planning functions work to enter data, upload it from Excel, or perform tasks and calculations in the system.

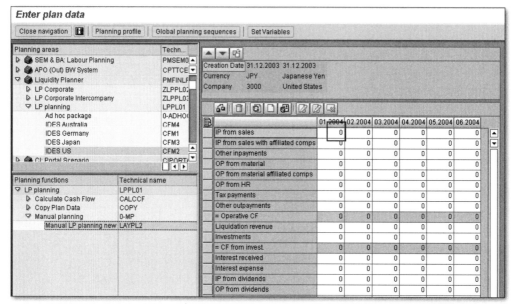

Figure 7.49 Manual Planning Function and Planning Layout

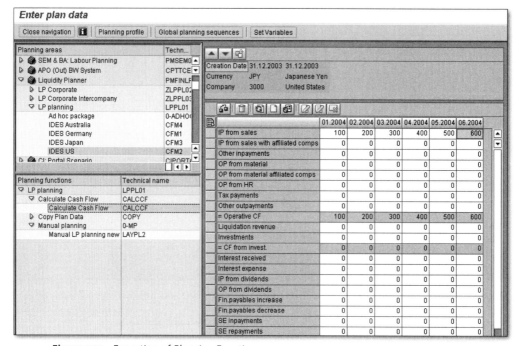

Figure 7.50 Execution of Planning Function

In Figure 7.51, you can see the manual planning function again — but this time the web application is being accessed through the web browser.

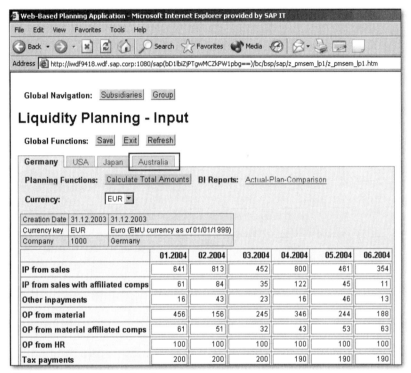

Figure 7.51 Web-Based Planning

In Figure 7.52, you can see a report being executed on the web application after manual data has been entered and the planning functions have been executed.

7.4.4 Reporting and Actual versus Plan Comparisons

One of the main goals of using Liquidity Planner is to be able to run actual versus plan comparisons, which enables you to see where your forecasts are off and gives you the opportunity to fine-tune your forecasting methods over time.

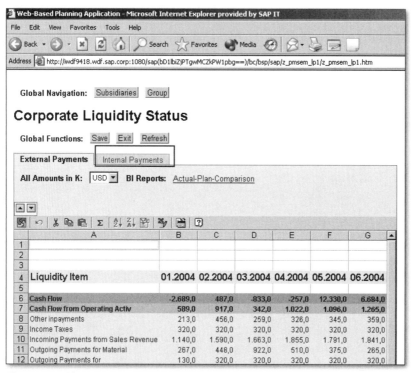

Figure 7.52 Planning Report

Forecasting the right way can allow the treasury department to make investment or borrowing decisions earlier and therefore improve the interest rate at which those are performed. This, in turn, increases the interest revenue or reduces the interest expense, both of which can affect the company bottom line.

To see this in practice, let's look at some examples. Figure 7.53 shows a list of liquidity items on the left and then columns for plan data and actual data.

As you can see, on top of the data section, there are multiple functions that can be performed for this report: filters, totals, sorting, graphics, and so on. For example, in Figure 7.54, we have filtered the report to only display Germany, United States, and Japan.

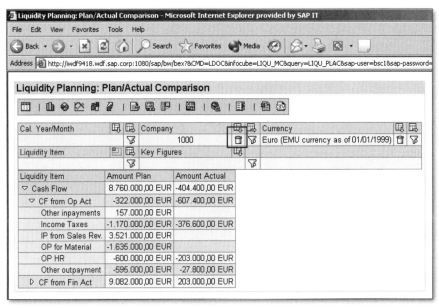

Figure 7.53 Plan versus Actual Comparison

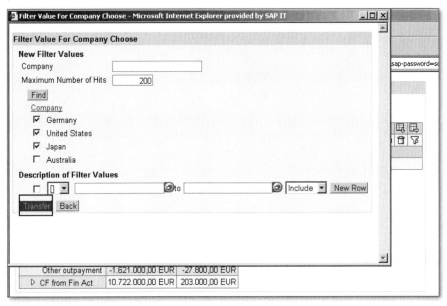

Figure 7.54 Filtering by Country

In Figure 7.55, you can see the report with subtotals per country per liquidity item, and with totals for the sum of the three countries.

Liquidity Planning: Plan/Actual Comparison

Cal. Year/Month		Company		Currency	
		Germany, United States, Japan		Euro (EMU currency as of 01/01/1999)	
Liquidity Item		Key Figures			

Liquidity Item	Company	Amount Plan	Amount Actual
▽ Cash Flow	Germany	8.760.000,00 EUR	-404.400,00 EUR
	United States	990.000,00 EUR	
	Japan	4.645.000,00 EUR	
	Result	**14.395.000,00 EUR**	**-404.400,00 EUR**
▽ CF from Op Act	Germany	-322.000,00 EUR	-607.400,00 EUR
	United States	820.000,00 EUR	
	Japan	3.275.000,00 EUR	
	Result	**3.773.000,00 EUR**	**-607.400,00 EUR**
Other inpayments	Germany	157.000,00 EUR	
	United States	600.000,00 EUR	
	Japan	1.478.000,00 EUR	
	Result	**2.235.000,00 EUR**	
Income Taxes	Germany	-1.170.000,00 EUR	-376.600,00 EUR
	United States	-1.500.000,00 EUR	
	Result	**-2.670.000,00 EUR**	**-376.600,00 EUR**
IP from Sales Rev.	Germany	3.521.000,00 EUR	
	United States	4.159.000,00 EUR	
	Japan	2.710.000,00 EUR	
	Result	**10.390.000,00 EUR**	
OP for Material	Germany	-1.635.000,00 EUR	
	United States	-1.920.000,00 EUR	
	Japan	-390.000,00 EUR	

Figure 7.55 Display of Filtered Report with Totals

In Figure 7.56, you can see the liquidity item list and hierarchy, the columns for each country, and a column for overall result.

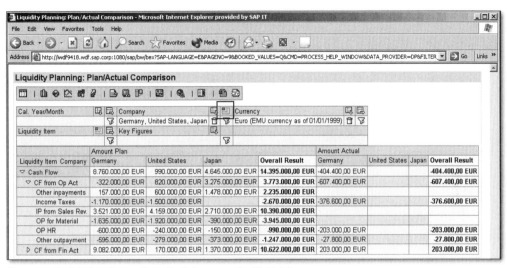

Figure 7.56 Display Comparisons in Columns and with Totals

In Figure 7.57, you can see a pie chart of plan amounts per country.

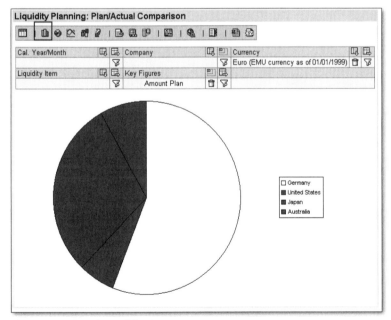

Figure 7.57 Pie Chart of the Data

285

Finally, Figure 7.58 shows a bar representation of the data for the plan amount by country.

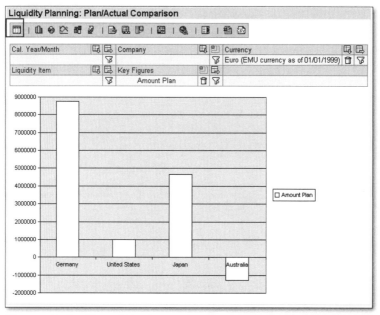

Figure 7.58   Bar Chart of Plan Amount by Country

These are just some examples of the possibilities of Liquidity Planning reporting.

7.5   Summary

In this chapter, we offered a business process description of the two functionalities available in Liquidity Planner: Cash Accounting and Liquidity Planning and Reporting. We also explained some of the shortcomings of the Cash Management functionality and how Liquidity Planner can be used to overcome them and to complement the Cash Management functionality.

Then we covered some of the differences between the Liquidity Planning functionality available in SEM-BPS and in Integrated Planning, and some of the differences between the functionality available in Integrated Planning and the functionality recently released in SAP BusinessObjects Planning and Consolidation.

We then explained the configuration and setup of the system. In this particular area, we concentrated on the Cash Accounting side of Liquidity Planner.

Finally, we provided demonstrations of how Cash Accounting works in SAP ERP, how data is extracted into SAP NetWeaver BW, how liquidity plans are created in Liquidity Planning and Reporting, and, how after all of these steps are completed, you can run actual versus plan comparisons and slice and present the data in multiple ways. In the next chapter, we cover the integration points between the Liquidity Forecast functionality and the rest of the SAP system.

The integration of the order-to-cash and procure-to-pay cycles and other financial processes in SAP ERP is essential to your Cash Management reports.

8   Integration with Procure-to-Pay, Order-to-Cash, and Other Financial Processes

Sales, purchases, AR transactions, AP transactions, fixed assets, financial risk management, foreign exchange transactions, and securities management all need to be reflected in the cash management reports as they flow through the order-to-cash and procure-to-pay processes. This chapter explains the integration of all of the components of these processes in SAP ERP and discusses how they are reflected in the cash position and liquidity forecast reports.

> **Note**
>
> We do not provide detailed configuration instructions for the entire cash position report in this chapter because Chapter 9, Global Cash Position Reporting and Management, is dedicated to this topic.

8.1   Integration Points for the Cash Position and Liquidity Forecast Reports

Although Cash Management is aimed at short-term planning — a maximum of 12 weeks — most treasurers are happy with an accurate forecast for the current and following week. An accurate forecast is difficult for many reasons; for example, in most companies, people outside of the treasury department tend to forget the cash implication of their actions. As a result, treasurers are constantly bombarded with last-minute requests to fund large payments, all of which distort any forecasting done previously. It takes more than configuration to get forecasting under control. You must educate all employees on the impact their actions have on liquidity; last-minute needs for borrowing will require your company to pay higher interest rates, and early redemption of investments are often associated with penalties or lower rates.

It is also necessary to establish and enforce policies requiring that cash flows be reflected in the system, via purchase orders, invoices, or memo records (a concept that will be explained in the next chapter) at least one week in advance. This helps treasurers better plan how to resolve their cash needs.

The cash position and liquidity forecast reports were designed to help treasurers see, in a single screen, all of the items that are due on a given day, week, or month. To make forecasted cash flows visible to treasurers, SAP developed ways to update the liquidity forecast report as business transactions happen. Up to SAP ERP 6.0, the following functionalities have the ability to do this:

▶ Sales and Distribution

▶ Accounts Receivable

▶ Purchasing

▶ Accounts Payable

▶ Transaction Management (investments, loans, securities, FX, etc.)

▶ SAP In-House Cash

In this section, we provide business process explanations and configuration instructions for each of those integration points.

8.1.1 Integration with Sales and Distribution

Figure 8.1 guides you through the order-to-cash and procure-to-pay processes, and demonstrates how they affect the liquidity forecast and cash position reports.

When you get a sales order from a customer, the order is supposed to be fulfilled on a certain delivery date, for a certain quantity, at a certain price — the combination of which results in an amount. The system assumes that it can submit the invoice on that delivery date, so it uses that as its baseline date. Then the system looks into the customer master record and finds the payment terms. Using the baseline date and the payment terms, the system then calculates the due date and updates the liquidity forecast and cash position reports with a cash inflow for that amount on that due date.

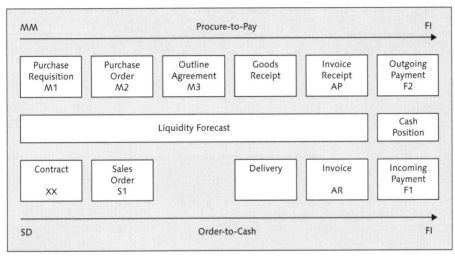

Figure 8.1 Integration of Procure-to-Pay and Order-to-Cash with Liquidity Forecast and Cash Position Reports

This integration requires the configuration of the planning levels for Logistics and is accessed via the following menu path: SAP CUSTOMIZING IMPLEMENTATION GUIDE • FINANCIAL SUPPLY CHAIN MANAGEMENT • CASH AND LIQUIDITY MANAGEMENT • CASH MANAGEMENT • STRUCTURING • DEFINE PLANNING LEVELS FOR LOGISTICS. When you access this path, the screen shown in Figure 8.2 appears.

Planning Levels
A *planning level* is an object used to group financial transactions that are used to facilitate cash flow analysis.

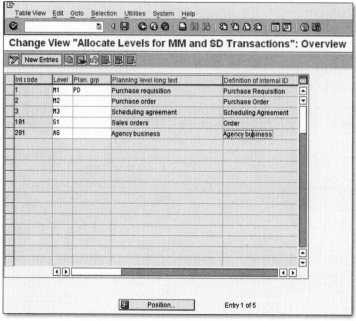

Figure 8.2 Planning Level for Sales Orders

As you can see in Figure 8.2, Internal Code 101 corresponds to sales orders in Sales and Distribution and can be assigned to a planning level to update the liquidity forecast and cash position reports. In this example, the planning level is S1.

8.1.2 Integration with Accounts Receivable

After the sales order is updated in the liquidity forecast and cash position reports, the processes of picking, packing, and shipping take place, followed by the invoice issue. It is not uncommon that the amount and due date in the invoice are different from the amount and due date calculated at the time the sales order was created. If the invoice is entered in the system in relationship to the sales order, the information entered at the time of the sales order is replaced with the information from the invoice. At this time, SAP ERP reads the baseline date and payment terms entered in the invoice and calculates the due date. This will be the date in which the inflow of cash is shown in the liquidity forecast report.

To access the configuration of the integration between the customer master record and the liquidity forecast and cash position reports, use the following menu path: SAP CUSTOMIZING IMPLEMENTATION GUIDE • FINANCIAL SUPPLY CHAIN MANAGEMENT • CASH AND LIQUIDITY MANAGEMENT • CASH MANAGEMENT • MASTER DATA • SUBLEDGER ACCOUNTS • DEFINE PLANNING GROUPS. When you access this path, the screen shown in Figure 8.3 appears.

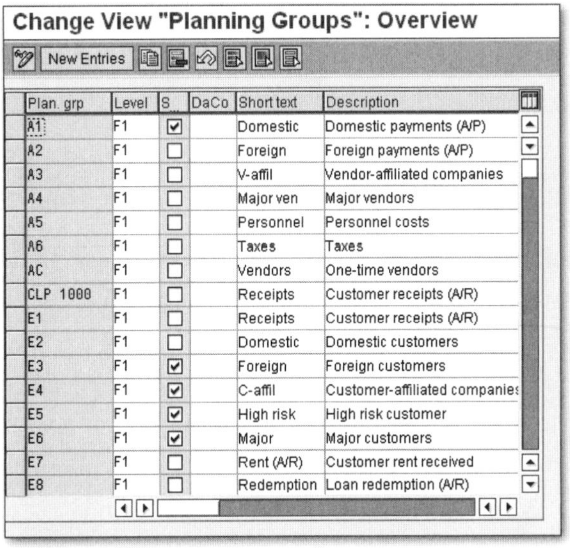
Change View "Planning Groups": Overview

New Entries

Plan. grp	Level	S	DaCo	Short text	Description
A1	F1	☑		Domestic	Domestic payments (A/P)
A2	F1	☐		Foreign	Foreign payments (A/P)
A3	F1	☐		V-affil	Vendor-affiliated companies
A4	F1	☐		Major ven	Major vendors
A5	F1	☐		Personnel	Personnel costs
A6	F1	☐		Taxes	Taxes
AC	F1	☐		Vendors	One-time vendors
CLP 1000	F1	☐		Receipts	Customer receipts (A/R)
E1	F1	☐		Receipts	Customer receipts (A/R)
E2	F1	☐		Domestic	Domestic customers
E3	F1	☑		Foreign	Foreign customers
E4	F1	☑		C-affil	Customer-affiliated companies
E5	F1	☑		High risk	High risk customer
E6	F1	☑		Major	Major customers
E7	F1	☐		Rent (A/R)	Customer rent received
E8	F1	☐		Redemption	Loan redemption (A/R)

Figure 8.3 Configuration of Planning Groups

Figure 8.3 shows planning groups, which are entered in the customer master record and update the AR invoices in the liquidity forecast and cash position reports. Once created, the planning groups are entered in the customer master record using Transaction FD02, as shown in Figure 8.4.

Planning Groups

Planning groups are created to facilitate the update of invoices from AR and AP into the liquidity forecast report.

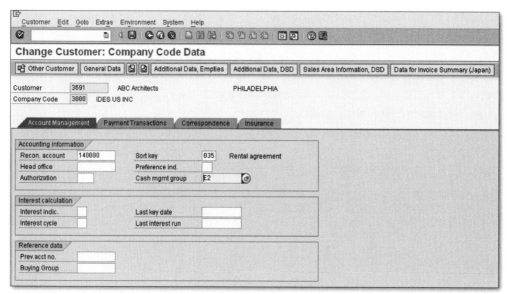

Figure 8.4 Cash Management Group (Planning Group) in the Customer Master Record

As you can see, the company code data section of the customer master record has an Account Management tab, which is where the cash management group (also called the planning group) is entered.

> **Note**
>
> For AR, the liquidity forecast and cash position reports are just estimating tools and tend to be inexact; just because you know when an invoice is due does not mean that it will be paid on that date, and, even if it is, the bank may take a few days cashing the check (or something else may cause a delay). In other words, when it comes to AR, the liquidity forecast is only a guide to what *could* happen, not a prediction of what *will* happen.
>
> The only place where the liquidity forecast and cash position reports offer certainty is in the Transaction Manager flows, which are described later in this chapter.

8.1.3   Integration with Purchasing

Recall the diagram, earlier in this chapter, that showed the integration between the cash position and liquidity forecast reports with the procure-to-pay process (reproduced in Figure 8.5).

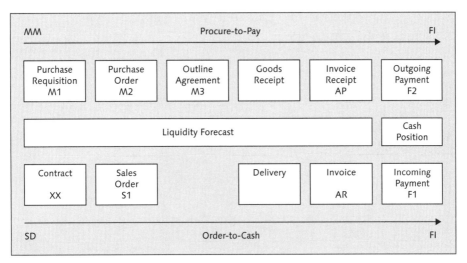

Figure 8.5 Integration with the Procure-to-Pay Process

As you can see in the figure, the procure-to-pay process has four stages that update the liquidity forecast and cash position reports. The first three are part of the Purchasing component, and the last one is part of the Accounts Payable component.

The first stage is purchase requisition, which is associated with a required delivery date. Based on this date and on the vendor payment terms, SAP ERP estimates the date of the cash outflow and shows it on the liquidity forecast and cash position reports. The second stage is the purchase order. The outline agreement works in a similar way, just with a different planning level.

To access the configuration of the integration between Purchasing and the liquidity forecast and cash position reports, use the following menu path: SAP Customizing Implementation Guide • Financial Supply Chain Management • Cash and Liquidity Management • Cash Management • Structuring • Define Planning Levels for Logistics. The screen shown in Figure 8.6 appears.

Just as you can with the sales order process, you use this screen to assign a planning level to each of the three stages of purchasing that are relevant to the liquidity forecast and cash position reports: the purchase requisition, purchase order, and scheduling agreement. Each stage of the process has to be entered with reference to the previous one; for example, the purchase order has to be linked to the purchase requisition so the system replaces one with the next and updates the dates and amounts as the process moves forward.

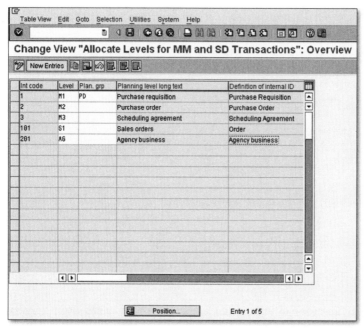

Figure 8.6 Planning Levels for Logistics

8.1.4   Integration with Accounts Payable

After the procure-to-pay process gets to the invoice stage, and assuming the invoice is entered with reference to one of the previous stages (e.g., the purchase order), the system updates the cash outflow with the invoice amount, and uses the baseline date and payment terms to calculate when the outflow will occur. To make this happen, you must configure a planning group. To do this, access the following menu path: Customizing Implementation Guide • Financial Supply Chain Management • Cash and Liquidity Management • Cash Management • Master Data • Subledger Accounts • Define Planning Groups. The screen shown in Figure 8.7 appears.

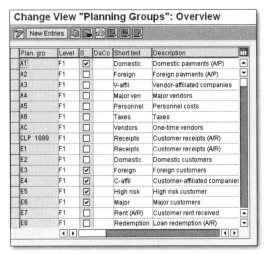

Figure 8.7 Planning Groups

Configure the planning groups (also called cash management groups) on this screen. After the groups are created, assign them to a vendor using Transaction FK02 (Figure 8.8).

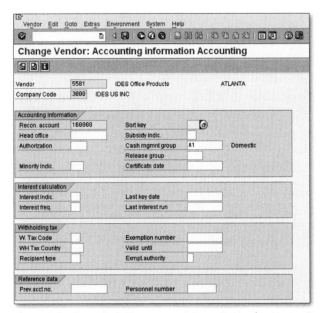

Figure 8.8 Enter Cash Management Group in Vendor Master Record

As you can see, the cash management group is entered in the Company Code Data section of the vendor master record.

8.1.5   Integration with Transaction Manager

Transaction Manager is a functionality of SAP Treasury and Risk Management and is where you enter trading deals related to money market transactions (such as fixed-term deposits and deposits at notice), securities transactions (such as stocks), foreign exchange transactions (such as spots), debt transactions (such as intercompany loans), and so on.

All of these transactions have a cash flow associated with them; for example, a loan has an original disbursement date, which is when you receive the funds, as well as annuity payments or interest and principal payments (depending on the repayment type). These cash flows should be visible to the treasurer so he remembers not only to plan on sending or receiving the funds but also to fulfill the companies' obligations on time; being late on a public transaction such as a bond can have an incredibly negative impact on the credit rating and valuation of the company stock. When a large corporation defaults on paying a bond, it usually makes headlines; this is something you have to avoid, which is where the liquidity forecast and cash position reports come in handy.

The liquidity forecast and cash position reports are also much more precise on these types of transactions than with those related to AR and AP because, in this case, the system knows the exact date in which the inflow or outflow of cash should occur (i.e., is due). In AR and AP, however, the payee controls the date of the payment.

To configure the link between Transaction Manager and the liquidity forecast and cash position reports, access the following menu path: SAP CUSTOMIZING IMPLEMENTATION GUIDE • FINANCIAL SUPPLY CHAIN MANAGEMENT • TREASURY AND RISK MANAGEMENT • TRANSACTION MANAGER • GENERAL SETTINGS • LINK TO CASH MANAGEMENT. The screen shown in Figure 8.9 appears.

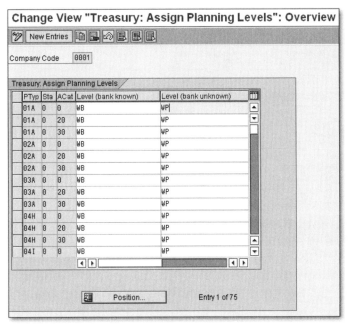

Figure 8.9 Assign Planning Levels to Product Types

To understand this configuration, there are two concepts with which you must be familiar:

▸ **Product type**
This is the type of transaction being processed in Transaction Manager. Examples are fixed term deposits, stocks, FX spots, and so on.

▸ **Activity category**
This is the stage of the transaction currently being processed. Most transactions start with a contract; however, some can go through a settlement phase, and some even more have additional steps.

In the screen shown in Figure 8.9, configure what planning level you want to display in the liquidity forecast and cash position reports for each of your product types and activity categories. You also have the option to show one product type if the bank is known and a different one if the bank is not known.

The following step, available on the same menu path, is the configuration of relevant update types as shown in Figure 8.10.

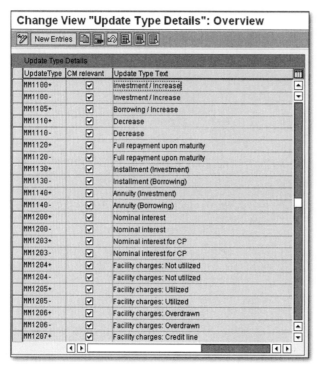

Figure 8.10 Update Types Relevant for Cash Management

The *update type* depends on the product type being processed and updates the status of the transaction and the remaining cash flow associated with it. For example, an investment increase, borrowing increase, annuity payment, or repayment on maturity would all be considered update types. You can choose whether to reflect this update type in the liquidity forecast and cash position reports, depending on whether the particular update is going to cause cash flow to occur.

8.1.6 Integration with SAP In-House Cash

In Chapter 6, In-House Banking with SAP ERP, we explained SAP In-House Cash and how it works. You'll recall that SAP In-House Cash processes result in multiple postings that happen inside the SAP In-House Cash component at the current account level. In other words, they happen in the cash subledger that SAP In-House Cash is in, but must then be updated in the general ledger in a separate step.

In the same way that a transfer to the general ledger takes place, a transfer to Cash Management needs to occur to keep the liquidity forecast and cash position reports in sync with the activity in the SAP In-House Cash component. To configure this transfer, access the following menu path: SAP CUSTOMIZING IMPLEMENTATION GUIDE • FINANCIAL SUPPLY CHAIN MANAGEMENT • IN-HOUSE CASH • PERIODIC TASKS • TRANSFER FINANCIAL STATUS TO SAP CASH MANAGEMENT • SET UP FINANCIAL STATUS. The screen shown in Figure 8.11 appears.

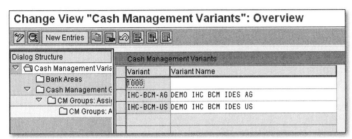

Figure 8.11 Definition of Cash Management Variants for SAP In-House Cash

The structure used to update Cash Management from SAP In-House Cash is called a cash management variant. In this example, we select Cash Management variant 1000 and click on Bank Areas, which results in the screen shown in Figure 8.12.

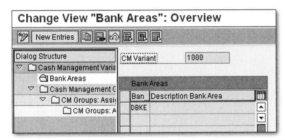

Figure 8.12 Cash Management Variant — Bank Areas Included

The system shows what bank areas are included in this cash management variant. In this case, there is only one: DBKE. Now click on Cash Management Groups, which is located under Bank Areas on the menu on the left. This results in the screen shown in Figure 8.13.

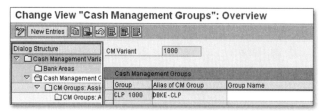

Figure 8.13 Cash Management Groups in Cash Management Variants

Now the system shows what cash management groups are included in this variant. In this example, the Cash Management group is CLP 1000. Now click on CM Groups: Assignment of Bank Area on the menu on the left. This results in the screen shown in Figure 8.14.

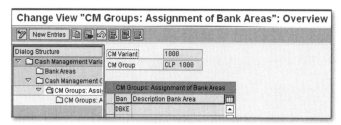

Figure 8.14 Assignment of Bank Areas to Cash Management Groups

As you can see, the bank area and the cash management group have been linked. Now click on CM Groups: Assignment of Accounts. This screen is shown in Figure 8.15.

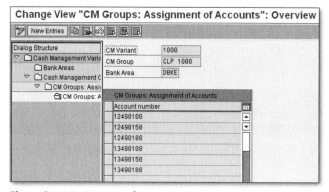

Figure 8.15 Assignment of Accounts

On this screen, you enter the specific general ledger accounts associated with the update of SAP In-House Cash in the general ledger. This will keep the sync between Cash Management and the general ledger for SAP In-House Cash postings.

On the same path (IMG • Financial Supply Chain Management • In House Cash • Periodic Tasks • Transfer Financial Status to SAP Cash Management • Check the Consistency of the Settings), you can find an IMG activity to check the consistency of the settings. Because there are several steps in this process, it is always a good idea to run this consistency check (Figure 8.16).

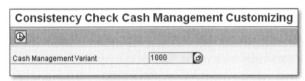

Figure 8.16 Consistency Check

Enter the Cash Management variant created in the previous step, which is 1000, and then click Execute. As you can see from Figure 8.17, the system finds that the settings are consistent. You can now be confident that SAP In-House Cash postings will be updated properly in the Cash Management system.

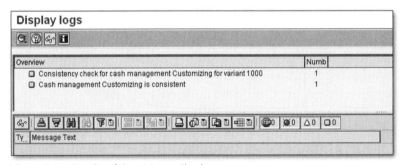

Figure 8.17 Results of Consistency Check

8.2 Forecasting in Liquidity Planner

Chapter 7, Global Liquidity Forecasting with Liquidity Planner, was dedicated to the Liquidity Planner, so we only briefly touch on it here. In the same way that the liquidity forecast and cash position reports are aimed at short-term planning, Liquidity Planner is aimed at mid- and long-term cash forecasting. However, the Liquidity Planner forecast is not associated with transactions happening in other components; rather, it's more like the budgeting process.

For example, let's consider a scenario where your sales forecast for the year is $12 million — $1 million per month. Of the sales in January, you estimate 50% will be paid for in cash, 25% will be paid for 30 days after purchase, and 25% will be paid for 60 days after purchase. Therefore, you would enter $500,000 of cash inflow in your January forecast, $250,000 in your February forecast, and $250,000 in your March forecast. Then do a similar exercise with all of the remaining months.

This planning is done in Liquidity Planner and was initially offered in SEM-Business Planning and Simulation (SEM-BPS); this functionality was replaced by Integrated Planning, and then Liquidity Planner was offered on it. SAP has since replaced Integrated Planning with SAP BusinessObjects Planning and Consolidation. At the time of this writing, this latest version of Liquidity Planner is about to be released to the public.

8.3 Summary

In this chapter, we discussed how the accuracy of cash planning is not only dependent on systems and configuration but also on educating the different departments of a company to understand the cash impact of their decisions and actions. We also explained that the sooner a transaction is entered in the system, via purchase order, invoice, memo record, or other methods, the better visibility and planning the treasurer will have. We then covered the different functionalities that integrate with the liquidity forecast and cash position reports, and how these functionalities are configured. Finally, we briefly discussed Liquidity Planner. In the next chapter, we cover the rest of the Cash Management functionality.

This chapter brings together all of the preceding chapter components and provides a visualization of the end result — managing daily cash positioning activity and reporting from a practical real-world perspective.

9 Global Cash Position Reporting and Management

We have covered multiple topics throughout this book, and now it is time to bring it all together to explain how these pieces fit into an integrated cash management process. Take a look at Figure 9.1 to see a diagram of the overall picture and each component we should consider:

To review, the overall process works like this:

- ► Every morning, the treasury staff loads the previous day's electronic bank statements into SAP ERP, which updates the initial cash balances for the day. This process can be monitored in the Bank Statement Monitor in SAP Bank Communication Management.

- ► Throughout the morning, the intraday electronic bank statements are loaded. They create memo records in the system to update last-minute cash deposits and payments.

- ► Entered sales orders and sales invoices update the expected cash inflows in the liquidity forecast report. Usually the treasurer uses a manual factor and multiplies it by this forecast to obtain an estimate for these cash inflows.

- ► Entered purchase orders, agreements, and vendor invoices update the expected cash outflows for the day. Most treasurers validate what items need to be paid as wires because these are more relevant for today's cash flows than other payment methods.

- ► Items captured in Transaction Manager for investments, securities, loans, and foreign exchange transactions update the liquidity forecast report.

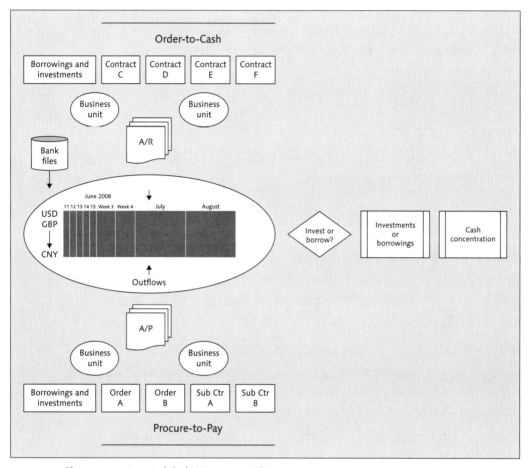

Figure 9.1 Integrated Cash Management Process

▶ Additional items not captured in the sources just mentioned can be entered manually using memo records.

▶ The cash position report is executed, with or without a liquidity forecast, using Transaction FF7B.

▶ If excess cash or additional funds are needed, they are invested or borrowed accordingly.

▶ Cash concentration is executed to fund the corresponding accounts in the cash position report.

- The required investments, borrowings, foreign exchange transactions, redemptions, and payments are processed using Transaction Manager.

- The cash position report is executed again to validate final balances.

- Optionally, the cash position report is uploaded into SAP NetWeaver BW and run from there.

We covered most of these processes in earlier chapters. In Chapter 3, Advanced Inbound Electronic Banking in SAP ERP, we covered inbound processes. Among those, we covered electronic bank statement processing, which is one of the first parts of the cash management process; it involves loading the previous day's electronic bank statement, which will provide the initial cash balances. Meanwhile, intraday bank statements provide same-day cash updates. In Chapter 4, Advanced Outbound Electronic Banking in SAP ERP, we covered cash concentration, one of the outputs of the cash position process. In Chapter 5, Overview of SAP Bank Communication Management, we explained SAP Bank Communication Management and how the Bank Statement Monitor can be used for the processing and status of electronic bank statements. In Chapter 8, Integration with Procure-to-Pay, Order-to-Cash, and Other Financial Processes, we explained the integration between the liquidity forecast and the procure-to-pay and order-to-cash cycles, and we covered how this information helps craft a short-term cash forecast. We also discussed the way Transaction Manager updates investments, borrowings, and FX transactions in the liquidity forecast, and how SAP In-House Cash updates the cash position report.

In this chapter, we cover a range of issues that we have mentioned throughout the book and explain how these affect the execution and configuration of the cash position report and the Cash Management component.

9.1   Introduction to the Cash Position Report

For most treasurers, the mark of a good treasury system is that it allows for a quick and effective preparation of the cash position report. Creating a cash position report is one of the most urgent business processes; if you don't complete it in time, you lose the opportunity to invest at the highest available rates in the market or borrow at the lowest possible rates.

In this section, we review how the cash position report addresses multicurrency and multicash considerations, and we discuss the main limitations of the report, some of which have now been addressed by SAP with the creation of the Liquidity Planner functionality.

One of the strengths of the cash position report is that it can be displayed in multiple currencies. It can also be configured so that it displays each individual bank, region, or company separately, or, alternatively, so that it displays a summary of all information in a single screen.

The report has some limitations, though. For example, some functionalities that many treasurers require are not possible with the cash position report. For example:

- Tracking actual cash flows the next day
- Running a comparative actual versus forecast report
- Carrying out long-term cash forecasting
- Tying each inflow or outflow of cash to an actual expense or revenue item

In the past few years, SAP started offering Liquidity Planner, a tool that allows all of the functions just listed. Users who implemented the old cash position report and are aware of its shortcomings should be aware that Liquidity Planner complements the Cash Management functionality; combining the two functionalities results in a very well-rounded and solid treasury workstation — similar to other treasury workstations that, for years, were considered best in class and better than SAP ERP.

9.1.1 Working with the Cash Position and Liquidity Forecast Reports

Here we explain how to use the cash position and liquidity forecast reports. To access the cash position and liquidity forecast reports, use the following menu path: SAP MENU • ACCOUNTING • FINANCIAL SUPPLY CHAIN MANAGEMENT • CASH AND LIQUIDITY MANAGEMENT • CASH MANAGEMENT • INFORMATION SYSTEM • REPORTS FOR CASH MANAGEMENT • LIQUIDITY ANALYSIS • FF7A – CASH POSITION.

When you access this path, the screen shown in Figure 9.2 appears. (Note: This is only the top half of the screen; the bottom half is shown in Figure 9.3.)

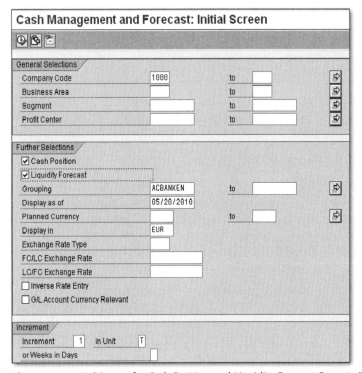

Figure 9.2   Initial Screen for Cash Position and Liquidity Forecast Reports (Top Half)

Enter the company code. If you are using business areas, segments, or profit centers, you can also use them as filters. From this screen, depending on which box you check, you can execute the cash position report, the liquidity forecast report, or both. Following are some of the important fields on this screen:

▶ **Grouping**

The Grouping field represents your settings for the report. We explain this topic in more detail in Section 9.2, Cash Management Configuration, but the basic idea is that the structure contains a group of general ledger accounts related to one or several banks and bank accounts. It also contains some planning levels and planning groups.

▶ **Display As Of**

The report displays multiple days, starting with a certain date. This date is entered in the Display As Of field.

▶ **Display In**

In this field, enter the currency in which you want to see the report.

▶ **Exchange Rate Type**

This is the exchange rate type you want to use when translating items in foreign currencies. You can also manually enter the exchange rates in the FC/LC Exchange Rate or the LC/FC Exchange Rate fields in this screen; the one you choose depends on whether you have a direct or indirect quotation.

▶ **G/L Account Currency Relevant**

If this box is checked, the report is displayed in the general ledger account currency.

▶ **Increment**

This field represents the interval for the columns in the report (e.g., an increment of 1 day will result in a daily display).

▶ **Unit**

This field is where you indicate whether you want to display the report for each day (T), for each week (W), or for each month (M).

Figure 9.3 shows the bottom half of the initial screen for the cash position and liquidity forecast reports.

There are several important fields on this screen:

▶ **Display Type area**

The Display Type area has several options. Cumulative Display adds today's transactions to the previous balances and shows a total. Delta Display shows the initial balances at the beginning, and then, for each day, shows its own transactions and the ending balance.

▶ **Scaling**
The Scaling field is where you choose how to display the cash amounts (thousands, millions, etc.). You can also choose how many decimal places you want to see.

▶ **Number of Columns**
The number of columns determines the number of days, weeks, or months that are displayed at once.

▶ **Shift Planned Amounts (for Increment in Days) area**
In this area, you can choose how to display weekend days.

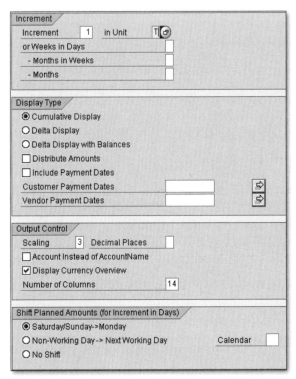

Figure 9.3 Initial Screen for Cash Position and Liquidity Forecast Reports (Bottom Half)

Figure 9.4 shows a cumulative display, in days, in thousands, using Euros.

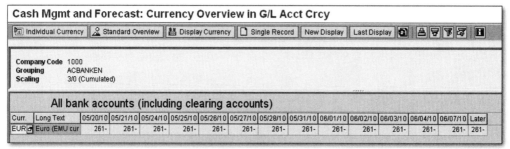

Figure 9.4 Example of Cumulative Display in Days and Thousands

Click on the New Display button. The screen shown in Figure 9.5 appears, and you can select the parameters again.

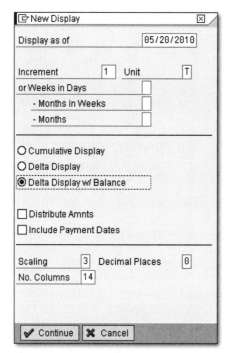

Figure 9.5 New Display Screen

Figure 9.6 shows the report again, but this time in weeks and using a delta display.

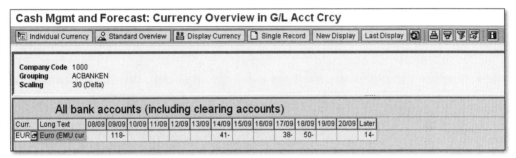

Figure 9.6 Delta Display in Weeks and Thousands

Finally, Figure 9.7 shows how the report looks with all of the different inputs from Transaction Manager for securities, commercial paper and loans, multiple planning levels for checks and EFTs, and domestic and foreign transactions, in day intervals and in thousands.

Cash Management and Forecast: Display Levels

Accounts | Single Record | New Display | Last Display

Company Code 1000
Display in EUR
Grouping BANKEN
Scaling 3/0 (Cumulated)

CITIBANK | **

Level	Short text	06.09.09	07.09.09	08.09.09	09.09.09	10.09.09	11.09.09	14.09.09	15.09.09	16.09.09	17.09.09	18.09.09	21.09.09	22.09.09	Later
AB	Advice, c.	1.339	1.339	1.339	1.339	1.339	1.339	1.339	1.339	1.339	1.339	1.339	1.339	1.339	1.339
B1	Out. check	1.884-	1.884-	1.884-	1.884-	1.884-	1.884-	1.884-	1.884-	1.884-	1.884-	1.884-	1.884-	1.884-	1.884-
B2	Dom trans	51.158-	51.158-	51.158-	51.158-	51.158-	51.158-	51.158-	51.158-	51.158-	51.158-	51.158-	51.158-	51.158-	51.158-
B3	For. trans	2.216-	2.216-	2.216-	2.216-	2.216-	2.216-	2.216-	2.216-	2.216-	2.216-	2.216-	2.216-	2.216-	2.216-
B4	Bank coll.	940	940	940	940	940	940	940	940	940	940	940	940	940	940
B5	Int posts	266.306	266.306	266.306	266.306	266.306	266.306	266.306	266.306	266.306	266.306	266.306	266.306	266.306	266.306
B8	Inc checks	80	80	80	80	80	80	80	80	80	80	80	80	80	80
B9	Cash rec	169.675	169.675	169.675	169.675	169.675	169.675	169.675	169.675	169.675	169.675	169.675	169.675	169.675	169.675
BV	Advice, c.	15	15	15	15	15	15	15	15	15	15	15	15	15	15
CB	CP ext. B.	10.000	10.000	10.000	10.000	10.000	10.000	10.000	10.000	10.000	10.000	10.000	10.000	10.000	10.000
D1	Cap banks	893-	893-	893-	893-	893-	893-	893-	893-	893-	893-	893-	893-	893-	893-
D5	Swap banks	1.445-	1.445-	1.445-	1.445-	1.445-	1.445-	1.445-	1.445-	1.445-	1.445-	1.445-	1.445-	1.445-	1.625-
D7	FRA banks	452-	452-	452-	452-	452-	452-	452-	452-	452-	452-	452-	452-	452-	452-
F0	Fl Banks	29.929	29.929	29.929	29.929	29.929	29.929	29.929	29.929	29.929	29.929	29.929	29.929	29.929	29.929
PR	Pay.Req.	245-	245-	245-	245-	245-	245-	245-	245-	245-	245-	245-	245-	245-	246-
TB	Deps/loans	307.352-	307.352-	307.352-	307.352-	307.352-	307.352-	307.352-	307.120-	307.227-	307.227-	307.227-	307.227-	307.227-	279.220-
WB	Securities	154-	154-	154-	154-	154-	154-	154-	154-	154-	154-	154-	154-	154-	167-
		112.486	112.486	112.486	112.486	112.486	112.486	112.486	112.719	112.611	112.611	112.611	112.611	112.611	140.424

Figure 9.7 Example with All Components Integrated

9.1.2 Memo Records

Even with all of the integration available in SAP ERP, there are always some items that are not automatically updated, for example, funding for real estate or company acquisitions, trading of commodities, and other types of transactions. To reflect changes such as these in the cash position report, you must enter a *memo record* by accessing the following menu path: SAP MENU • ACCOUNTING • FINANCIAL SUPPLY CHAIN MANAGEMENT • CASH AND LIQUIDITY MANAGEMENT • CASH MANAGEMENT • PLANNING • MEMO RECORD • FF63 – CREATE. The screen shown in Figure 9.8 appears.

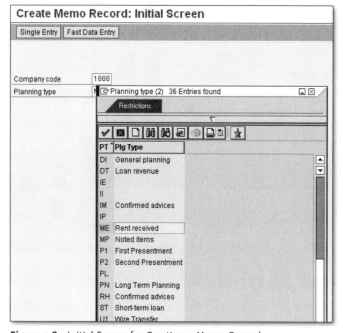

Figure 9.8 Initial Screen for Creating a Memo Record

On this screen, select the company code and the planning type. (The planning type often reflects the type of inflow or outflow expected.) Then select Enter, which brings you to the screen shown in Figure 9.9. Here, enter a value date (which is the date in which you want the memo to be displayed), the bank account name, the currency, the amount, and a description of the reason for the expected cash flow in the Text field. Save the record.

Figure 9.9 Create Memo Record Screen

After you save the memo record, you can execute the cash position report. As you can see from Figure 9.10, the memo record now appears on it.

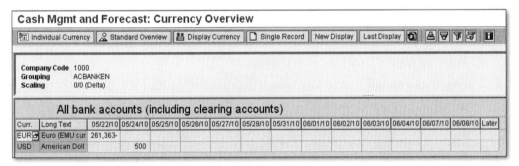

Figure 9.10 Cash Position Report Showing Entered Memo Record

As you can see in Figure 9.11, if you double-click the memo record, it shows you the planning type (which was Rent, as shown in Figure 9.9).

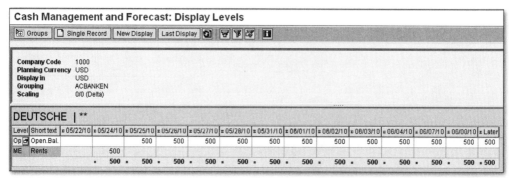

Figure 9.11 Cash Position Report After Drilldown to Planning Type

If you keep drilling down, you are able to see the original memo record and who entered it. In this example, you can see memo record ID 1000000135 (Figure 9.12).

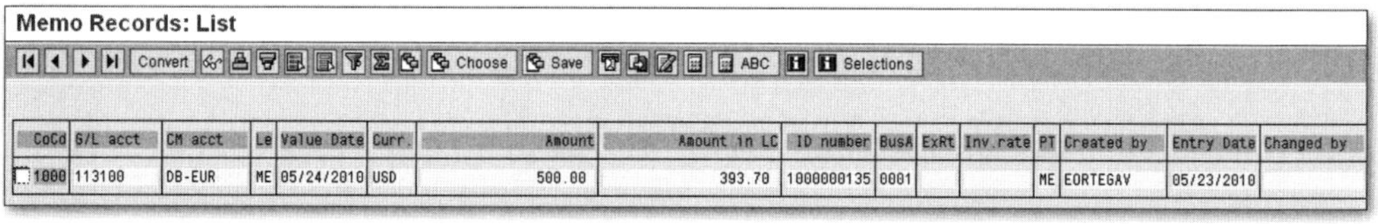

Figure 9.12 Drilldown to Original Record

Entering Memo Records Collectively

If you don't want to enter memo records individually, and have a large amount of them, you can upload them from Excel using the following menu path: SAP MENU • ACCOUNTING • FINANCIAL SUPPLY CHAIN MANAGEMENT • CASH AND LIQUIDITY MANAGEMENT • CASH MANAGEMENT • INCOMINGS • MEMO RECORD • RFTS6510 – LOAD FROM FILE. The screen shown in Figure 9.13 appears.

To load the memo records successfully, you need your Excel file to adjust to a specific layout. If you want to know and understand this layout, click on the Information icon to the right of the Execute button. This tells you to look at structure FDES_IMPORT, which you can see in Transaction SE11 (Figure 9.14).

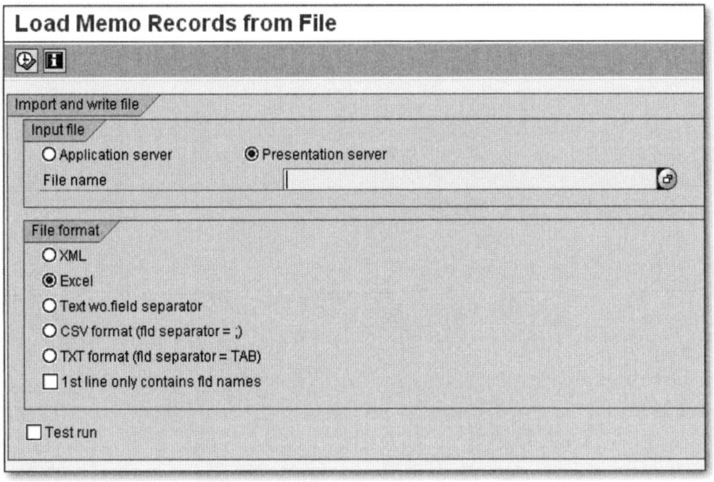

Figure 9.13 Load Memo Records from File Screen

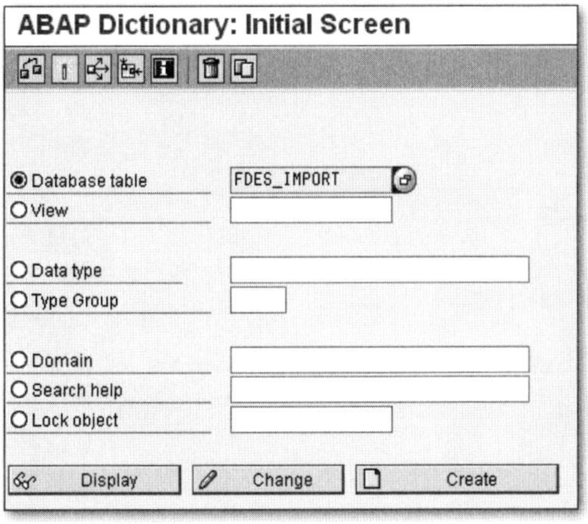

Figure 9.14 Review Structure Using Transaction SE11

In the screen for Transaction SE11, enter the structure name in the Database Table field, and then click on the Display button. The screen shown in Figure 9.15 appears. For you to successfully load your Excel file into SAP ERP, it must have the same sequence of fields (columns) with the same column widths as on this screen.

Structure	FDES_IMPORT		Active				
Short Description	Structure for Importing TR-CM Memo Recs (Pyt Advs/Plan Itms)						

Attributes Components Entry help/check Currency/quantity fields

Predefined Type   1 / 39

Component	RTy	Component type	Data Type	Length	Decim	Short Description	Group
BUKRS	☐	BUKRS	CHAR	4	0	Company Code	
BNKKO	☐	SKPSK	CHAR	10	0	G/L account/internal Cash Mgmt account	
GRUPP	☐	FDGRP	CHAR	10	0	Planning Group	
EBENE	☐	FDLEV	CHAR	2	0	Planning level	
DISPW	☐	DISPW	CUKY	5	0	Planned currency for cash management and forecast	
DATUM	☐	FDTAG	DATS	8	0	Planning date	
GSBER	☐	GSBER	CHAR	4	0	Business Area	
.INCLUDE	☐	FDIES	▭▭	0	0	Include cash management memo records	
DMSHB	☐	DMSHW	CURR	15	2	Amount in local currency	
WRSHB	☐	WRSHW	CURR	15	2	Amount in planned currency	
KURST	☐	KURST_CURR	CHAR	4	0	Exchange Rate Type	
XINVR	☐	XKURSINV	CHAR	1	0	Indicator: inverted rate entry	
DSART	☐	DSART	CHAR	2	0	Planning type	
USRID	☐	USRID	CHAR	12	0	User who created the record	
HZDAT	☐	HZDAT	DATS	8	0	Date on Which Record Was Created	
AENUS	☐	AENUS	CHAR	12	0	Last user to make a change	
AENDT	☐	AENDT	DATS	8	0	Date of last change	
AVDAT	☐	AVDAT	DATS	8	0	Archiving or automatic expiration date	

Figure 9.15 Structure FDES_IMPORT

Archiving and Activating Memo Records

If you need to delete Memo Records either individually or collectively, you can use the following menu path: SAP MENU • ACCOUNTING • FINANCIAL SUPPLY CHAIN MANAGEMENT • CASH AND LIQUIDITY MANAGEMENT • CASH MANAGEMENT • PLANNING • MEMO RECORD • FF6B – CHANGE USING LIST. The screen shown in Figure 9.16 appears.

As you can see, you have multiple parameters here. Pay particular attention to the Archiving Category field. If you enter A in this field and then execute the program, you will see only *archived* memo records. If you leave it blank, you will see all active memo records.

In our example, let's execute the program for company code 1000, which is the one we used for our earlier memo record. In this example, we leave the Archiving Category field blank. The result is shown in Figure 9.17.

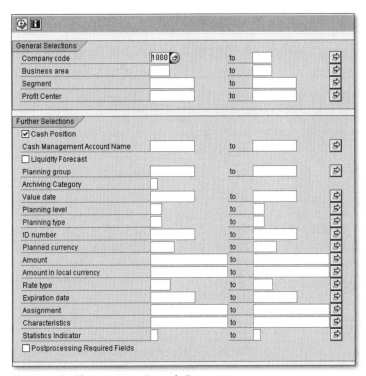

Figure 9.16 Change Memo Records Screen

	CoCd	G/L acct	CM acct	Le	Value Date	Curr.	Amount	Amount in LC	ID number	BusA	ExRt	Inv.rate	PT	Created by	Entry Date	Changed by
☐	1000	113100	DB-EUR	ME	05/24/2010	USD	500.00	393.70	1000000135	0001			ME	EORTEGAV	05/23/2010	

Memo Records: List

Figure 9.17 Memo Records List

If you want to archive a memo record on this screen, click on the checkbox on the left of the record row, then click on the Convert button at the top of the screen; it is removed from the list and from the cash position report.

To reactivate memo records, execute this program, and enter an "A" in the Archiving Category field. You will see archived memo records that match your parameters. If you click Convert, they will become active again.

9.2 Cash Management Configuration

In the previous chapter, we looked at configuration specific to the liquidity forecast report. In this chapter, we focus on all of the options that weren't covered in the previous chapter (because they were more specific to the cash position report than to the liquidity forecast report). In this section, we specifically look at value dates, master data, source symbols, planning levels, bank accounts, account names, structures, and more.

9.2.1 Activating the Default Value Date

To activate the default value date, access the following menu path: SAP CUSTOMIZING IMPLEMENTATION GUIDE • FINANCIAL SUPPLY CHAIN MANAGEMENT • CASH AND LIQUIDITY MANAGEMENT • CASH MANAGEMENT • BASIC SETTINGS • DEFINE VALUE DATE DEFAULT. The screen shown in Figure 9.18 appears.

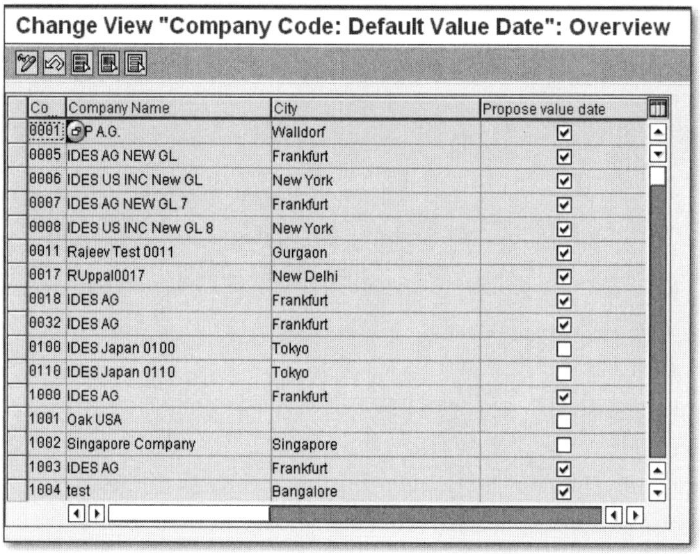
Change View "Company Code: Default Value Date": Overview

Co	Company Name	City	Propose value date
0001	P A.G.	Walldorf	☑
0005	IDES AG NEW GL	Frankfurt	☑
0006	IDES US INC New GL	New York	☑
0007	IDES AG NEW GL 7	Frankfurt	☑
0008	IDES US INC New GL 8	New York	☑
0011	Rajeev Test 0011	Gurgaon	☑
0017	RUppal0017	New Delhi	☑
0018	IDES AG	Frankfurt	☑
0032	IDES AG	Frankfurt	☑
0100	IDES Japan 0100	Tokyo	☐
0110	IDES Japan 0110	Tokyo	☐
1000	IDES AG	Frankfurt	☑
1001	Oak USA		☐
1002	Singapore Company	Singapore	☐
1003	IDES AG	Frankfurt	☑
1004	test	Bangalore	☑

Figure 9.18 Default Value Date Screen

The default value date is a very important setting that affects multiple transactions across the system. Selecting the box means that whenever you try to post an account where the Value Date field is available for entry, the system proposes the current date as the value date.

9.2.2 Configuring Source Symbols

Another basic setting for Cash Management regards the source symbols, which are the areas in the system from where Cash Management information is generated. Standard sources are as follows: BNK for Bank Accounting, IHC for In-House Cash, MMF for Materials Management, PSK for subledger accounting (AR and AP), and SDF for Sales and Distribution. Figure 9.19 shows these sources. Typically, you won't add to the list here; you will only determine which of the sources you want to display in the cash position report, and which ones you want to display in the liquidity forecast report. Most people leave the default settings.

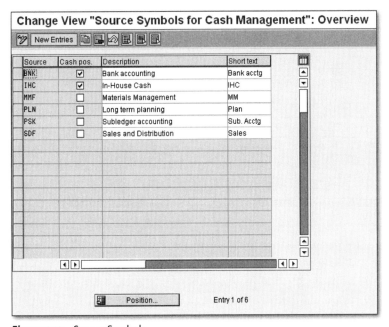

Figure 9.19 Source Symbols

9.2.3 Configuring Planning Levels

A *planning level* is an object that controls the display in the cash position report based on certain characteristics and is assigned to general ledger master data. Although it is freely definable, you should follow naming conventions. To configure planning levels, access the following menu path: SAP CUSTOMIZING IMPLEMENTATION GUIDE • FINANCIAL SUPPLY CHAIN MANAGEMENT • CASH AND LIQUIDITY MANAGEMENT • CASH MANAGEMENT • MASTER DATA • G/L ACCOUNTS • DEFINE PLANNING LEVELS. The screen shown in Figure 9.20 appears.

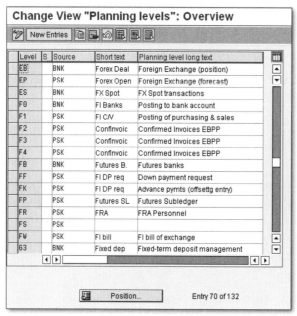

Figure 9.20 Planning Level Configuration

As you can see, the planning level is associated with a source symbol; it has a short description and a long text. Planning levels define the cash flow with which they are associated; for example, for wire payments, you might have a planning level called Outgoing Wires (or something similar). In Chapter 3, Section 3.1, Business Process Overview, we explained how the planning levels and the numbering of general ledger accounts facilitate cash reconciliation and cash position reporting; please review that section for a better understanding of this material.

For the planning levels to work properly, you must set up your general ledger master record as shown in Figure 9.21, which depicts Transaction FS00.

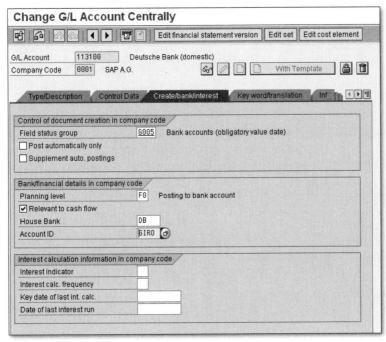

Change G/L Account Centrally

| Edit financial statement version | Edit set | Edit cost element |

G/L Account 113100 Deutsche Bank (domestic)
Company Code 0001 SAP A.G. With Template

Type/Description | Control Data | Create/bank/interest | Key word/translation | Inf

Control of document creation in company code
Field status group 6005 Bank accounts (obligatory value date)
☐ Post automatically only
☐ Supplement auto. postings

Bank/financial details in company code
Planning level F0 Posting to bank account
☑ Relevant to cash flow
House Bank DB
Account ID GIRO

Interest calculation information in company code
Interest indicator
Interest calc. frequency
Key date of last int. calc.
Date of last interest run

Figure 9.21 Planning Levels in General Ledger Accounts

As you can see, in the company code data of the Create/Bank/Interest tab, in the Bank/Financial Details in Company Code section, you can enter the planning level. You can also select the Relevant to Cash Flow indicator, which allows you to enter the house bank and account ID with which that account is associated.

Create another session while you are working on this step, and execute Transaction FI12 (Figure 9.22). This brings you to the configuration of the house bank and account ID.

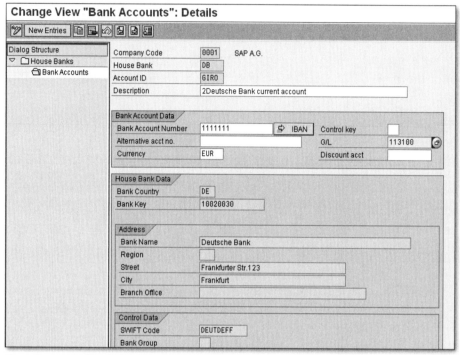

Figure 9.22 Configuration of Bank Accounts

In the G/L field, make sure that the general ledger account entered is consistent with the previous step. (In this example, the account is 113100, the house bank is DB, and the account ID is GIRO.)

9.2.4 Configuring Cash Management Account Names

Sometimes, instead of displaying the house bank and account ID or the bank account number (which is sometimes confidential), you want to have a cash account name, which can be used for reporting and to distinguish which account you are referring to without disclosing the specific bank account number. This Cash Management account name is also displayed in the cash position report. To configure this, access the following menu path: SAP CUSTOMIZING AND IMPLEMENTATION GUIDE • FINANCIAL SUPPLY CHAIN MANAGEMENT • CASH AND LIQUIDITY MANAGEMENT • CASH MANAGEMENT • STRUCTURING • DEFINE CASH MANAGEMENT ACCOUNT NAME. The screen shown in Figure 9.23 appears.

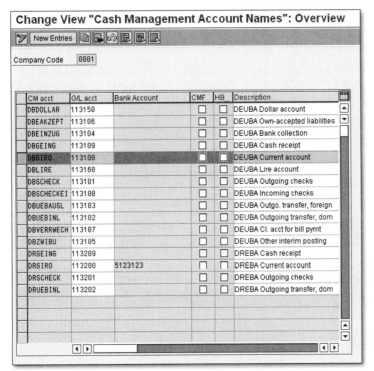

Figure 9.23 Cash Management Account Name Configuration

> **Note**
>
> If you correctly executed the steps in Section 9.2.3, the bank account number will appear on this screen after you enter the general ledger account; otherwise, it will show as blank, and may not display properly in reports. The exception to this if you want to use the CMF box, which we explain in the next paragraph.

There are three important fields on this screen. The Bank Account field can be populated or empty. The CMF box is used for one-time transactions; for example, if you have a fixed-term deposit, and you want this option available without creating general ledger postings, you would click the CMF box (which makes the option for use with Cash Management only). The third field is the HBPR column. If checked, this means that the Cash Management account name can be used for payment requests that don't have complete bank details.

9.2.5 Configuring Planning Groups

Let's briefly talk about Cash Management's relationship to subledger accounts and how this affects the cash position report. Although subledger accounts (e.g., AR and AP) are where you can configure customer and vendor details such as account groups and field status, this information is not specific to Cash Management, so we will not discuss it here. Rather, the information specific to Cash Management is the creation of planning groups. Access the following menu path: SAP CUS-TOMIZING AND IMPLEMENTATION GUIDE • FINANCIAL SUPPLY CHAIN MANAGEMENT • CASH AND LIQUIDITY MANAGEMENT • CASH MANAGEMENT • MASTER DATA • SUB-LEDGER ACCOUNTS • DEFINE PLANNING GROUPS, and the screen shown in Figure 9.24 appears.

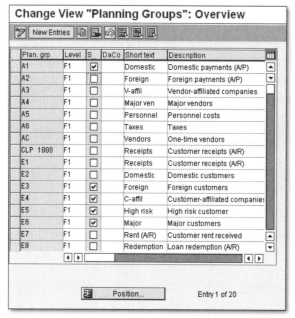

Figure 9.24 Configuration of Planning Groups

On this screen, enter the group, the planning level that is associated with it, and the short- and long text description. If you select the Screen Control checkbox, after the level column, you can enter a different planning level and date when entering a transaction. After you've created your planning groups, you need to link them to the vendor and customer master records (using Transactions FK02 for vendors and FD02 for customers), as shown in Figure 9.25.

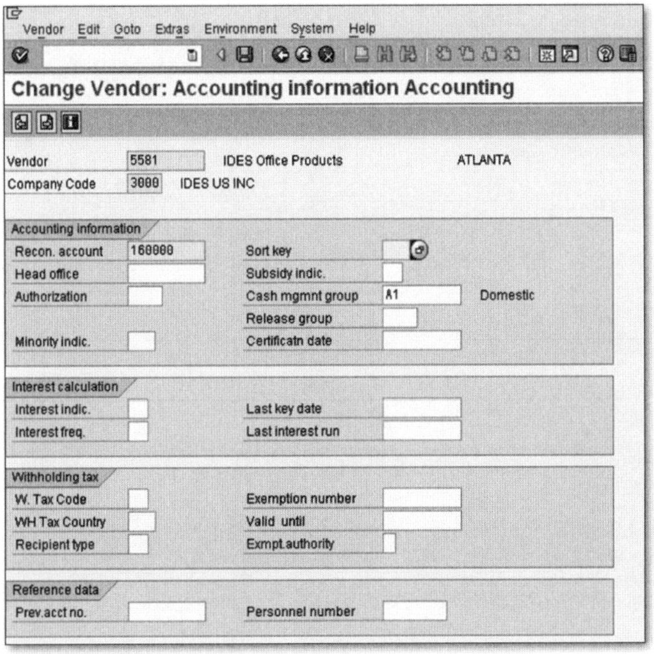

Figure 9.25 Enter Planning Group in Vendor Master Record

> **Note**
>
> Recall from Chapter 8 that the planning group is often called the cash management group in the vendor and customer master record screens.

9.2.6 Structuring the Cash Position Report

The structure of the cash position and liquidity forecast reports is based on a *grouping*, which, in simple terms, is a number of planning levels, planning groups, and master data presented together for cash analysis. For a grouping to work, it should contain at least one level and one group. To establish the structure of your cash position report, access the following menu path: SAP CUSTOMIZING AND IMPLEMENTATION GUIDE • FINANCIAL SUPPLY CHAIN MANAGEMENT • CASH AND LIQUIDITY

MANAGEMENT • CASH MANAGEMENT • STRUCTURING • GROUPINGS • DEFINE GROUP-
INGS AND MAINTAIN HEADERS. The screen shown in Figure 9.26 appears.

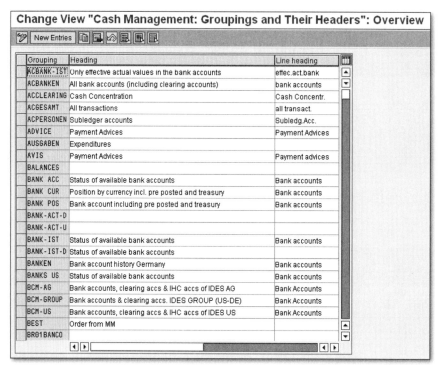

Figure 9.26 Maintain Groupings and Headers

Create the name of the grouping, and enter its heading, which is what will appear
at the top of your cash position report when you use this grouping.

Now, in the screen in Figure 9.27 (IMG • FINANCIAL SUPPLY CHAIN MANAGEMENT •
CASH AND LIQUIDITY MANAGEMENT • CASH MANAGEMENT • STRUCTURING • GROUP-
INGS • MAINTAIN STRUCTURE), enter the levels and groups you want to include. For
the level, use E; for the group, use G (this is standard SAP ERP procedure). Note
that master data, such as general ledger accounts, are entered as G, and that leading zeros must be added to the general ledger account number. Sometimes, you
may notice plus signs (+) listed in the Selection column; this is a wildcard that
searches for any character.

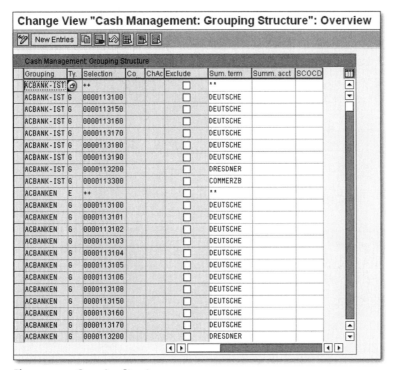

Figure 9.27 Grouping Structure

In your group, include all of the general ledger accounts, planning levels, and planning groups that you want to see on the same screen when you run the cash position and liquidity forecast reports. Customers and vendors are also entered as groups (again, with leading zeros).

9.2.7 Configuring the Distribution Function

Now let's discuss the distribution function, which you can access using the following menu path: SAP CUSTOMIZING AND IMPLEMENTATION GUIDE • FINANCIAL SUPPLY CHAIN MANAGEMENT • CASH AND LIQUIDITY MANAGEMENT • CASH MANAGEMENT • STRUCTURING • DEFINE DISTRIBUTION FUNCTION. The resulting screen is shown in Figure 9.28.

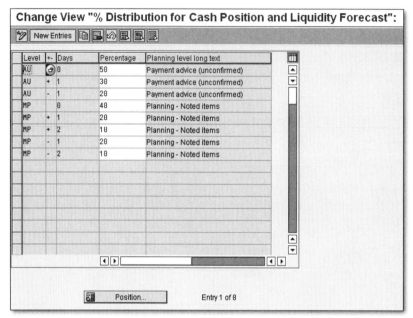

Figure 9.28 Distribution Function

Sometimes, for a certain payment method, the bank may clear the funds over a period of two days. Using the distribution function, you can enter the planning level associated with that payment method in this configuration screen and then enter the specifics about the time for clearing. For example, you can enter +0 and 50%, meaning that 50% of the funds will clear the same day, and then +1 and 50%, meaning that the other 50% of funds will clear one day later. This will make the flows shown in your cash position report more accurate.

For this to work when you run the cash position report in Transaction FF7B, you must select Distribute Amounts, as shown in Figure 9.29.

9.2.8 Configuring Archiving Categories

The next step is to configure the archiving categories, which is done via the following menu path: SAP CUSTOMIZING AND IMPLEMENTATION GUIDE • FINANCIAL SUPPLY CHAIN MANAGEMENT • CASH AND LIQUIDITY MANAGEMENT • CASH MANAGEMENT • STRUCTURING • MAINTAIN ARCHIVE RETENTION PERIOD. Access this menu path, and the screen shown in Figure 9.30 appears.

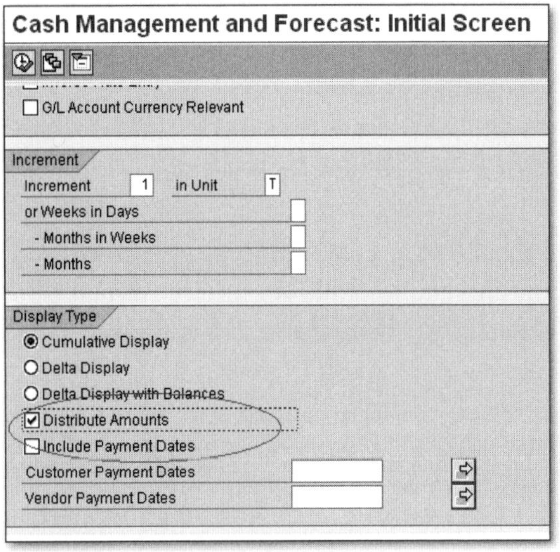

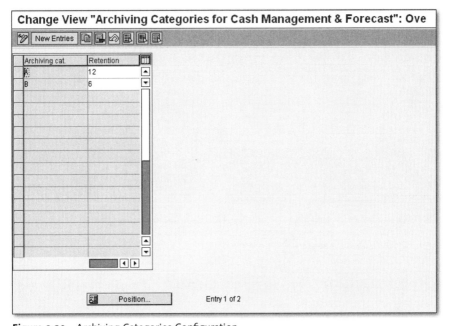

Figure 9.29 Distribute Amounts Field

Figure 9.30 Archiving Categories Configuration

Enter the archiving category and then the number of months that this category will remain in the system after it expires. As you will see in Figure 9.32, the archiving category, is used when configuring a planning type.

9.2.9 Configuring Memo Records

The first step in configuring memo records is to create number ranges; as with any document in SAP ERP, memo records are required to have consecutive numbers. The path to configure this is the following: SAP CUSTOMIZING AND IMPLEMENTATION GUIDE • FINANCIAL SUPPLY CHAIN MANAGEMENT • CASH AND LIQUIDITY MANAGEMENT • CASH MANAGEMENT • STRUCTURING • MANUAL PLANNING • DEFINE NUMBER RANGES. The resulting screen is shown in Figure 9.31.

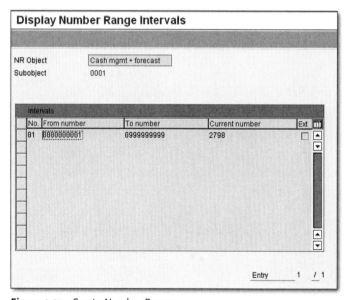

Figure 9.31 Create Number Ranges

Enter the relevant company code, and create the number range just as you would in any other part of the system.

Now you must configure the planning type, which you can understand as a memo record type (though that is not the official SAP ERP term). This screen is shown in Figure 9.32. Enter the type, planning level, archiving category, and whether you want the memo record to automatically expire. This automatic expiration is a very important feature because it allows you to arrange your process so that you don't accidentally duplicate the cash information when the actual cash flow occurs. Then enter the number range and planning type text in the appropriate fields.

Change View "Planning types": Overview

Plg Type	Plg level	Arch.cat.	Auto expir	Number rng	Planning type text
00	00	A	☑	01	Opening Available
01	01	A	☑	01	Opening Ledger
02	02	A	☑	01	Current Available
03	03	A	☑	01	Closing Available
04	04	A	☑	01	Closing Ledger
05	05	A	☑	01	0 Day Float
06	06	A	☑	01	1 Day Float
07	07	A	☑	01	2+ Day Float
AB	AB	A	☐	01	Confirmed advices
AC	AC	A	☐	01	Outgoing advices
AU	AU	A	☐	01	Unconfirmed advices
BV	BV	A	☐	01	Confirmed advices
C1	C1	A	☐	01	All bank fields
C2	C2	A	☐	01	All bank fields
CD	CD	A	☑	01	CDA items
CL	CL	A	☑	01	Bank-acct clearing
DE	DE	A	☐	01	Loan revenue

Figure 9.32 Planning Type Configuration

9.2.10 Defining Levels in Payment Requests

In the previous chapter (Sections 8.1.1, Integration with Sales and Distribution, and 8.1.3, Integration with Purchasing), we described the use of planning levels for Logistics, so we won't repeat it here. To configure planning levels in payment requests, access the following menu path: SAP CUSTOMIZING AND IMPLEMENTATION GUIDE • FINANCIAL SUPPLY CHAIN MANAGEMENT • CASH AND LIQUIDITY MANAGEMENT • CASH MANAGEMENT • STRUCTURING • DEFINE LEVELS IN PAYMENT REQUESTS.

Several treasury processes create payment requests. Two important cases are in Transaction Manager, for investments and borrowings, where the system creates a payment request that is later paid using Transaction F111. Another example is in SAP In-House Cash; when you approve a payment order, the system creates a payment request. The configuration shown in Figure 9.33 defines how these payment requests are shown in the cash position report.

Change View "Payment Request Levels": Overview

Level	Cty	P	PR level	Level	Pay.Method	Payment request level
B1			PR	Out. check		Pay.Req.
B2			PR	Dom trans		Pay.Req.
B3			PR	For. trans		Pay.Req.
B4			PR	Bank coll.		Pay.Req.
B5			PR	Int posts		Pay.Req.
B5	DE	Z	PR	Int posts	Bank Trans	Pay.Req.
B6			PR	Liability		Pay.Req.
B7			PR	Cl. bill		Pay.Req.
B8			PR	Inc checks		Pay.Req.
B9			PR	Cash rec		Pay.Req.
F0			PR	FI Banks		Pay.Req.

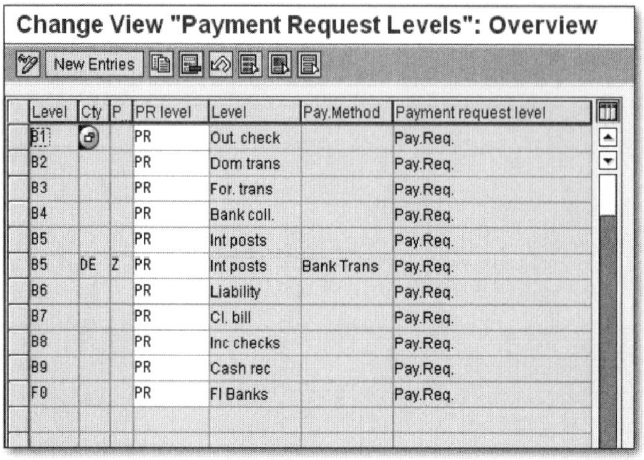

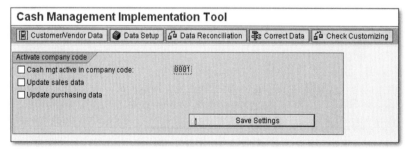

Figure 9.33 Configuration of Planning Levels on Payment Requests

Enter the planning level of the payment method and then the planning level of the payment request.

9.2.11 Configuring Production Startup and Reorganization

The last two steps in Cash Management configuration are the production startup and the reorganization, which are accessed via the following menu path: SAP Customizing and Implementation Guide • Financial Supply Chain Management • Cash and Liquidity Management • Cash Management • Tools • Prepare Production Startup and Data Setup. Figure 9.34 shows the production startup screen.

Figure 9.34 Production Startup Screen

On this screen, enter the company code, whether Cash Management should be active, and whether you want to update Sales and Purchasing data. Then click the Save Settings button.

After using the cash position report for a long time, you may need to correct it — because of a reorganization of general ledger accounts or company codes, for example. The reorganization report is used to retroactively update the cash position report and (and the liquidity forecast report). To access this report, use the following menu path: SAP Customizing and Implementation Guide • Financial Supply Chain Management • Cash and Liquidity Management • Cash Management • Tools • Reorganize Cash Management. The screen shown in Figure 9.35 appears.

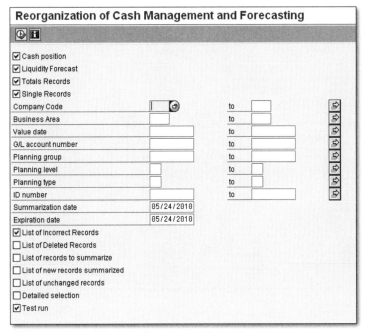

Figure 9.35 Reorganize Cash Position and Liquidity Forecast Reports

On this screen, select the appropriate parameters, and execute the program. If desired, you can do a test run to validate the results.

9.3 Summary

In this chapter, we explained how multiple sections in previous chapters relate to the cash position report. The chapter served as a complement to Chapter 8, in which we explained Cash Management integration with the liquidity forecast report. We also covered the Cash Management configuration details that weren't described in the previous chapter. In the next chapter, we discuss project considerations, methodology, and lessons learned.

This chapter is particularly relevant to organizations that are considering migrating standalone treasury workstations or manual systems to SAP ERP-based Cash and Liquidity Management. It will cover key considerations, project methodology, and lessons learned for migration.

10 Building an Integrated SAP ERP Treasury System

In this chapter, we talk about the main implications of implementing treasury applications from SAP. In Section 10.1, Treasury Workstations Versus ERP Systems, we discuss the differences between standalone treasury workstations and ERP systems. In Section 10.2, Migrating Standalone Treasury Workstations to SAP ERP, we discuss migration considerations and issues. Finally, in Section 10.3, Implementing SAP Treasury Applications, we review methodology, roll-out approach, budget aspects, and lessons learned.

10.1 Treasury Workstations Versus ERP Systems

In this section, we discuss the topic of treasury workstations and ERP systems. A *treasury workstation* is typically a standalone application that enables treasury processes, such as the following:

- **Electronic banking**
  The treasury workstation serves as a loading, analysis, and accounting interface for electronic bank statements.

- **Cash position**
  Based on initial cash balances, commitments, and cash forecasts for the day, the treasury workstation calculates whether investments or borrowings are required.

▶ **Liquidity forecast**
The treasury workstation is involved in the manual or automatic feed of wire and ACH payments, the manual entry of cash forecast items for the day, and the Excel upload of cash forecasts.

▶ **Analysis of actual cash flows**
Based on the bank statement, the invoices and other FI postings, the treasury workstation calculates actual cash flows by category.

▶ **Forecast versus actual comparison**
To refine forecasts, it's necessary to compare previous forecasts to the actual cash flows that took place.

▶ **In-house banking**
The treasury workstation enables a virtual bank to provide financial services without using an external bank.

▶ **Portfolio management**
The treasury workstation can be used to perform the booking of financial instrument trades for investments and borrowings.

▶ **Foreign exchanges**
The treasury workstation can be used to manage trades and the hedging of foreign currencies.

> **Note**
>
> Some treasury workstations offer all of these functionalities, while others are more limited. In Chapter 2, Section 2.2.1, Treasury Technology Platforms, we provided a list of some of them.

An important characteristic of these types of applications is that they are not integrated in real time with the accounting or AP systems. As a result, a company has to enter the same data in several systems (e.g., a vendor invoice using a wire transfer has to be booked at the bank website, then in the company accounting system, and then in the AP system). This lack of integration results in a process with fewer controls; for example, if someone completes a rush payment via wire transfer and also turns in an invoice to AP for a check payment, there is no easy way to avoid paying it twice. The lack of integration also results in less data security and integrity because manual data entry results in a greater risk for errors and inconsistencies and has more room for a misuse of the information. In addition, the month-end closing is lengthy because the cash reconciliation department has to work with multiple departments and applications, and must reconstruct the entire transaction as it flows through different nonintegrated systems.

In contrast, an ERP system integrates many front-office and back-office applications into a single platform and database, resulting in real-time accounting for many processes and in a secured environment in which treasury, AR/AP, cash reconciliation, and accounting processes are integrated, and resulting in an audit trail for every transaction. Implementing an ERP system results in great efficiency because there is no duplication of data entry, less manual typing and thus fewer errors, more controls due to the enhanced visibility of the entire transaction flow, availability of better reporting for decision making, and a faster month-end closing due to an easier reconciliation of data.

10.2 Migrating Standalone Treasury Workstations to SAP ERP

In many cases, an SAP treasury implementation project represents significant challenges, some of which are unique to treasury projects:

▶ If a treasury department is using a good treasury workstation, they may perceive it as best-in-class and may feel little incentive to switch to an ERP system.

▶ In a standalone environment, there is little visibility of the implications of the nonintegrated processes of cash reconciliation, AP, and accounting; as such, the efficiencies and gains for the overall company may not be obvious or perceived as important by the treasury department.

▶ A treasurer's job is to validate and secure information, not to trust others and share information openly. Although this skepticism and wariness serves well the needs of a treasury department, it is not always beneficial when working on a project. Thus, it may take some time for a treasury analyst to adapt to project work, which means that more investment in change management and support will be required.

▶ Treasury departments are usually very lean, so securing a full-time person to work on an implementation project is not always possible.

▶ Because of the high cost of making mistakes in the treasury department, there is more anxiety in treasury team members about the risk of a poor design or a malfunction in the new system.

▶ Banking and brokerage institutions have their own timelines when testing transactions, which may not adjust to a project timeline. It's important to consider this when creating a project plan.

▶ It is difficult to find experienced, knowledgeable treasury consultants who not only know SAP processes and terminology but also know treasury language and processes, and who can thus relate to treasury users.

▶ Data conversion can be complicated because data that exists in different applications (e.g., cash reconciliation, accounting, AP/AR, and treasury workstations) have to be migrated to a single application. You must use a good data conversion specialist with specific experience in migrating treasury applications.

Mitigating and resolving all of these challenges requires good planning to secure internal and external resources and estimate timelines and budgets, good change management and communications to obtain internal buy-in from the treasury department, training to reduce anxiety and to avoid mistakes, and a very good consultant that can earn the trust and respect of the treasurers.

10.3 Implementing SAP ERP Treasury Applications

In this section, we discuss the main considerations of an implementation of treasury applications from SAP ERP, including the methodology and roll-out approaches, budget aspects, and lessons learned.

10.3.1 Project Methodology

There are many system implementation methodologies, but the most famous one, and the one which serves as a base for most others, is known as the *ASAP methodology*. This methodology was created by SAP as a way to focus investment and efforts in those project activities that are essential for an implementation project and avoid those that are "nice to have" and which often result in increased time, resources, and budget. Figure 10.1 shows the phases of the ASAP methodology.

Figure 10.1 Phases of the ASAP Methodology

Let's take a look at what each of these phases mean in more detail:

▶ **Project preparation**
The project plan and organization chart is created, document templates and standards are defined, hardware and software requirements are validated and timelines for their installation and support are established, and workshops are planned.

▶ **Business blueprint**
The business process master list is defined, business requirements and process design workshops take place, functional specifications are started, configuration plans are defined, and business process procedure lists are produced. This is probably the most important phase because critical business requirements and major gaps in functionality should be identified. Sandbox and development environments are installed during this phase.

▶ **Realization**
The design created during blueprint materializes. System configuration, program development, scenario and scripts testing, business process procedures formation, unit testing, integrated testing, and user acceptance testing all take place here. The quality assurance environment is made available during this phase.

▶ **Final preparation**
All of the deliverables are refined, and both the system and the organization for the new processes and systems are prepared. Training materials are completed,

system documentation is created, cutover plans are defined and executed, the production environment is installed, end-user training takes place, and security and user access is finished.

▶ **Go-live and support**
The production support organization becomes operational, the production environment is working, troubleshooting and minor fixes take place, a transition from the project team to the support organization occurs, and consulting companies get final sign-off.

Each major consulting firm has its own variation of this methodology. In recent years, some firms added threads to the phases, where all threads ran across all phases in parallel. Each thread is handled by a subteam; some of the common threads are listed here:

▶ **Project Management**
Verifies the execution of the project plan, controls time and resources, and facilitates issue resolution.

▶ **Change Management**
Evaluates organizational readiness for change and creates plans to facilitate business buy-in of the project.

▶ **Functional Thread**
In charge of business processes and system configuration and testing.

▶ **Security and Controls Thread**
In charge of system security and often Sarbanes-Oxley act requirements.

▶ **Technical Thread**
In charge of hardware and software sizing, and planning and installation. It often runs program development as well.

▶ **Data Conversion Thread**
Maps legacy and SAP ERP data and enables data conversion.

▶ **Quality Assurance**
In charge of making sure the project meets the expectations of the client and that the project remains on time and budget.

In recent years, many niche players have been established to handle each of these threads and complement the efforts of large consulting firms.

10.3.2 "Big Bang" or "Phased Roll Out"

When embarking on a project as complicated as a global treasury redesign, it is important to define a scope that is achievable and doesn't incur too much risk, while also avoiding too much throwaway work. This creates the need to decide whether to implement the system in every company at the same time, which is known as a *big bang*, or to implement some first and then continue to others, which is known as a *phased roll out*.

It's difficult to make a global statement about which of these approaches is better; in reality, each situation is unique. However there are some particular situations in which a big bang approach make sense:

▶ When Shared Services have been implemented and the process to be implemented in SAP ERP is already centralized

▶ When the project includes centralization as part of the process redesign

▶ When all of the companies to be considered are in the same region or country, under the same set of regulations (or nonregulation), and operating in the same system or set of systems

These situations are more suitable for a big bang because a phased roll out would require two different processes at the same time for the same group of people (Shared Services employees), or having two sets of systems (legacy for some companies, and SAP ERP for companies included in the phase's scope).

Having two sets of systems at the same time is very likely to require you to create temporary interfaces with some legacy systems. These interfaces are likely to be discarded when the remaining companies move into SAP, and therefore become the throwaway work we mentioned before.

Situations in which a phased roll out makes more sense are as follows:

▶ When the processes to be implemented in SAP are de-centralized; i.e., performed at each individual subsidiary.

▶ When the companies in the group are in different systems.

▶ When the companies where SAP will be implemented are under different regulations.

▶ When the companies are in different regions or countries.

▶ When the companies are already part of a phased roll out for other SAP functionalities when the decision to bring treasury into SAP is made.

In these scenarios, you are unlikely to have two different processes for the same group of people, and temporary interfaces would either not be needed or would have been created anyway. Also, when companies are in different regions and time zones, it makes sense to bring them into SAP ERP separately, so that focused support efforts in the appropriate time zone are in place.

If you take a phased roll-out approach, you will need separate unit and integration testing, and separate cutover and go-live support, for each phase. This will inevitably make the project more expensive. Usually, when a company decides in favor of a phased roll-out approach, the company is trying to avoid risk or is bound by other restrictions that would make a big bang unfeasible or impractical.

10.3.3 Time and Resources

This is another subject for which it is very difficult to suggest a general approach. Each project is different depending on the scope (functionality), size of the company, and process complexity. We can, however, offer some guidelines that may or may not apply to your individual situation.

If you are implementing the entire treasury set of processes, we recommend dividing the work as follows:

▶ Inbound processes, such as electronic bank statements, lockboxes, Bank Statement Monitors in SAP Bank Communication Management, and cash reconciliation

▶ Outbound processes, such as AP payments for checks, positive pay files, wire and ACH payments, Batch and Payment Monitor, and approval processes in SAP Bank Communication Management

▶ Cash position processes, such as the cash position report, the liquidity forecast report, and analysis of actual cash flows in Liquidity Planner

▶ Transaction Manager processes, such as money market transactions, securities transactions, foreign exchange transactions, and so on

- Long-term forecasting in Liquidity Planner

- Reporting and risk analysis

- SAP In-House Cash (if it is contained in the scope of the project)

Depending of the size and complexity of each topic, we would suggest one to two consultants, and two to three client team members, working on each. If the scope of functionalities is reduced, and the company is small, you can combine two functions in a single team.

Timelines are another difficult topic. The average SAP ERP treasury project is about a year; however, the number of functionalities in the project scope, the size of the company, and the overall complexity of the project can cause it to require up to two years. If you are using a one-year timeline, we suggest four months for the project preparation and blueprint phases, six months for the realization phase, and two months for the final preparation phase. Remember, too, that you must also consider the timelines of the banks involved. Each bank has its own requirements for testing, and you must account for this in your plan. Never assume that they will stick to your own timeline.

10.3.4 Lessons Learned

Experience with SAP treasury implementations can teach you a number of valuable lessons. The following are some of the most important:

- **Make sure the process owners are committed to the project.**
  If they are not, they will make your job more difficult than it has to be, or they simply won't use the system in the end. If you sense that they are not committed, either invest in change management to win them over or stop the project altogether.

- **Do not speculate about what certain functionality does or does not do.**
  Get the proper training before starting your project. It is devastating to your credibility if you assume the system will behave a certain way, and then discover your mistake when you start configuring or unit testing.

- **Understand as-is processes and business requirements.**
  Even if your project methodology doesn't call for a deliverable related to the as-is business process, nothing gives you a better understanding of the business

requirements than understanding the current process and the reasons behind it. This will put you a step ahead when designing the to-be process and making sure it covers all of the requirements. It will also help you prepare better training materials.

▶ **Use experienced consultants.**
A nonexperienced consultant that is learning SAP and your company at the same time won't be able to determine the correct scope and won't be able to correctly assess complexity. You can waste months by having the wrong consultant working on your project.

▶ **Decide the scope first, or as quickly as possible.**
Adding extra components to the scope in the middle of the blueprint or realization phase will often require you to significantly modify your design; the sooner the scope is ready, the less throwaway work is necessary. In the past decade, most companies do a *scoping and planning* project before they do the actual implementation; this helps determine critical requirements, major gaps, staffing needs, timelines, and scope, which in turn will help you avoid surprises and last-minute changes.

▶ **Keep the scope reasonable.**
Try to eliminate "nice to have" requirements and focus on the most important ones. A treasury project is very complicated already, so don't make it more complicated than it needs to be.

▶ **Make sure you include people from the AR, AP, and accounting departments on your team.**
Due to the integration between their tasks and the treasury department, it's impossible for an SAP treasury project to succeed without them.

▶ **Obtain copies of your legacy reports at the beginning of the project.**
This will help you understand better your reporting requirements in SAP ERP.

▶ **Be careful with data.**
There's no room for mistakes or indiscretions in bank data. This is the type of data that requires secure handling because losing it or revealing it can cost a significant amount of money. The conversion of data should be perfect.

▶ **Include bank timelines in your own project timeline.**
Most banks take weeks or months from the time you tell them you need them

to test something to the time they are ready to start. They usually need signatures from key stakeholders and then also need to set up a test system and a test team for you. Never assume that they will stick to your timeline; ask them about their own and budget accordingly.

▸ **Do not alienate your business or IT counterparts.**
This rule is so basic that it almost seems silly to include it here; however, it is important because if you alienate your counterparts, almost anything of value that you come up with later will be ignored. If you alienate them, apologize and make amends — there is no other way to survive a project.

10.4 Summary

In this chapter, we covered the differences between a standalone treasury workstation and the integrated SAP ERP applications for treasury, as well as some of the reasons such an implementation is particularly difficult. We then covered the methodology of an implementation project; in particular, we discussed the ASAP methodology and the multithread approach that most large consulting firms are taking today. As part of this discussion, we explained in which situations it makes sense to take a big bang approach, and in which it makes sense to take a phased roll-out approach. We also provided some examples of how to staff a project, and a typical timeline for an SAP implementation. Finally, we discussed some important lessons learned from years of implementing treasury applications from SAP ERP. In the next chapter, we cover architecture, tools, and enhancements for the treasury applications of SAP.

This final chapter provides a functional overview and explanation of the latest tools and technologies offered in SAP ERP.

11 Leveraging Tools and Enhancements

In this chapter, we review architecture options, technical tools offered by SAP ERP, and sources for information on enhancements as they get released to the public.

> **Note**
>
> This is intended to be a functional book, not a technical one, so we won't get into the minute details of these tools. Our purpose here is to point you in the right direction, not offer explicit instruction. If you need more information on any of these topics, refer to SAP PRESS's other offerings at *www.sap-press.com*.

11.1 Architecture Options for SAP FSCM

When you implement SAP Financial Supply Chain Management (SAP FSCM) treasury applications, you can decide to do it in the same SAP ERP instance as your other SAP ERP applications, or on a different instance (Figure 11.1).

There are three main reason why you may want to, or have to, implement this application in separate instances:

- You have multiple companies that have been acquired and are in different SAP ERP instances.

- Your group of companies conducted several regional SAP ERP implementations, and you haven't integrated them all.

- You want or need to have the latest version and enhancement packs for SAP FSCM, and your other systems are not at the same level, so you chose to have a separate box for SAP FSCM.

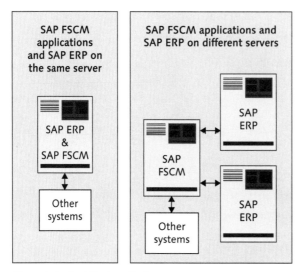

Figure 11.1 Architecture Options

In addition to communications between SAP ERP instances and components, you might also need to interface to other systems, for example, information vendors such as Reuters, credit agencies such as Moody's, trading systems, banking systems, and so on. Doing so will require you to use SAP NetWeaver Process Integration (SAP NetWeaver PI) or some of the tools discussed in Section 11.2, Tools and Architectures of SAP ERP.

11.2 Tools and Architectures of SAP ERP

In this section, we discuss the Business Architecture Framework (BFA) and SAP NetWeaver PI. These will be needed in your project if you have requirements that can only be supported using BAPIs, if you have to connect the system to external partners such as banks or trading agencies using SAP NetWeaver PI, or if you have to connect to separate instances of SAP ERP using ALE.

> **Note**
>
> As this is a functional book, the topics here are discussed only briefly. If you require additional information, please consult online documentation.

11.2.1 Business Framework Architecture (BFA)

SAP created the BFA to allow integration and communication between both SAP components and non-SAP components (Figure 11.2).

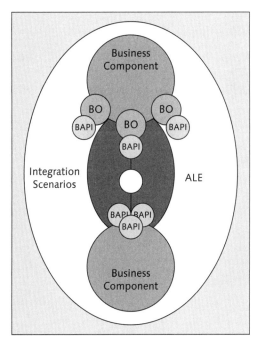

Figure 11.2 Business Framework Architecture

The main components of the BFA are as follows:

▶ **Business components**
These can be understood as the different components of SAP, for example, Human Resources and Sales and Distribution.

▶ **Business object types**
A business object type represents one business element, for example, an employee.

▶ **Business Application Programming Interfaces (BAPIs)**
A BAPI is a connection to an SAP business object type with its own methods and properties.

▶ **Application Link Enabling**
ALE allows the distribution of business object types across systems to enable the execution of business processes that happen in different systems.

▶ **Integration scenarios**
These scenarios describe how business components, business object types, and BAPIs interact to support business processes.

11.2.2 SAP NetWeaver Process Integration (SAP NetWeaver PI)

SAP NetWeaver Process Integration (SAP NetWeaver PI) is a tool used to design, configure, and implement processes that require the exchange of messages between different systems, and that have not yet been automated (these are often known as *collaborative processes*). SAP NetWeaver PI is very useful in creating interfaces using graphics instead of code. Figure 11.3 shows the architecture of SAP NetWeaver PI.

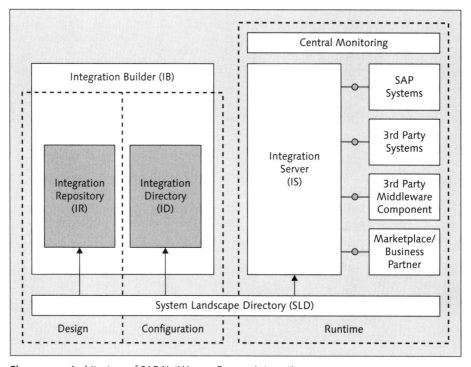

Figure 11.3 Architecture of SAP NetWeaver Process Integration

The integration repository is used to design the collaborative process and enter all of its components, systems, and interfaces. After you move into the configuration phase, you determine the message flow for all of the relevant objects in the integration directory. After your process goes live, all messages are stored in the integration server, which can be used to monitor all interfaces.

11.3 SAP Enhancement Packs and New Treasury Functionality

With the latest platform, SAP ERP Central Component 6.0, SAP will no longer produce new versions, at least for a few years. Instead, it will provide *enhancement packs*, which allow you to keep a stable version while still having the option to enable new functionality. Figure 11.4 describes the main functionalities added during the enhancement packs since SAP ERP Central Component 6.0 was launched in June of 2006.

	Enhancement Package 2	Enhancement Package 3	Enhancement Package 4	Enhancement Package 5 and beyond
TCI/TCO Reduction	Bank communication	Collaboration with TPT	Exposure management	Improved payment advice handling
Functions & Features	ISO20022 support	Commodity paper deals	SWIFT correspondence monitor	Commodity SWAPS and OTC-options
Compliance	SWIFT integration	Hedge management	Hedge management commodities	Update SEPA rules, commodity hedging
Usability/ Analytics	Bank statement monitor	New value at risk key figures	IFRS 7 reporting	Cash and risk Xcelsius dashboards

Figure 11.4 Enhancement Packages and New Treasury Functions

There is extensive documentation on each of these enhancement packages. Some of them, such as SAP Bank Communication Management and the integration package for SWIFT, have entire chapters in this book; others are covered in SAP online documentation and other books. However, given the dynamic nature of the subject, we want to give you the resources you need to find information, rather than give you specific details that will likely soon be outdated. With this in mind, Figure 11.5 outlines all of the websites where SAP provides continuous news and updates on enhancement packages, upgrades, and new functionalities.

SAP ERP
- Homepage: *http://service.sap.com/erp*
- SAP EHP News: *http://service.sap.com/erp-ehp*
- Release Notes: *http://service.sap.com/releasenotes*
- Release Strategy: *http://service.sap.com/releasestrategy*
- Maintenance Strategy: *http://service.sap.com/maintenance*
- Scenario & Process Component List: *http://service.sap.com/sci*
- Upgrade Information Center: *http://service.sap.com/upgrade*
- SAP EHP Consulting Services: *http://service.sap.com/ufg*

SAP NetWeaver
- Homepage: *http://service.sap.com/netweaver*
- NetWeaver Administrator: *http://service.sap.com/nwa*
- System Landscape Directory: *http://service.sap.com/sld*
- System Lifecycle Manager: *http://service.sap.com/slm*

Figure 11.5 SAP Links to Upgrade and Enhancement Package News

11.4 Summary

In this chapter, we covered some of the architecture options for SAP FSCM treasury applications, provided a brief description and summary of SAP ERP integration functions, provided a list of the main treasury functionalities offered in the different enhancement packages, and included a list of links where you can obtain additional information.

The Author

 **Eleazar Ortega Van Steenberghe** is a Senior Manager of Capgemini, LLC (*www.capgemini.com*), one of the largest global firms that provides consulting, technology, and outsourcing. With almost 20 years of experience in finance and treasury, he has spent the last 16 years providing SAP and business process consulting services to many global Fortune 500 companies, such as Nike, Aflac, Target, Smurfit, and several others, including large private corporations around the world. He is also an active blogger on *www.insiderlearning-network.com* and has created LinkedIn groups for SAP In-House Cash, SAP Bank Communication Management, and SAP Liquidity Planner.

Before joining Capgemini, Eleazar worked as a Senior Manager for Deloitte Consulting, and, in 2005, he founded Experthink, Inc. (*www.experthink.com*), a company that specializes in the implementation of treasury applications from SAP. He holds a Masters in Business Administration from the University of Miami. He has done multiple presentations at SAP Financials conferences in America and Europe, and has written an article on Shared Services for *SAP Info* magazine. To learn more about Eleazar and this book, view his profile at *linkedin.com* or check out his website at *www.eleazarvansteenberghe.com*.

Index

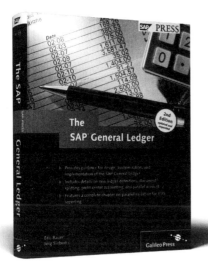

Provides guidance for design, customization, and implementation of the SAP General Ledger

Includes details on new ledger definitions, Document Splitting, Profit Center Accounting, and parallel accounting

Features a complete chapter on parallel valuation for IFRS reporting

Eric Bauer, Jörg Siebert

The SAP General Ledger

This book gives you complete overview of the SAP General Ledger, including all of the new features like Document Splitting, Profit Center Accounting, parallel accounting, and Balanced Scorecard. It also includes a complete chapter on the SAP General Ledger's role in reporting for IFRS, including parallel valuation. A must-have for all finance professionals who have migrated or are migrating to the SAP General Ledger, this book is a resource that can be used in both daily work and at the implementation level.

approx. 505 pp., 2. edition, 79,95 Euro / US$ 79.95
ISBN 978-1-59229-350-6, Aug 2010

>> www.sap-press.com

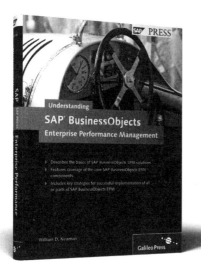

Provides key stakeholders and decision-makers with a practical functional overview of SAP BusinessObjects EPM solutions

Features coverage of the core EPM components, including BPC, FIM, SM, and SPM

Includes key strategies for successful implementation of all or parts of EPM

William D. Newman

Understanding SAP BusinessObjects Enterprise Performance Management

This book provides decision-makers with guidance on implementing and using the SAP BusinessObjects Enterprise Performance Management solutions, including Strategy Management, Financial Information Management, Spend Analytics, XBRL and more. Readers will benefit from the strategic, high-level overviews of the various products in the EPM application, and develop an understanding of the best practices for implementation, integration, and use. The scenario-based approach should appeal to a broad range of stakeholders, from executives to functional department heads and managers.

282 pp., 2010, 69,95 Euro / US$ 69.95
ISBN 978-1-59229-348-3

>> www.sap-press.com

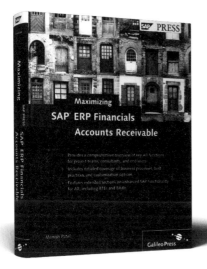

Provides a comprehensive overview of key AR functions for implementation teams, consultants, and end-users

Includes detailed coverage of business processes, best practices, and customization options

Features extended sections on enhanced SAP functionality for AR, including BTEs and BAdIs, among others

Manish Patel

Maximizing SAP ERP Financials Accounts Receivable

Are you using SAP ERP Financials Accounts Receivables to its maximum capability? If not, this book will give you a roadmap for ensuring that you are, whether you're an implementation team member, executive, functional or technical user, or an end-user. The book will teach you how to maximize the use and potential of the Accounts Receivable component and increase the ROI of your implementation. You'll also develop knowledge and strategies for enhancing the use of the AR component and integrating it with other SAP services and components.

505 pp., 2010, 79,95 Euro / US$ 79.95
ISBN 978-1-59229-303-2

>> www.sap-press.com

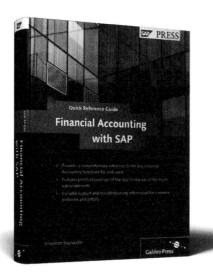

Provides a comprehensive reference to the key Financial

Accounting functions for end-users

Features practical coverage of the day-to-day use of the major sub-components

Includes support and troubleshooting information for common problems and pitfalls

Vincenzo Sopracolle

Quick Reference Guide: Financial Accounting with SAP

If you use SAP ERP Financials on a daily basis, this definitive, comprehensive guide is a must-have resource. You'll find practical, detailed guidance to all of the key functions of the Financial Accounting component, including troubleshooting and problem-solving information. You'll find easy-to-use answers to frequently asked questions in the core areas of the SAP General Ledger, Asset Accounting (AA), Accounts Payable (AP), Accounts Receivable (AR), Banking (BK), and Special Purpose Ledger (SPL). In addition, the book includes quick-reference material such as lists of transaction codes, tables, and menu paths.

665 pp., 2010, 69,95 Euro / US$ 69.95
ISBN 978-1-59229-313-1

>> www.sap-press.com

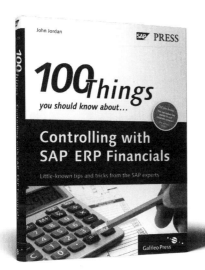

Provides 100 little-known time-saving tips and workarounds for SAP Controlling users, super-users, and consultants

Features a practical, highly-visual, easy-to-use 2-page spread for each topic area

Includes access to a companion e-book or online updates that will be kept current with new tips contributed by readers

John Jordan

100 Things You Should Know About Controlling with SAP ERP Financials

Have you ever spent days trying to figure out how to generate a report in SAP ERP Financials only to find out you just needed to click a few buttons. If so, you'll be delighted with this book—it unlocks the secrets of Controlling in SAP ERP Financials. It provides users and super-users with 100 tips and workarounds you can use to increase productivity, save time, and improve overall ease-of-use of SAP ERP Financials Controlling. The tips have been carefully selected to provide a collection of the best, most useful, and rarest information.

approx. 300 pp., 49,95 Euro / US$ 49.95
ISBN 978-1-59229-341-4, Oct 2010

>> www.sap-press.com